Chinese Astrology

2019

Year of the
Earth Pig

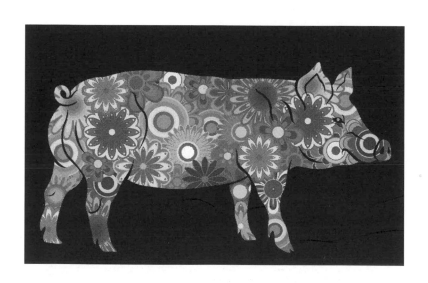

Donna Stellhorn

Published by ETC Publishing
Carlsbad, California
WWW.ETCPUBLISHING.COM

First Edition, First Publication 2018

ISBN: 978-1-944622-24-4

Cover design by Gary Dunham and Donna Stellhorn

Concepts presented in this book derive from traditional Chinese,
European, and American metaphysical and folk lore. They are not
to be understood as directions, recommendations or prescriptions
of any kind. Nor does the author or publisher make any claim
to do more than provide information and report this lore.

Contents

Introduction

On February 5, 2019, we enter the Year of the Earth Pig, the
last year of the natural 12-year cycle. This is a time when family and friends come together to support each other and to look back on the experiences, good and bad, of the past 12 years. It's a time when we are drawn home to celebrate with food, drink, and laughter.

If we were to consolidate this 12-year cycle in order to think of it from the perspective of a single year in farming, this Year of the Earth Pig would represent the last period of Winter, the time of year when the world goes on outside without our direct participation; the snow is piled up against the door. We're snuggled together in the house with the fire going in the hearth or a pot of soup bubbling on the stove. We are on a well-deserved break after the long period of planting, tending our fields, and harvesting.

Now we are taking time to rest and reflect on the past year, this previous 12-month cycle. It's a time of contentment. Yet, even though we're all a little tired of winter, possibly feeling bored with having to economize (and eat the same healthy food day after day), we have the time to think and talk to friends and family about future plans, and what we'll do this coming Spring.

If we look at the 12-year cycle as if it were the lunar cycle, this Earth Pig year would be the balsamic period, a time when there is no visible moon. There's no moonlight to light our way at night. However, in the darkness we can see so many more stars when the Moon's glow is not visible to us. We are reminded to look past what's near and familiar, to see what's out there—the vast Universe of potential.

Pig years are festive, offering many reasons to celebrate. But there's also a reminder to avoid being lulled into a deep sleep following the festivities. We may dream the party will go on every night, everything and everyone will continue to be happy and celebrate, maintaining their party mood all year long. We may imagine we will wake up in the morning and just be our usual thoughtful and aware selves. What seems right may just prove to be a superficial gloss, and a closer look will reveal many things going on below the surface. Those who stay awake will make plans, and those who party until they fall asleep could potentially lose out.

Earth Pig years are the more spiritual years when we feel more connected to the Universe and the powers that be. It is a time when we feel prosperous because our pantries are full and the refrigerator is stocked (even if our retirement accounts are lacking). We have loads of entertainment at our fingertips and we can avoid thinking if we want to. We feel we can relax after the hard work of the past 11 years; it's easy to fall asleep.

We tend to overindulge at this time. In Earth Pig years, we are likely to overspend, overeat, and take up habits that aren't so good for our health. There's a desire to play today and let tomorrow take care of itself. While living in the present can be a good thing, we must stay mindful of the debt we will have to pay for our actions tomorrow.

2019 is a good year to learn meditation, to expand your intuitive ability through practice, to study yoga or tai chi, to try painting or to make pottery. Through these activities we can learn more about ourselves, we can clear away personal blocks to reaching our goals.

It's a good time to look around your house and get rid of the excess, keeping only the things that make us happy. Pass on unneeded items to someone who does need them. Charity and benevolent actions are in harmony during Earth Pig years.

This is a good year to complete projects, especially ones you've been working on for a long while. Finish up degrees, get businesses off the ground, get designs patented, complete the book you've been writing. Or if you can't complete a project, think about what may be blocking your progress. Is there an obstacle in our path? Or, is this the excuse we use to procrastinate?

Earth Pig years are good for businesses whose focus is on making people comfortable at home and in other areas of their lives. This will be a profitable year for businesses and service providers who can help bring people together for a celebration; who assist people in selling off unwanted stuff; and who offer to help individuals finish projects, or gain a degree or certification qualifying them for future success. Spiritual and alternative businesses can do very well offering support, training, and techniques to help people get in touch with the inner self. Creative companies also get a boost this year as people are drawn to explore color, design, and things that make them happy.

In 2019 it will be much better for each of us to take prudent, well thought out action, rather than indulge in out-and-out risk-taking. For example, angrily storming out of your current job in haste would not be a good idea. A much better approach would be to carefully craft your new and updated resume, connect with headhunters, negotiate an excellent salary, then securing a new position—while still working at your old job. This would be the best way to change jobs during an Earth Pig year.

In Earth Pig years, good advice suggests we plan long term. Earth energy is a very stable, calm element which reminds us to look out into our future, not to months ahead, but years ahead. Where do you want to be in six years? What is your vision for yourself 12 years from today?

Overall, Earth Pig years can be delightful, filled with the pleasure of celebrating life with the people we love. To enjoy the best this year has to offer, balance this joy-filled energy with mindfulness and an awareness of your bigger goals. Create work/life balance, and apply yourself to pursuing what you want to achieve. Leave the comfortable familiarity of home often, get out of your comfort zone; brave the Winter storms now and you can gain much. Do this, and you will find joy and prosperity during the coming years.

In this installment of my Chinese Astrology series, I offer predictions for each month of the year. There are also sector predictions for love, money, career, education, health and more. There are several Feng Shui cures suggested for each Chinese Zodiac sign to help you focus and bring in positive energy. At the end of this book, you'll find sections on Feng Shui principles, the upcoming eclipses, Mercury retrograde, Flying Star. There is also a large section on compatibility.

This year, I've included the addition of "Lucky Days." On these days, plan to take important or significant actions, make vital phone calls, send emails. These are days when your energy and luck (both positive and negative) are high, and the most significant happenings of the month will occur. The more positive action you take on these days, the better your overall results and satisfaction will be.

I hope you enjoy this book and it's useful for you. Please take a moment and review it on Amazon, so more people can find this book.

Celebrating Chinese New Year

The biggest holiday of the year in China is Chinese New Year. Based on the lunar calendar, Chinese New Year falls on a different day each year—most often on the second New Moon after the Winter Solstice. The Winter Solstice is on December 21, so Chinese New Year is about two months later.

Occasionally, the Chinese New Year will fall on the third New Moon after the Winter Solstice. We will next experience this in the year 2033. In historical China, emperors were in charge of keeping time and telling the people when important dates would happen. Emperors marked these important dates with festivals. Chinese New Year is one such festival.

There's a legend in China, the tale of a "Nian," a fearsome creature with the head of a lion and the body of a bull. Every winter the Nian would grow very hungry and finding nothing to eat, he would come down into the villages to snack on the villagers. But over time, the villagers learned that the Nian was afraid of loud noises, fire, and the color red.

One night, the Nian was spotted coming down from the mountains, so the villagers lit fires, waved red flags, and made lots of noise by banging gongs and setting off firecrackers. Their village was spared, and to this day, New Year's is celebrated with lots of firecrackers and red banners.

Before New Year there is much to do. The house must be thoroughly cleaned to sweep away any of the remaining bad luck from last year. Lots of special foods are prepared. The night before New Year, it is considered "lucky" to stay up past midnight—to symbolize enjoying a long life. At midnight the firecrackers start popping.

On the first day of the New Year, everyone wears their best clothes, and everyone says only positive things to one another to secure good luck for everyone. Red envelopes are filled with money and given to children.

This begins a multi-day holiday. At Chinese New Year there is the dance of the Golden Dragon (sometimes called the Lion Dance). This dragon is decorated with representations of the five elements, lights, silver, and fur. It can take as many as a hundred people to carry the Golden Dragon through the streets. At the end of the route, the dragon is met with firecrackers and cheers from the crowds.

On the second day of the New Year, there is a vegetarian feast, after which people go and visit relatives, bringing them oranges to wish them a prosperous new year. People eat long noodles, the longer the better, to symbolize a long life. They indulge in Nian Gao—which is a cake made of rice flour, brown sugar, and oil—to bring prosperity.

I offer a series of videos on the subject of what to do before and during the New Year's Celebrations to bring luck. Here's the link: https://www.youtube.com/c/DonnaStellhorn

Find Your Chinese Zodiac Sign

The annual Chinese Zodiac sign changes each year in January or February. If you were born in January or February of any year, check the date carefully to make sure you find your correct animal sign. Below I've also listed the element and Yin or Yang quality for the year. If you have any difficulty determining your sign, element, and Yin or Yang quality, please email me at donnastellhorn@gmail.com with your birth date, and I will help you find your sign.

2/20/1920 to 2/7/1921 Yang Metal Monkey

2/8/1921 to 1/27/1922 Yin Metal Rooster (or Cock)

1/28/1922 to 2/15/1923 Yang Water Dog

2/16/1923 to 2/4/1924 Yin Water Pig (or Boar)

2/5/1924 to 1/24/1925 Yang Wood Rat

1/25/1925 to 2/12/1926 Yin Wood Ox

2/13/1926 to 2/1/1927 Yang Fire Tiger

2/2/1927 to 1/22/1928 Yin Fire Rabbit (or Hare)

1/23/1928 to 2/9/1929 Yang Earth Dragon

2/10/1929 to 1/29/1930 Yin Earth Snake

1/30/1930 to 2/16/1931 Yang Metal Horse

2/17/1931 to 2/5/1932 Yin Metal Sheep (or Goat or Ram)

2/6/1932 to 1/25/1933 Yang Water Monkey

1/26/1933 to 2/13/1934 Yin Water Rooster (or Cock)

2/14/1934 to 2/3/1935 Yang Wood Dog

2/4/1935 to 1/23/1936 Yin Wood Pig (or Boar)

1/24/1936 to 2/10/1937 Yang Fire Rat

2/11/1937 to 1/30/1938 Yin Fire Ox

1/31/1938 to 2/18/1939 Yang Earth Tiger

2/19/1939 to 2/7/1940 Yin Earth Rabbit (or Hare)

2/8/1940 to 1/26/1941 Yang Metal Dragon

1/27/1941 to 2/14/1942 Yin Metal Snake

2/15/1942 to 2/4/1943 Yang Water Horse

2/5/1943 to 1/24/1944 Yin Water Sheep (or Goat or Ram)

1/25/1944 to 2/12/1945 Yang Wood Monkey

2/13/1945 to 2/1/1946 Yin Wood Rooster (or Cock)

2/2/1946 to 1/21/1947 Yang Fire Dog

1/22/1947 to 2/9/1948 Yin Fire Pig (or Boar)

2/10/1948 to 1/28/1949 Yang Earth Rat

1/29/1949 to 2/16/1950 Yin Earth Ox

2/17/1950 to 2/5/1951 Yang Metal Tiger

2/6/1951 to 1/26/1952 Yin Metal Rabbit (or Hare)

1/27/1952 to 2/13/1953 Yang Water Dragon

2/14/1953 to 2/2/1954 Yin Water Snake

2/3/1954 to 1/23/1955 Yang Wood Horse

1/24/1955 to 2/11/1956 Yin Wood Sheep (or Goat or Ram)

2/12/1956 to 1/30/1957 Yang Fire Monkey

1/31/1957 to 2/17/1958 Yin Fire Rooster (or Cock)

2/18/1958 to 2/7/1959 Yang Earth Dog

2/8/1959 to 1/27/1960 Yin Earth Pig (or Boar)

1/28/1960 to 2/14/1961 Yang Metal Rat

2/15/1961 to 2/4/1962 Yin Metal Ox

2/5/1962 to 1/24/1963 Yang Water Tiger

1/25/1963 to 2/12/1964 Yin Water Rabbit (or Hare)

2/13/1964 to 2/1/1965 Yang Wood Dragon

2/2/1965 to 1/20/1966 Yin Wood Snake

1/21/1966 to 2/8/1967 Yang Fire Horse

2/9/1967 to 1/29/1968 Yin Fire Sheep (or Goat or Ram)

1/30/1968 to 2/16/1969 Yang Earth Monkey

2/17/1969 to 2/5/1970 Yin Earth Rooster (or Cock)

2/6/1970 to 1/26/1971 Yang Metal Dog

1/27/1971 to 2/14/1972 Yin Metal Pig (or Boar)

2/15/1972 to 2/2/1973 Yang Water Rat

2/3/1973 to 1/22/1974 Yin Water Ox

1/23/1974 to 2/10/1975 Yang Wood Tiger

2/11/1975 to 1/30/1976 Yin Wood Rabbit (or Hare)

1/31/1976 to 2/17/1977 Yang Fire Dragon

2/18/1977 to 2/6/1978 Yin Fire Snake

2/7/1978 to 1/27/1979 Yang Earth Horse

1/28/1979 to 2/15/1980 Yin Earth Sheep (or Goat or Ram)

2/16/1980 to 2/4/1981 Yang Metal Monkey

2/5/1981 to 1/24/1982 Yin Metal Rooster (or Cock)

1/25/1982 to 2/12/1983 Yang Water Dog

2/13/1983 to 2/1/1984 Yin Water Pig (or Boar)

2/2/1984 to 2/19/1985 Yang Wood Rat

2/20/1985 to 2/8/1986 Yin Wood Ox

2/9/1986 to 1/28/1987 Yang Fire Tiger

1/29/1987 to 2/16/1988 Yin Fire Rabbit (or Hare)

2/17/1988 to 2/5/1989 Yang Earth Dragon

2/6/1989 to 1/26/1990 Yang Earth Snake

1/27/1990 to 2/14/1991 Yang Metal Horse

2/15/1991 to 2/3/1992 Yin Metal Sheep (or Goat or Ram)

2/4/1992 to 1/22/1993 Yang Water Monkey

1/23/1993 to 2/9/1994 Yin Water Rooster (or Cock)

2/10/1994 to 1/30/1995 Yang Wood Dog

1/31/1995 to 2/18/1996 Yin Wood Pig (or Boar)

2/19/1996 to 2/6/1997 Yang Fire Rat

2/7/1997 to 1/27/1998 Yin Fire Ox

1/28/1998 to 2/15/1999 Yang Earth Tiger

2/16/1999 to 2/4/2000 Yin Earth Rabbit (or Hare)

2/5/2000 to 1/23/2001 Yang Metal Dragon

1/24/2001 to 2/11/2002 Yin Metal Snake

2/12/2002 to 1/31/2003 Yang Water Horse

2/1/2003 to 1/21/2004 Yin Water Sheep (or Goat or Ram)

1/22/2004 to 2/8/2005 Yang Wood Monkey

2/9/2005 to 1/28/2006 Yin Wood Rooster (or Cock)

1/29/2006 to 2/17/2007 Yang Fire Dog

2/18/2007 to 2/6/2008 Yin Fire Pig (or Boar)

2/7/2008 to 1/25/2009 Yang Earth Rat

1/26/2009 to 2/13/2010 Yin Earth Ox

2/14/2010 to 2/2/2011 Yang Metal Tiger

2/3/2011 to 1/22/2012 Yin Metal Rabbit (or Hare)

1/23/2012 to 2/09/2013 Yang Water Dragon

2/10/2013 to 1/30/2014 Yin Water Snake

1/31/2014 to 2/18/2015 Yang Wood Horse

2/19/2015 to 2/7/2016 Yin Wood Sheep (or Goat or Ram)

2/8/2016 to 1/27/2017 Yang Fire Monkey

1/28/2017 to 2/15/2018 Yin Fire Rooster (or Cock)

2/16/2018 to 2/4/2019 Yang Earth Dog

2/5/2019 to 1/24/2020 Yin Earth Pig (or Boar)

01/25/2020 to 2/11/2021 Yang Metal Rat

2/12/2021 to 1/31/2022 Yin Metal Ox

2/1/2022 to 1/21/2023 Yang Water Tiger

1/22/2023 to 2/9/2024 Yin Water Rabbit

2/10/2024 to 1/28/2025 Yang Wood Dragon

1/29/2025 to 2/16/2026 Yin Wood Snake

Where Are You in the 12-year cycle?

In 2019, Year of the Earth Pig, we are in the last sign of the 12-year cycle of the Chinese Zodiac. However, you may not personally be experiencing the last sign energy in your own life. Your personal 12-year cycle is based on your birth year.

First, let's define the cycle itself. We can compare the 12-year cycle to a single year on a farm in the following manner: three months of the year = three years of the 12-year cycle.

Therefore, the first three years of the Chinese zodiac represent the three months of Spring, bringing the farmer the opportunity to plant seeds. The next three-year segment brings a similar type of energy as the three months of Summer, where the farmer would be tending the growing plants, weeding the garden, and protecting his fields.

This period is followed by the three-year segment representing the three months of Autumn, and harvest time. This period is marked by significant achievements but also hard work. The cycle ends with a three-year segment representing the three months of Winter, a time when the farmer finishes up tasks he didn't have time to complete during the other busy months of the year, as he plans for the future. He eats from his storehouse of food and waits for the next Spring planting season to begin.

If you are born in the Year of the Pig (sometimes known as the Year of the Boar), this year marks the beginning of your personal Springtime, a time which will last for the coming three years. During this period you will want plant lots of seeds by trying new things, meeting new people and going to new places. Anything new you do could sprout into real opportunities during this three-year period and during the three following years.

For Rat, you are in your last year of Winter. You have been through some busy years, and it's time to think about what needs catching up, what to release or let go, what plans you need to put in place now to make it easier for you to plant new seeds and start new things in 2020.

Ox natives are in your second year of Winter, and it's time to take stock of what you have accomplished over the past ten years.

Where are the investments of your time and energy still paying off? It's a good time to think of beginning to let go of what isn't working, and of how you can accumulate more with less effort.

Tiger natives are in the first year of Winter. Your storehouse and pantry are as full as they will get. To accumulate more, you will have to be energetic and clever in identifying and gathering the final bits of the harvest missed by others. This is the year you begin your time of rest and recuperation. You need to take care of yourself and your body.

Rabbit (or Hare) is in their last year of Autumn, and the harvest is underway. Take everything you have learned so far, and let the world know about your skills and what you have to offer. Demand to be paid what you are worth. This is a time when you can accumulate more.

Dragon natives, you are in your second year of Autumn, and the harvest is in full swing. Opportunities abound but require you to be out in the world in order to gather them up. Think big, connect with people who can help you gather even more.

Snakes, your Autumn is beginning, and you must adjust to the new workload. That said, now is the period when you can easily gather what you want and need. Don't be shy. You can accumulate much with just a little effort.

Horses, you are in the final year of your three-year Summer. It's time to focus in on the aspects of your life which are working the way you want them to! Don't put effort into things in your life that are not bringing results. You also want to take steps to gather as many people around you as you can this year, people who will help you with your harvest in the coming three-year period.

Sheep (or Goat or Ram) natives, you are in the middle of your Summer. You see the results of the effort you've made over the past few years. There's still time to make decisions and point your life in a more fruitful direction. It's good to identify and find ways to protect what's yours, as well as to weed out anything less desirable.

Monkey natives, you are at the beginning of your Summer. There are sprouts taking root everywhere. Many things you have tried now begin yielding results. This is the year you need to be discerning, and try not to be everything to every person; nor should you try to take on every project alone. A good manager knows when to delegate.

Rooster (or Cock), you are in your last year of Spring. You have planted many new seeds over the past couple of years. Look at what is sprouting and determine if you're happy with it. You still have time to try new things, reinvent yourself, and make progress on your goals.

Dog natives, you are entering your second year of Spring. You are creating new options for yourself, but may not yet see much in the way of results. This is an excellent time to study and improve your skills. Follow your heart and plant seeds for what you want to do with your life. The sprouts are coming soon.

Rat

January 31, 1900–February 18, 1901: Yang Metal Rat

February 18, 1912–February 5, 1913: Yang Water Rat

February 5, 1924–January 24, 1925: Yang Wood Rat

January 24, 1936–February 10, 1937: Yang Fire Rat

February 10, 1948–January 28, 1949: Yang Earth Rat

January 28, 1960–February 14, 1961: Yang Metal Rat

February 15, 1972–February 2, 1973: Yang Water Rat

February 2, 1984–February 19, 1985: Yang Wood Rat

February 19, 1996–February 6, 1997: Yang Fire Rat

February 7, 2008–January 25, 2009: Yang Earth Rat

January 25, 2020–February 11, 2021: Yang Metal Rat

Rat Personality

I am a Rat. It's hard to admit. I really wanted to be one of the cute animals. But after exploring so much about the 12 different Chinese Zodiac signs, I have come to love and appreciate being a Rat.

Rats are very hard working, ambitious, and thrifty. The Rat individual is very focused on getting ahead. They want to achieve things in their life, and they want to get to the top first. They have a frugal reputation, but they are generous with those they love. They do love a bargain, and are good not only at saving money but making money as well.

In the traditional stories about the animals who make up the Chinese Zodiac, little Rat ran ahead of the other animals to be named the first of the Chinese Zodiac. This drive to move quickly is indicative of people born under this sign, and they desire to get there first and to be noticed.

Rat natives want positive recognition for their work and to be awarded honors for their achievements. That said, they also just love a challenge—but once the award is won, it's easily tossed aside as Rat focuses on taking the next step up the ladder.

Even though Rat may not be the cutest of the Chinese Zodiac menagerie, they are very well liked. They may start out acting in a reserved manner but become more social when they feel more comfortable in their surroundings (it's perfectly under-standable to be cautious when you're a little mouse...). You'll find Rat to be more talkative when topics relating to business and money are involved.

Rat makes a good friend. They may not have a lot of close friends, but those who make it to Rat's inner circle will be looked out for and supported. People born in the year of the Rat will gravitate to other successful people. They have trouble tolerating lazy people, and can't be bothered with anyone who wants a free ride.

Reading a Rat's feelings is easy. When they are upset (and they are easily irritated), they can be critical. They also tend to compare and contrast everything. This helps them identify and locate the best of everything—from bargains to loyal friends. Rats are good at writing and communication. They have excellent memories and are always asking questions.

Rats like to accumulate, although it varies from Rat to Rat what exactly they are collecting. Some Rats accumulate money, others material things, and still others gather social or business contacts. Rat is adaptable and has good intuition, so they can quickly determine whether there will be a benefit in any specific situation.

Because Rat is the smallest of the animals of the Chinese Zodiac, safety and self-preservation are considered paramount. They can sense danger, but Rat finds it hard to heed the warnings if they simultaneously smell opportunity and potential success. Rat needs only to follow their gut and finish what they start to end up the wealthiest of any of the signs.

How to use your Lucky Days: *On these days plan to take important actions, make vital phone calls, send emails. These are days when your energy and luck are high.*

Rat: Predictions for 2019

January: *[note: This month there is a Solar Eclipse on January 5th, and a Lunar Eclipse on January 21st. Check out the section on Eclipses for more details. Your Lucky Days are 6, 12, 18, 24 and 30.]*

The year begins with a need to sit quietly and formulate your plan. Rat natives are quick to take action but unplanned action usually yields small results. This month consider taking up daily meditation, or brainstorm .with a group of friends once a week. Join a mastermind group to get outside input.

A person in a position of power will notice you're doing a good job.

Finances are improving this month. You feel you need to shift how you are using your resources (or how others are spending your money). This month watch for unauthorized charges on bank cards. Your fast action will save you lots.

In relationships it's time for you to put yourself and your needs first. Others may balk at this and even call you selfish—though you are nowhere near deserving that label. This is your opportunity to acknowledge you are valuable and worthy of love.

A prediction you made last month about a teacher or education matter comes true.

February: *[note: Happy Lunar New Year on February 5th. Your Lucky Days this monh are 5 (super lucky day), 11, 17 and 23.]*

As February rolls around, you find the plans you carefully crafted last month are falling apart. Don't worry, this is part of the process. Like any hike up a mountain, there will be switchbacks. Sometimes seeing what's not working helps you find your path forward. Continue your meditations and prayers.

A wrong turn on the way to a meeting reveals an opportunity. You may be determined this month to "invest in yourself." It may be prudent to make purchases which help you become more educated or qualified in the context of your work or to spend to make connections (perhaps by attending a conference or seminar.) Get creative and ask yourself if there's a way to achieve your goal without spending the money—or is it possible you can have someone else pay for it?

Part of a dream you recall actually happens to a friend of ours.

In matters of the heart, you feel a little bruised. However, your needs have been noticed by others, and you will see friends and family members come to your aid (even if they are not exactly the person you were hoping would come to your aid.) If you're looking for love, be out in the world where you can be seen. Love is looking for you too.

March: *[note: Mercury is retrograde from March 6th to March 29th. See the section on Mercury retrograde for more information. Uranus moves into Taurus on March 6th – Time for change. Your Lucky Days are 1, 7, 13, 19, 25 and 31.]*

Now things are starting to take shape. You're seeing progress on your big goals, and also able to see where you've been playing it too small. Despite what's going on the world you have all the resources you need to make what you want happen. Picture what you want and you will see it manifest.

Your actions lead to money this month. You may feel things have been slow out of the gate this year, but now you're starting to see the results you have envisioned. Career opportunities are available (if you want them). You can consider a job change or the offer of a promotion within your company. If you own a business, some unexpected publicity helps you a lot.

You receive heart-warming compliments from a stranger (wearing a hat).

In your love life, positive energy is flowing toward you. However, there could be an aspect of the relationship one or both of you have decided needs to change to make things better.

April: *[note: Jupiter goes retrograde on April 10th, Pluto goes retrograde on April 24th and Saturn goes retrograde on April 29th. Your Lucky Days are 6, 12, 18, and 30.]*

Taking care of your body is highlighted this month. Often personal appearance affects how you feel about yourself. This month simply acting with more confidence makes you more attractive. Stand up straight, walk tall, and you'll be noticed and supported by the right people.

An unexpected invoice throws your finances for a curve this month. This could be something like a blown water heater, a friend who needs a loan, or a last minute trip (fun, but an unplanned expense). You may need to do some overtime or move some money from one account to another. Dust off your Feng Shui cures for prosperity to bring in extra cash.

You make an impulsive phone call and it leads to something you've been seeking for some time.

Love is brewing but not yet revealed this month. The walls you surround yourself with for safety are coming down, and love will be walking in your door before you know it. Keep in mind what you want in a relationship. There's no need to compromise on what's important to you. Love is coming.

If you're already in a relationship, you will sense your partnership growing stronger now.

May: *[note: Your Lucky Days are 6, 12, 18, 24, and 30.]*

There's a lot of motion in your life now. You had an idea—it just popped into your head—and now your life feels as if it's been turned upside down. And you're loving it! This new idea may affect your career or your home life, or it may be such a significant change that every aspect of your life will be different from now on. Congratulations! You've had a breakthrough.

Letting go of a cherished item brings a windfall.

Love is here and you're too busy to notice. Because Rat natives can be motivated by both a desire for success and a fear of failure, you're focused on other aspects of your life now. This has left your partner feeling lonely and a little bit neglected. Show up with a small gift and you'll see a smile again.

If you're not in a relationship and want to find love, don't toss out that party invitation. It's time now to schedule being out in the world meeting new people.

A compliment you pay someone else comes back to you three-fold.

June: *[note: Neptune goes retrograde on June 21st. Your Lucky Days are 5, 11, 17, 23, and 29.]*

This month you are in inclined to have a falling out with a sibling or neighbor. Often times internal stress can make you outwardly irritable leading to you voicing your complaints a little too loudly. Rat natives are known to be smooth talkers, this is a time to use that ability.

Handle family heirlooms with care. Move something to a place where it will be safe from accidents.

Money opportunities are within your grasp this month. You would do well to meditate, visualize, pray or light candles to give this energy a boost. Focus your energy on your goal of money coming in.

Resist the temptation for extra spending this month. Even if the deal sounds amazing, it's better to concentrate on money flowing in rather than resources flowing out.

Love is patiently waiting for you to catch up. Your partner sees how hard you're working, and appreciates you being in their life. The words may not always be spoken, but Rat Natives can feel the love just by looking around and seeing everything the people who love you are doing for you.

If you're looking for love, it's waiting for you behind a friendly face. Ask your friends (especially a brown-haired individual who cares about you) to introduce to you their friends.

July: *[note: Mercury is retrograde from July 8th to August 1st. See the section on Mercury retrograde for more information. There's a Solar Eclipse on July 2nd and a Lunar Eclipse on July 16th. Check out the section on Eclipses for more details. Your Lucky Days are 5, 11, 17, 23, and 29.]*

This month you feel a strong desire to let go of everything that's no longer working for you. This likely includes habits you've had for years, but it could also be behavioral and response patterns you formed in childhood. You finally realize how these ideas have imprisoned you. You feel like a person being fully aware of your world for the first time; you suddenly understand how you've been limiting your own potential. Now you are free.

At the beginning of the month, money seems to be playing "hide-and-seek" with you. However, in a week or two the steady flow returns with increased pressure.

If you own a business, you could notice a sudden increase due to some word of mouth advertising. Take a small portion of this extra money and go have some fun.

Communication is a little off this month, and this could create some bumps in your relationships. All this can be avoided if you do some active listening and make a little extra effort to understand what is going on in the lives of the important people in your life. Don't waste energy on blame, instead make a little effort to imagine yourself in their shoes; when you have the full picture, love will prevail.

This month marks the ending of a family tradition (or an old family curse). Relief or release paves the way for something new and wonderful to come into your life.

August: *[note: Mercury moves forward again on August 2nd. Both Jupiter and Uranus move forward again August 11th. Your Lucky Days are 4, 10, 16, 22, and 28.]*

This is quite a challenging month. The work you've been focused on as part of the process of manifesting your goals for the future is blocked by your current responsibilities. This is the classic "not enough time" scenario.

Some of the tasks in front of you now can be delegated, but some of your obligations just have to be done by you alone. This means that whatever you're attempting to bring into being—whether a business, art project, home repair, or investment—just simply has to wait right now.

Forgiving an individual (most likely an older relative) lifts a big burden from your shoulders, and gives you the freedom to move forward.

Those who take risks have the greatest possibility of gain, and Rat natives are risk takers (at least when it comes to taking well-calculated risks, nothing foolhardy). This month, fortune favors the bold. You can ask for the sale, set up the meeting, negotiate for the job. Think big and follow up with contact or a contract. This is an opportunity you don't want to miss.

Romance is in the air. If you're looking for love, you have a high probability of finding it this month. Ask out people you're interested in. Say "yes" when you are asked.

If you're already in a relationship, it's time to schedule a date night. Do something you find fun. Go dancing, attend a party, or walk on the beach—absolutely get out of the house!

September: *[note: Saturn moves forward again on September 18th. Your Lucky Days are 3, 9, 15, 21, and 27.]*

This month you receive recognition for a job well done. You're naturally a hard worker, and are generally satisfied with the material rewards, but it's nice every once in a while to receive credit where credit is due. For a change welcome the acknowledgment of your success; don't wave it away. Recognition like this brings more success in the future.

If you're in business, it may be time to raise your prices. If you are employed, consider negotiating for a pay increase. If you're looking for a job, this is the month it manifests.

A trip to a park—actually any place out in nature—reminds you of the abundance all around you in the world. Meditating on or feeling grateful for the beauty all around you helps you attract abundance for yourself and for your family.

'Happiness' is the right word to choose to describe your relationship now. You feel content with every circumstance and aspect of your relationship, these days, no matter what.

If you've been looking for love, this is the month you become fully aware of the benefits of being single; indeed you wonder why you've been considering giving it all up in search of a partner. That's when love shows up.

October: *[note: Pluto moves forward again on October 3rd. Your Lucky Days are 9, 15, 21, and 27.]*

You're working hard this month with single-minded focus on decluttering, organizing, and being more efficient with your time. Other people may try to distract and dissuade you from all of this effort, but you're on a mission (and a beneficial one at that). By the end of the month, you've made great strides in eliminating paper clutter, selling off unneeded items, and letting go of time-wasting projects and people. Way to go!

Self-criticism is nothing more than a bad habit. Let it go now.

Money is flowing in at a steady pace. There's a chance of a small bonus or unexpected payment in the middle of the month.

If you have a business, prepare to expand. If you're employed, notice what jobs are available now—especially within your field or organization.

As usual Rat natives put relationships on the back burner when there's work to do. But this month it's wise to schedule time to spend with loved ones. You value companionship and cooperation, so making a little extra effort to accommodate them is worth it.

If you're looking for love, it can show up for you via a business contact or through an old friend. Make sure people know you're looking for love so they can introduce you to new people.

November: *[note: Mercury goes retrograde from November 1st to November 21st. See the section on Mercury retrograde for more information. Neptune moves forward again on November 27th. Your Lucky Days are 2, 8, 14, 20 and 26.]*

This is a month of significant change. As a result of the meditation or inner work you've been doing, you've uncovered some fantastic insights to change your life. This is a month to let go of resentments and grudges so you can move forward. The action of releasing past ill feelings will accelerate your progress moving forward through blocks which previously held you back. People around you will be surprised and impressed.

Spend even just 10 minutes appreciating and valuing your self-worth; don't be surprised when a new opportunity shows up in less than a week.

Career energy is intense this month. You may have been having issues with a boss or team leader. This situation comes to a head this month and will fall in your favor if you respond with the end game in mind. Don't focus on short-term goals just to satisfy your ego. Respond diplomatically and you will win this game.

Love is all around you this month. You have opportunities to meet a wonderful match. Make sure you're out in the world.

If you're already in a relationship, you will find yourselves drawing closer together. Your individual lives may not be that smooth, but together you form a united front and will succeed.

December: *[note: There is a Solar Eclipse on December 26th. Check out the section on Eclipses for more details. Your Lucky Days are 2, 8, 14, and 20.]*

This is a high activity month because of the solar eclipse—even more so because it's December. There are projects to be finished and lots of people who need your input or an answer NOW.

You will receive a message about your life path this month. It likely comes in the form of a TV show episode or a passage in a book.

Your finances act like a bucking bronco this month, up and down and up again. There are surprise wins and unexpected losses. It's okay to take risks this month, just don't bet the farm.

Rat natives are known for their generosity around the holidays, but try to keep spending in check. A shiny object has enchanted you. But there's no need to start the next year with debts from the last.

Romance is centered around the bedroom this month for Rat natives, for both those in a long-term relationship, and those who are just dating at this point. You have a chance of greater intimacy and understanding.

If you're looking for love this month, check out comedy clubs, nightclubs and places where you can dance until dawn.

January 2020: *[note: There is a Lunar Eclipse on January 10th. Check out the section on Eclipses for more details. Uranus moves forward again on January 11th. Your Lucky Days are 1, 7, 13, 19, 25, and 31.]*

January marks the last few weeks of your 12-year cycle. This is the time to release any old stuff so you can welcome in your new cycle with a clean slate. Besides decluttering, it's a good idea to cut cords with those people who don't support you. Remove the negative energy from your life. Look to keep that which enriches you and brings joy, and leave the rest behind.

Your thoughts create your reality. This month make sure the positive thoughts outnumber the negative.

Finances are good this month. However, some related aspects benefit from your attention. It's a good idea to change passwords on financial accounts. See whether you can get a better deal on interest rates. Increase your automatic savings plans so more money is being transferred into savings every month. This will help you start the new year off in prosperity mode.

This is the strongest month of your year for moving an intimate relationship forward. If you've wanted to take a new relationship to the next level, you can now bring the subject up.

If you're already in a love relationship, it's time to bring back the romance. Even something as simple as taking a hike to a new place will spark some romantic excitement.

Attract New Love

The lightning bolt of love can strike this year. This is a sudden, unexpected connection because you're open and willing to take a chance. To be "ready" for the surprise make sure you look your best when you're out and about. Even when just running errands be ready to meet new people and make connections. If you're hiding behind dark glasses, you could miss opportunities for love.

There is a chance you have already met the person, and an up-until-now platonic relationship can explode with sparks of love. This is again dependent on your general openness to love. Write out a list of the pros and cons of being in a relationship.

Cut the list in two and keep the list of pros in your pocket or wallet. Take the list of cons and start to work through these issues. As you find solutions to what you think will be problems you remove the blocks to what you want.

You may think you want to find your forever person, but if you've been looking for a while consider the next person you meet may just be a transition relationship, helping you move towards a long-term situation. Rat natives often talk about the security they want in a long-term relationship, but this type of relationship grows organically. They can't usually be spotted on the first date.

Burn a red candle in your bedroom about once a month to really stimulate the energy for bringing a love relationship into being. You can use a tea light or votive candle for this purpose, or you can choose a large pillar candle to burn over a series of days.

Burn the candle for an hour or two each night until the candle burns out. So, a large pillar candle or a jar candle could take all month to finish. But that's okay, the act of burning the candle over many days strengthens the energy. As you light the candle, visualize happy times together for the two of you in your new relationship.

If you don't feel comfortable burning candles in your home, you can use a battery operated or electric candle. Choose one that has a red base. Because this type of candle is not as powerful a cure as a real candle, it's helpful to "light" this candle each day. You don't need it on at night, as that might disturb sleep, instead keep it on during the day.

Enhance Existing Love

Overall the energy is positive for Rat natives when it comes to your love relationships. However, there may be periods when you feel out of step with your sweetheart. There may be times when you're working different schedules or business travel sends one of you away.

These apart times are challenging, and you may wonder if this is what your relationship will be like going forward. You weigh the risks of staying together while having this feeling of being disconnected. But what's really needed is your leadership in bringing the two of you together.

You are noticed by others and this draws the attention of your partner in perhaps a worried way. Your popularity can be seen as a threat now, where it may have been seen as cute before. There might be someone at work who is paying you more attention than usual.

Your partner is feeling uncertain, and this is putting a strain on the relationship especially around June or July. You would do well to give your special someone some reassurance by showing them your full attention at home.

There is a lot of energy helping you weather the mid-year storm, but you have to want to stay together. Sit and visualize how your relationship could be better. What changes would you and the other person need to make? Start by changing yourself. Later, when things improve you can gently suggest the changes you want your partner to make.

To bring greater harmony into your love life find a red, heart-shaped box. Place the box on your dresser in your bedroom and put small objects inside the box to represent different aspects of your relationship. You may place shells to remind you that this relationship makes you feel protected and at home. You may put mementos of past dates with your spouse (such as ticket stubs) in the box. You can find pictures of recent vacations together or places you want to travel to. Keep changing up the things you place in and take out of the box to keep the energy fresh.

Looking to Conceive?

What could be a sweeter fertility symbol than honey? The ancient Egyptians associated honey with love, happy marriage, and fertility. Honey was considered a gift from the divine.

To enhance fertility this year, place a jar of honey in your bedroom near the entrance (on a dresser or shelf), and pair it with a silver spoon. Give your partner a taste of honey to set the mood and attract conception energy. From Donna Stellhorn's eBook, A Path to Pregnancy: Ancient Secrets for the Modern Woman)

(From Donna Stellhorn's book, A Path to Pregnancy: Ancient Secrets for the Modern Woman)

Family and Kids

While you don't feel completely satisfied with your living situation or the house you're in, you will probably stay in this place for a while longer. This may be because you haven't really formed a vision of what's next. You are at the end of your 12-year cycle and it doesn't quite feel like the right time to let go. Signs and opportunities will show up from time to time all year tempting you to explore your choices. This may be because you need to travel to a possible new location to live; or you may hear from distant relatives, sharing information about all of the benefits of living nearer to them. For the most part, this year will bring thoughts and ideas, rather than the necessity of actually packing the moving boxes.

The end of a full cycle, such as this 12-year cycle, can bring losses. This is to help clear the way for new things to grow. Perhaps adult children are leaving home or going away to University. This would give you a chance to let go of "treasures" you've held onto for years (perhaps decades). Now, maybe you'll be thinking about a future where you want to downsize.

Be mindful of the people in your life, mend fences where you can, and visit loved ones who are older than you. These are all good things to do at the end of a major life cycle.

There is good energy this year around having a business at home. If you already have one going, look to expand either by adding an employee, contracting out some work, or bringing in a family member to help you. Consider rearranging the furniture in your office, and how you could use other rooms in your home to make money on the side.

To clear old energy out of your home and bring in positive family energy consider using Smudge Spray this year. Smudge Spray, also called Sage Spray, can be made by making a tea from white sage leaves and putting it in a spray bottle. This spray will stay fresh in your fridge for about three days. Smudge Spray you make yourself will smell very woodsy like sage. You can also find commercially sold Smudge Spray created by some very good herbalists. This Smudge Spray usually has an alcohol base and a light floral scent. It lasts a long time and doesn't need to be refrigerated.

Use the spray at least once a month. Spray around doorways, especially the front and back door. Also, use it in the bedroom. Be careful spraying around delicate fabrics. Using Smudge Spray will help you clear the energy and bring in positive health vibes.

Money

It will be no surprise for you to hear you'll feel like you're chasing money this year. This is an energy Rat natives are very familiar with. You feel close to a breakthrough with this issue. But there are still a block or two you must overcome to make it big.

Think about how you create value for yourself in the marketplace. How do you present yourself to the world? It's less about your website and more about how you see yourself. How do you process your internal thought patterns? Confidence wins more deals than a good resume.

That said, you are on display this year. You have been working hard in your field and steadily rising to the top. You have opportunities you can parlay into real money. Don't gloss over these factors this year, because the opportunities coming up now may not be available to you next year (especially since this is the last year of your personal 12-year cycle—the last year to harvest whatever remains from the work of the past 12 years). So go BIG this year.

You also show income possibilities from side jobs and investments. In fact, Rat natives could make money through several sources this year. It's a good idea to take time each day and visualize opportunities coming to you. This way when chance shows up, or the person arrives with the deal, you'll notice and be ready.

Gold Flakes remind us of the accumulation of wealth and abundance through seemingly small actions. You can attract positive money energy by placing a vial of real gold flakes on a table near your front door. (Gold flakes are available in gem and mineral shops and online.)

Write out your money goals and place them under the vial of gold flakes. Every few days as you pass the table pick up the vial and shake it; watch the gold flakes sparkle in the light and think about your goals for a moment. This will increase the positive money energy.

Job or Career

While there are numerous opportunities for you in your career, you may feel a bit rudderless this year. You may sense you need a change, or the profession you're in is changing. There are constant demands for you to keep up with new developments at all times.

It's possible you face a situation where your industry is being phased out due to new technology or automation. This is a closing cycle for you, and this can mean that in a year or so you may be doing something different. It's not necessarily a completely new job, but you can expect significant aspects of what you do now to change and the income from your position may be adjusted.

But as mentioned previously there are many opportunities for the wise, restless Rat native who wants to push the boundaries of what you think you are capable of. Generally, you are cautious but in this last year of your 12-year cycle, now is the best time to take a big step out of your comfort zone and reach for the stars.

It's important to focus on your own efforts. Don't sit by the phone waiting for someone to ask you. Don't wait for headhunters or HR reps to connect with you. It's up to you to make the call, or check out the appropriate job search websites, check your social media sites, and keep an eye on what is going on in your industry. By March things will start to really pop, and though there may be a small setback in July, you will be rolling forward again by September.

In choosing a Feng Shui cure, remember the universal rule: "Like attracts like." This concept allows us to use representations of things to attract the real thing. For example, as you are looking for your new job, visualize that you will be showered with money when they make you the offer.

To complete the picture, find a wind chime made of Chinese coins. Choose a chime with many coins—This is to represent a shower of money.

Hang the wind chime outside your front door or if you're in an apartment, hang it from your balcony/patio. As you hear the coins tinkle and chime in the breeze, imagine the sound of raindrops showering money on your roof and your windows.

While it's best to hang the chime outside your front door, if this isn't a viable option where you live, hang your wind chime on your back porch or balcony.

Education

Time to sign up for work-related and technology classes this year. Any degrees you complete will give a boost to your career. In fact, this year it's wise to try to finish any degree you've been working on for more than five years. Mostly you will want to sign up for practical, hands-on classes which are (or could be) directly related to your industry. Look for certification programs you can do quickly and inexpensively. You might even be able to avail yourself of free University classes online.

There may be some difficulty about obtaining or expanding your student loan debt this year; much can be resolved if you take action, connect with people who can answer your questions or address your concerns, and pay attention to the details of your process. You may need to complete some paperwork, or there may have been a change in the status of a loan.

Be wary this year of paying for expensive classes (of any kind) especially to private education firms, online colleges or extensively hyped courses offered by "experts in the field..." Look for free options this year. Remember, you can also learn what you need to know just by watching videos on YouTube.

Legal Matters

You are lucky in legal matters and contracts this year. While this doesn't mean you can sign without reading the fine print—always read the contract—you can negotiate better terms for the agreements you're making. This includes leases, real estate contracts, and employment agreements. You can consider licensing agreements, book, and representation contracts as well.

Health and Well-Being

You enjoy good health energy this year. You have been taking better care of yourself and the results have been beneficial.

You've seen improvement on all levels. This year you will have more energy and vitality than you've had in previous years. It's as if you're getting younger! That's not to say you can't slip back into old, bad habits—be especially mindful of this in July and December. It's easier to stay on a path then to leave it for a while and then try to return.

You'll have opportunities for more physical exercise, perhaps offered as a benefit at your work, or as a side benefit of the work you do. Your company might offer a health club membership or monthly free massages for employees. Perhaps you've chosen a standing desk or treadmill desk, and now you're putting in extra miles every day. You may consider getting together with work colleagues and going to yoga class together.

Finding and maintaining your work/life balance can be the primary source of stress for Rat natives this year. There are so many great opportunities for you, but you can't sign up for everything and expect to also have time for rest and recuperation. Your work schedule has been infringing on your home and family life for some time. It's time to restore balance by adjusting your schedule and learning to say "No."

Palo Santo is a fragrant wood from a particular tree that grows on the coast of South America. Its name means "Wood of the Saints." When burned, this wood (Bursera graveolens) creates a delightful scent—a mix of lemon and pine, with just a hint of mint. Palo Santo wood comes in the form of little sticks and can be found in spiritual shops and online.

Burn Palo Santo wood in your kitchen, family room or bedroom to bring healing vibrations into the house. It's excellent to burn before doing meditation or when resting. The people of the Inca empire believed that burning this magical wood removed negativity and brought good fortune. It will help bring good energy to your home.

Ox

February 19, 1901–February 7, 1902: Yin Metal Ox

February 6, 1913–January 25, 1914: Yin Water Ox

January 25, 1925–February 12, 1926: Yin Wood Ox

February 11, 1937–January 30, 1938: Yin Fire Ox

January 29, 1949–February 16, 1950: Yin Earth Ox

February 15, 1961–February 4, 1962: Yin Metal Ox

February 3, 1973–January 22, 1974: Yin Water Ox

February 20, 1985–February 8, 1986: Yin Wood Ox

February 7, 1997–January 27, 1998: Yin Fire Ox

January 26, 2009–February 13, 2010: Yin Earth Ox

February 12, 2021–January 31, 2022: Yin Metal Ox

Ox Personality

Slow and steady, the Ox is always making progress towards success and prosperity. Ox is the hardest working of all the signs of the Chinese Zodiac. Once they accept a task, they toil and toil until it's done. They like to finish one thing before starting another. Often, new projects will sit and gather dust while Ox completes any previous obligations—no matter how exciting, or how potentially profitable or beneficial the new project may be.

Those born in the year of the Ox are highly intelligent and resourceful, although these qualities may not be apparent as the Ox native is often introverted and shy. Well, the truth is, they're shy until the need to be otherwise arises—then we will see them stand up in front of a group and take on a leadership role. As an Ox, one of the largest and strongest animals of the Chinese Zodiac, he or she is never intimidated and rarely at a loss for words.

Ox individuals like a routine. They will stick to a certain way of doing things and may find it extremely difficult to make a change. In some ways, this is the key to Ox's success. They use tried and true methods and hard work to create the outcomes they want to manifest.

Ox never jumps in, or relies on "luck" to succeed in their endeavors (or worse, simply "wings it"). Their tenacity and dedication to a specific outcome are what bring Ox the most satisfaction and the most success.

Those born in the year of the Ox are patient and understanding with others. They take pride in being a good and loyal friend. On the other hand, they are not particularly good at being a romantic partner; it wouldn't occur to them to fly you off to Paris at a moment's notice to enjoy a weekend vacation. However, once Ox does fall in love and marries, they are in it for the long haul. They are faithful and prove to be good partners.

Ox, like buffalo, cannot be stopped once they begin moving. If an Ox person gets angry, expect to be run over. On the other hand, the Ox native can get stuck. They can walk the same path, doing the same things for so long that they wear a rut so deep they can't climb out of it.

This can occur in the course of their career or their daily work, but the same pattern can also show up in their personal or intimate relationships. An Ox can hold onto grievances far longer than any other sign. You can easily identify an unhappy Ox: they work all the time.

Because Ox is so self-disciplined, they expect similar behavior from other people in their lives. Ox will patiently instruct others, but should someone refuse to listen or pay attention to their good advice, Ox will turn away, head out, and never look back.

Ox doesn't believe in shortcuts, not for others and definitely not for themselves. They tend to build things that last, designs that are copied around the world. Everything Ox receives, he or she has earned, and no one can say otherwise.

Those born in the year of the Ox do not like to be in debt. They want to settle accounts as soon as possible, preferably never get into debt in the first place! When they receive something as a gift, their gratitude overflows. That being said, Ox is also likely to remember an injustice for a very, very long, long, long time.

How to use your Lucky Days: *On these days plan to take important actions, make vital phone calls, send emails. These are days when your energy and luck are high.*

Ox: Predictions for 2019

January: *[note: This month there is a Solar Eclipse on January 5th and a Lunar Eclipse on January 21st. Check out the section on Eclipses for more details. Your Lucky Days are 1, 7, 13, 19, 25 and 31.]*

It's time for a new beginning. You're seeing a mostly clear path towards what you want to do. Unfortunately, Ox natives don't usually like change. You're more than willing to make small shifts, but it never seems practical to get rid of things you've spent so much time creating. However, this month there will be a significant change involving home and family; it will bring happiness, Take the plunge.

This month you have good luck in the realm of money. You feel motivated to make more, and it's flowing in. You reduce spending, cut bills, and eliminate extra costs—all of this contributes to you feeling more abundant. This is a good month to ask for a raise or to secure a bonus.

If you own a business, this is a good time to advertise.

Romance is in the air this month. You and your honey may lock yourselves in the bedroom and not come out. If you're in a new relationship this month, you may seal the deal, taking it to a whole new level.

Your sexual attraction is high this month. If you're looking for love, you are likely to find it.

February: *[note: Happy Lunar New Year on February 5th. Your Lucky Days are 6, 12, 18, and 24.]*

As the new Lunar New Year officially begins, you feel ready for change. You're decluttering and toss out all the things that haven't brought you joy (this includes some people/clients/customers). This is a good thing. The more change you create in your life this month, the more benefits you will receive all year.

Money owed to you is flowing in. You may be receiving benefits from projects you worked on in the previous year. You may even pay off some large debt this month. Any progress in that area is worth celebrating.

This is a good month to start a side business or expand your current business. It's also wise to hire help this month as this will help you grow more quickly.

The intense sexual energy you were enjoying last month continues. The seeds planted previously are sprouting into a very pleasant routine of more physical contact and shared experience.

It's easy to meet a new love this month if that's on your list, especially if you go to new places and start meeting new people. Visualize what you want and then see how quickly the Universe brings it to you.

March: *[note: Mercury is retrograde from March 6th to March 29th. See the section on Mercury retrograde for more information. Uranus moves into Taurus on March 6th—Time for change. Your Lucky Days are 2, 8, 14, 20, and 26.]*

This is a very strong month for travel. This could be an actual trip, but you could also be expanding your mind through reading or accessing visual media. You might be contacted by people who live far away, possibly traveling to visit. People from your past reach out to you to make contact again.

This is another good month for finances. Be sure to write in your gratitude journal about what's been good so far this year.

If you own a business, you'll find word-of-mouth advertising is working well. Rethink your marketing material but don't order anything new until Mercury is out of retrograde motion.

If you're employed, you are receiving some very positive recognition that could lead to a better position later this year.

If you're looking for a job, you'll have some great opportunities. Don't waste time wondering if you're qualified, instead just apply and see what they say.

When it comes to romance, you are looking for a change. This doesn't necessarily mean a break-up, but you'd like to sit down and have a heart-to-heart.

If you haven't found your special someone, it's time to have the talk with yourself. Do you really want a relationship? Or, is staying single just too tempting?

April: *[note: Jupiter goes retrograde on April 10th, Pluto goes retrograde on April 24th and Saturn goes retrograde on April 29th. Your Lucky Days are 1, 7, 13, 19, and 25.]*

This month you feel like indulging yourself and that, of course, is fine as long as it doesn't upset the good habits you've established. One night out or an extra scoop sundae won't throw you off track if you are mindful about what you're doing.

This month lots of friends are looking to connect with you. Consider accepting an invitation to attend a party or social gathering, even though most Ox natives are homebodies.

Back up your technology this month just to be on the safe side. A storm in April or local power issues could mess with your tech.

When it comes to money-making, you have more energy than usual. Your thoughts are full of new ideas. It's a good idea to set your ideas in motion and see what they bring. Look for help with social media or websites to get yourself up and running. Outside financing is also a possibility.

Lots of friendship energy this month surrounds you this month, less so for one-on-one relationships. This is a good month to meet new people and allow the time to have something blossom.

If you're in a relationship, it's time to remind each other why you're friends as well as being a couple. Compliment each other and do it often. Watch your relationship grow.

May: *[note: Your Lucky Days are 1, 7, 13, 19, and 25.]*

After so much social activity last month you welcome some alone time now. You want to just curl up on the sofa and watch some favorite TV shows. Meditation, yoga, and long walks are also excellent this month to help you feel more balanced again. Consider a trip to a beach, lake, or river to rejuvenate your soul.

You feel like being a free spender this month—something highly unusual for Ox natives. Some of what you're buying are things which have been needed for a long time, and other indulgences are going to make wonderful additions to your life.

This month it's a good idea to spend some time meditating on your career and/or business. Get a clear vision of where your industry is heading so you can see if this is where you should be putting your energy, or whether it might be time to look for an exit.

You're want to sit back and watch old, romantic movies, think about the past and eat chocolate this month. You could be soothing hurt feelings or just feeling lonely but either way, this just isn't the best plan. Try to get out among friends. Reach out to your contacts on social media. Take a class. Things will be better soon.

June: *[note: Neptune goes retrograde on June 21st. Your Lucky Days are 6, 12, 18, 24, and 30.]*

Time for a new look. Go ahead and change hairstyles, make some new fashion choices, or even go as far as to have plastic surgery. A change will do you good. Look over some new exercise routines and diet and see if you would benefit from some changes there. Ox natives can get stuck in routines. This month you have both opportunity and desire to take the leap.

You feel happy as money flows in. Except for a blip here and there you've been very prudent with your money. It would be a good idea to check investments and see if you need to shift funds. This month you show money from several sources. This could be a side job or selling something of value.

Clear the energy of resentment this month with smudging or journaling. It's a waste of your time to hold on to this negativity anymore.

Your relationship is back on track. Whatever kept you feeling lonely last month has passed and you feel connected again. You and your lover are spending time at home. Communication between the two of you is good.

If you're looking for love, this is a fine month to join an online dating site or a social meetup. Your powers of attraction are high this month. Don't waste it doing the same old thing. Try something new.

July: *[note: Mercury is retrograde from July 8th to August 1st. See the section on Mercury retrograde for more information. There's a Solar Eclipse on July 2nd and a Lunar Eclipse on July 16th. Check out the section on Eclipses for more details. Your Lucky Days are 6, 12, 18, 24, and 30.]*

After making changes in yourself last month, you are interested in helping others change. Not all of your suggestions will be appreciated, so be gentle or better yet, lead by example.

While finances are good this month, you want them to be better, so you're keeping a sharp eye on what can be cut from the budget. You want to put a larger portion of income into savings.

You have opportunities to sell some of your creative work be. You could also sell some possessions. Nothing is more enjoyable than having cash in hand, except perhaps having cash in the bank. You can declutter your stuff and sell it on eBay, but wait until your family is ready to declutter their stuff too before you start selling it off.

You feel a strong need to have a conversation with your partner about how they treat you in this relationship. Sometimes you feel like you're doing more than your share. Ox natives can be self-contained, leaving little for another person to do for them. Remember, the one who gives is the one who bonds.

August: *[note: Mercury moves forward again on August 2nd. Both Jupiter and Uranus move forward again August 11th. Your Lucky Days are 5, 11, 17, 23, and 29.]*

Home life is highlighted this month. You may have decided to sell your home, or other changes may be happening, such as someone moving in or moving out (pets count here, too). If you've been unhappy with your dwelling, you will find a great new place. Or you may consider a renovation project to make your current place a home you love. After a bunch of work and shifting things around, everything works out.

Money is not your focus this month so you may not be your usual careful self when it comes to your pocketbook. It's okay, it's only once in a while, but sometimes, especially after Mercury retrograde, you can discover things like banking and receipts have piled up instead of being in their proper place. It's time to get everything deposited, filed or posted. Also, check to see if insurance needs to be upped or changed.

You feel happy and satisfied about the energy exchange with a person younger than yourself. This is a friendship that will last.

The strong pull of home is keeping you and your partner there. You may be doing projects together. Your love is strong, and sharing the process of finding or making a home is bringing you closer.

If you're looking for love, however, you have to face the challenge of not wanting to leave the house. Look for love in your neighborhood by taking walks, meeting the neighbors, or organizing a street sale.

September: *[note: Saturn moves forward again on September 18th. Your Lucky Days are 4, 10, 16, 22, and 28.]*

Ox natives are tireless workers so when the inner call to have fun happens, it's an excellent idea to heed it. This month is the time to do something you enjoy. It might be a good idea to brainstorm some ideas with friends and family. They would love to see you put down your work for a little while and join in their social activities.

You're not really a risk taker. In fact, to get you to step out on a limb, you need to hear a really compelling argument. This month, some opportunities require a calculated risk. Small risks this month could bring you a large reward later this year.

Your inner guidance system is working well this month. Trust yourself to make the right choices.

You're seeing your partner in a whole new light. It's like falling in love again. Old arguments may still be there but, you're above petty stuff and you accept your spouse/lover for who they are… shortcomings and all.

If you're looking for love, this is one of the best months of the year to get yourself out there. Use all possible means to let the world know you are ready to have the right person in your life.

A light-eyed stranger or celebrity gives you inspiration in pursuing your life's work.

October: *[note: Pluto moves forward again on October 3rd. Your Lucky Days are 4, 10, 16, 22, and 28.]*

You can be quite the creature of habit, from your morning routine to the brand of nut butter you buy. This month, it's a good idea to examine your habits and see if you might benefit from a change.

Consider something simple like journaling, and give yourself five minutes a day to jot down what you're grateful for. Or try getting up 30 minutes earlier than usual and taking a walk. Shut off the news for a week and see how you feel. Look at how you can change your routine and you'll be amazed at the results.

This month a small windfall is possible. This could be money owed to you, perhaps a royalty or found money. This shows you're lucky this month, and this fortunate energy applies to your career in general. Look to have a meeting with your boss about your future with the company.

If you own a business, consider negotiating a partnership with a compatible company to do cooperative advertising.

You're feeling a little grumpy about the household chores this month. It may be because you're doing them all by yourself. This could be because your partner is too busy with their job or travels. A conversation late in the month will yield good results.

Clear intent sends a message to the Universe. Choose a day to focus on visualizing your goals once an hour for five hours. Positive results will happen.

November: *[note: Mercury goes retrograde from November 1st to November 21st. See the section on Mercury retrograde for more information. Neptune moves forward again on November 27th. Your Lucky Days are 3, 9, 15, 21, and 27.]*

Travel and visits from friends and relatives are at the top of your list this month. With Mercury retrograde nearly all month, things can be chaotic with lost luggage, missed communications, and random arguments. Thank goodness you have the patience of an Ox native. Remember to maintain flexibility in your plans (and to purchase travel insurance). Things get better towards the end of the month.

Finances get a boost as a result of a chance meeting. Try networking, or reach out to someone you don't know who is in your industry.

While your relationship is holding together because you're a devoted lover, you're at the end of your tether about how stuck your partner is in some area of their life. You can't seem to find a way to encourage them to move forward. The secret this month is: they are your mirror! As you get unstuck, they magically get unstuck too.

This goes for the single Ox natives too. If you've been looking for love all year and not finding it, look for your mirror in your single friends and uncover your own roadblocks.

There is some truth in a critique you have received from a distant relative or acquaintance. Find the piece of it that's true before discarding their comments and opinions.

December: *[note: There is a Solar Eclipse on December 26th. Check out the section on Eclipses for more details. Your Lucky Days are 3, 9, 15, 21, and 27.]*

There is a lot of energy around spirituality this month for you. You are a practical person and sometimes you don't take the time to hear the music of the Universe. This month the melody is loud and clear. It will give you the answers to your questions if you listen. Write down your questions and place them under your pillow. In a day or two, you will wake up with the answers.

This month your finances could improve if you would just promote yourself. Ox natives are known for their self-effacing nature. They would prefer their talents and accomplishments to be noticed by others. But this month putting yourself forward either via a resume or by raising your prices will bring you rewards.

People love you right now. Realize this energy and enjoy.

This is a grand month for all types of relationships if you are willing to do a little work (to sing the Native Ox's favorite song). Sometimes self-reflection helps you figure out why a relationship is not going as smoothly as you would like. You'll have a realization, and it will change how you see your partner's behavior; things get better as a result.

If you're looking for love, take a chance and ask someone to coffee. There's no reward for procrastination.

January 2020: *[note: There is a Lunar Eclipse on January 10th. Check out the section on Eclipses for more details. Uranus moves forward again on January 11th. Your Lucky Days are 2, 8, 14, 20, and 26.]*

Your reputation precedes you this month and helps open the doors so you can make a new acquaintance, someone of considerable power. This accomplished individual can assist you with your goals.

There is a lot of energy around education this month. You may be asked to teach a class, or to take one (perhaps as part of continuing education at work.) You feel motivated to jump right in. This can lead to meeting interesting people and/or adding to your skills in the context of new technology.

An attractive person with wild wisps of hair gives you information to help move you forward in a business or legal matter. Make a note of what the advice they offer, or the things they say.

Even though you both sit on the same sofa, you don't feel as connected as usual to your partner. Something is on their mind, something they're not willing to talk about...yet. Just hold the space for them until they're ready. Once they start communicating their thoughts, things will improve.

If you're looking for love, you're projecting a lot of charisma! Go, be in places where you can be noticed.

Attract New Love

Love comes in the form of a friendly face for you this year. This may mean you already know the person who wants to be in a relationship with you. Or, something seems very familiar about a new person you meet. This kind of connection—a spiritual bond—is possible now. In your busy world, it can take a considerable amount of patience to search for this type of love, but Ox natives are more than up for the challenge.

This year it's okay to trust the right person will find you. But this means you can't hide at home or spend all your time at work the way you might prefer. You must be out in the world, being social. Ox natives love their routines, but this well-worn path hasn't brought you what you've wanted up until now in the area of love. It's time to venture into new places. Perhaps you need to have lunch at new restaurants, shop in different malls, even take a new route to work; be aware of places you might want to visit at another time.

Ox natives are known for their strength and resolve. However, you have probably been hurt in the past, and are now both looking for love while simultaneously trying to protect yourself. It's hard to move forward when you are afraid of finding yourself in pain. You may not even realize you're not as vulnerable as you were in the past. Much of the pain you felt before was because everything happened so unexpectedly. It won't happen again this year; you are much more watchful and aware of negative signs.

To start the flow of new love coming into your life hang a mobile in your bedroom. A mobile is hanging art that moves at the slightest breeze. You can find one with hearts or one that allows you to attach pictures or small pieces of paper with affirmations on them. Hang the mobile in your bedroom in a place where you won't hit your head on it. Or for a very simple mobile, you can make yourself, hang colorful hearts from pieces of thread suspended from the ceiling. Choose an odd number of hearts for the most potent energy.

Enhance Existing Love

While there are challenges to your love life this year, you are sticking it out through thick and thin. Yes, sometimes your partner drives you crazy. You like things the way you like them, and you have a well-thought-out plan for moving forward (in your own time). So why you're beloved insists on doing things their way makes no sense to you—especially with regard to a contract, legal matter, or travel situation. Arguments can occur, then the energy dissipates and you will both feel happy again.

Recognize some of the struggles you face are a result of your resistance to new ideas. Your partner may suggest things that don't sit well with you, but their suggestions are based in love. Consider that before stomping around the house, demanding they acknowledge you are right.

Between arguments, there will be plenty of happy times and ts of joy this year. You feel more spiritually connected to your partner. The Year of the Earth Pig increases your intuition and, you seem, at times, to be totally in sync with your beloved. Make a note of these times, journal about them, and talk to your friends about how you feel. Do this and you will be able to return to this feeling over and over.

You can use little stuffed animals—especially teddy bears—this year when you want to attract more love into our life. Teddy bears have long been associated with comforting love.

When you're ready to enhance love in your life, take a sheet of paper and write down the three qualities you find important in your partnership. You may have more on your mind but start with three. A quality would be something like "they show me kindness," or "they do the dishes without me asking," or "they ask me how my day went." Do not list vague qualities like, "open-hearted," or "generous," or "loving," because these are too hard to quantify.

Take the sheet, roll it up, and use a ribbon to tie it to the paw (or the waist) of a soft teddy bear. Get a second bear and place them both, either sitting on your bed or nightstand, in an embrace or side by side.

Looking to Conceive?

In many parts of China women who want to conceive place a bowl of uncooked rice under their bed. If you would like to test this traditional approach to becoming pregnant, take a decorative bowl made of porcelain or china, and fill it about two-thirds full of uncooked rice (white rice is traditional). Place the bowl in the center, underneath the bed. Do not disturb the bowl until the baby is born.

(From Donna Stellhorn's book, A Path to Pregnancy: Ancient Secrets for the Modern Woman)

Family and Kids

There are irritating changes in the neighborhood or in your apartment complex causing you to consider moving. It usually takes a lot to get patient, steady Ox to start contemplating a major change like this.

The energy will decrease and you can enjoy peace again if you will just make a few changes in your routine—or, if you shift the way you use the space in your home or the way you use the rooms in your home. Also, consider that the more things you let can go of (decluttering), the more you will both clear the energy in your current space, and make a future move a lot easier.

You experience a lot of activity around family. There are big changes with extended family; people may be moving, or there may be losses related to older relatives. Arguments in the family often happen as you sit back and observe. There's no need for you to get in the middle of these discussions. A family legal matter or contract will need your attention but you are up for the challenge.

There's a lot of business or work activity in your home this year. You may have a business at home or bring work home from the office. You may be up late at night working on a hobby or side hustle. It's also possible to turn your home into a money-making machine by renting out a room or charging rent of adult children who are still there but now working.

The Chi-Lin is a magical creature, a chimera, part horse, part dragon with the scales of a fish. Statues of this creature are displayed in the living room or dining room to protect the home and family. Place him up high where he can watch over everyone. The statue need not be large but it should be a size that can be seen on its high shelf. The Chi-Lin can be plain or colorfully decorated.

Money

You show money opportunities from several sources but somehow you don't seem so thrilled about it. This could be related to skills you have but don't enjoy doing anymore. Ox natives are practical and don't like leaving money on the table. If you're interested in filling up your bank account, you may want to continue doing these tasks as they will bring you money.

You will be spending a little more money than usual. This could be connected to a trip or something dealing with a foreign country. You may consider importing goods to sell. You could travel to a faraway place to do a business deal or to teach a language. Or you might just need a vacation, so you have to open your bank book in order to make it happen.

Your investments are performing well this year. The more money you can place in safe, secure investments, the better you will do in the long run. If you're not sure about how to make passive income, this is a good year to study or read up on this subject. Avoid signing up for scammy video courses on the subject and instead choose books by noted authors.

There is a gemstone that brings luck with money, it's called aventurine. It's a light green form of quartz that is translucent and shimmers in the light. You can find inexpensive pieces tumbled into smooth stones. You can carry a few stones with you or put them on your desk. If you play the lottery, store the stones with your tickets.

Job or Career

This is an outstanding year for you regarding your career. You can keep a job you like or find one better suited to your tastes. Often when given a choice, Ox natives decide to continue with what they've been doing. You might think you've invested so much time and energy into this path, why change directions at this point? But you can hear the distant rumblings of change in your industry. Deep down you know how future technological advances will disrupt the type of job you hold.

This means it's time to visualize a long-term future for yourself. At first, you may get frustrated with the idea of having to make these adjustments in your future. You may not be clear on what changes you need to make, but it's certain you will have to make them. When you look out to the future, the horizon might seem stormy. You need only ask the Universe for insight.

Many opportunities will drop unexpectedly into your lap this year. An Ox native who's looking for options will see them clearly. Have your resume ready, a mental picture of what you're ideal job is, a list of contacts in your pocket and you will do just fine. These are the things helping you prosper this year.

When it comes time for Pig natives to look for a new job, the Feng Shui cure I suggest is to take a wooden box; place a list of what you want in the new job inside the box. Add a few coins to the box, along with some leaves or needles from a tree.

Close up the box and place it on a table near your front door. Once your wish for the new job has been realized, open the box and take out that piece of paper; replace it with a new wish. (Just make sure you also add some fresh leaves or pine needles.)

Education

There is a lot of education energy around you now. You may be teaching, but even so, you are probably studying something as well. It may have been a while since you spent time in a classroom as a student. It's a challenge to get into the swing of things at first but soon you have homework and going to class has become a familiar part of your regular schedule.

You are very fortunate with teachers this year. You'll find talented and helpful instructors. The classes are interesting and you find attending is the high them to be a high point of your week. These may not be classes in a formal setting, perhaps they are exercise classes at a gym, acting classes at a local studio or music lessons where the teacher comes to you.

There is protection surrounding past student loans. Make sure you investigate whether your payments are correct and if you might qualify for some student loan forgiveness.

Legal Matters

There is a lot of energy around legal matters for you this year. This could mean you are signing contracts for sales, representation or employment. It can mean you need to take legal action against someone—though the whole thing may be resolved by obtaining a letter from your lawyer. Because there's an energetic emphasis on legal items, you should take legal matters seriously. Inspect any paperwork you receive from lawyers and read contracts carefully. Take the utmost care with contracts or lawsuits in December.

Health and Well-Being

This year you have new energy in the area of health. You may have experienced a healing this past year, or you may have received a diagnosis, or been pursuing a course of treatment during 2018 and have plans for The Year of the Earth Pig. Even though you're at the beginning point, you still need to be kind to your body and give yourself the time and attention needed for complete healing. However long you think it will take for you to heal, your body may need longer.

When it comes to your eating habits, a book or video brings you life-changing information. You've found something that resonates with you and you're running with it. This information creates a profound shift for you and now you have no desire to turn back to the old ways of doing things.

For you this year, stress is centered around travel and transportation. It's possible the traffic and congestion around you are becoming unbearable. Or you may need to travel to help a friend or relative but there are aspects of the trip (the expense, the time, the energy it takes) causing you more stress than in previous years. Ox natives like their home. Even ones who are experienced travelers will opt for staying on the sofa when they can. But this year try to mentally prepare yourself for a trip or two.

The Feng Shui gourd is a symbol related to health, longevity, and well-being. The gourd can be made of wood, metal, glass, or stone. It can also be a natural gourd that's been painted or otherwise decorated. Gourds like these can be found in Asian markets and art & crafts festivals.

The gourd can be placed in the bedroom or family room. You can tie a red ribbon around the center of the gourd to increase the energy. But do this only if no one living in the house is ill. If someone in the house is recovering from illness, place the gourd in the family room and not a bedroom.

Tiger

February 8, 1902–January 28, 1903: Yang Water Tiger

January 26, 1914–February 13, 1915: Yang Wood Tiger

February 13, 1926–February 1, 1927: Yang Fire Tiger

January 31, 1938–February 18, 1939: Yang Earth Tiger

February 17, 1950–February 5, 1951: Yang Metal Tiger

February 5, 1962–January 24, 1963: Yang Water Tiger

January 23, 1974–February 10, 1975: Yang Wood Tiger

February 9, 1986–January 28, 1987: Yang Fire Tiger

January 28, 1998–February 15, 1999: Yang Earth Tiger

February 14, 2010–February 2, 2011: Yang Metal Tiger

February 1, 2022–January 21, 2023: Yang Water Tiger

Tiger Personality

There are two ways to think about Tiger. First and most obvious, consider the beautiful beast in its jungle habitat, hiding in the tall grass, patiently waiting for his prey. A herd of antelope comes loping into view, pausing at the local waterhole. The Tiger watches and waits until one not too bright antelope wanders away from the herd. Lunchtime!

But that's only one aspect of the Tiger. There is also an impatient side, the "bounce-bounce-bounce energy" we saw in Tigger, the Tiger of Winnie the Pooh fame. This Tiger is the impulsive, leap-before-you-look energy.

Those born during the year of the Tiger have a personality with a combination of these two aspects. They are both patient and spontaneous. For instance, they can be very patient when they are stalking something they want. But when they find it they jump in, completely committing themselves to having it, with no thought to the consequences.

The Tiger is a powerful sign, the second most powerful (and second most popular) of all of the Chinese Zodiac. People born under this sign are rebellious and unpredictable, but they do command our respect. They are ready for anything. Overall, they love life, and they want to experience it fully. Sometimes this sits well with the people around them, and sometimes it doesn't.

Those born in the Year of the Tiger are suspicious. They don't trust easily. When their suspicions are confirmed, they are quick-tempered and will say whatever is on their mind. Be cautious of a Tiger's temper—after all, they have sharp claws.

There is also a gentle side to the Tiger. Tigers are very affectionate and tend to devote themselves to those they care about. They can hug, snuggle and purr, just like a soft, little kitten.

Tigers are dreamers and artists at heart. At the mere suggestion of it, they are ready to fly off to Bali with you. They will join your band. They will audition when the reality show comes to town looking for contestants. Everything is possible!

Tiger people may spend their whole lives running after exciting adventures, or they may have short periods of rebellion when they quit their job, leave their relationship, and throw caution to the winds. Quietly, the rest of us watch and hope the Tiger succeeds.

Tigers are emotional; their highs are really high and their lows are very low. When the low periods happen, Tiger needs a shoulder to cry on. Others will be tempted to offer advice, but Tigers won't listen. As a Tiger, you've learned it's better just to stick with who you are, and know that tomorrow is another day.

Tigers can be very charismatic and easily influence others when they put their mind to it. They make compelling speakers, teachers, and politicians. Tigers are charming; potential lovers easily fall for their flattery. The passion will burn hot—at least for a while.

But when the initial excitement is over, Tiger can fall out of love just as quickly as they fell into it, and just drift away. If on the other hand, the object of their attention starts to stray away from them, Tiger is quickly back on the hunt, eager to renew the chase.

How to use your Lucky Days: *On these days plan to take important actions, make vital phone calls, send emails. These are days when your energy and luck are high.*

Tiger: Predictions for 2019

January: *[note: This month there is a Solar Eclipse on January 5th and a Lunar Eclipse on January 21st. Check out the section on Eclipses for more details. Your Lucky Days are 2, 8, 14, 20, and 26.]*

A new year and a fresh start, you feel things are flowing and moving in the right direction. Find some happy, prosperous friends, have dinner and exchange ideas. Look to be around people who are filled with joy.

Home seems more settled and happy. It's a good idea now to freshen up the energy by decluttering a little bit. Clearing out a drawer or cupboard will help attract opportunities. Clear out a whole room and many things will start happening.

Relationships—including your romantic one—are getting better. You have better communication now. You still fight occasionally, you are a Tiger after all. But as long as you focus on the other person's behavior and not their character, you'll be fine.

Those Tiger natives looking to meet a significant other have a lot of positive opportunities this month. There seems to be an opportunity for love coming from your past.

Since it's the New Year, it's time to review your finances. Figure out your goals for the year and beyond. Don't look so much at numbers. Instead, look at what you want to accomplish. Do you want to buy a house? Do you want to travel? Are you paying down student loans? Look at your goals to motivate yourself to make more money and curb impulsive spending.

February: *[note: Happy Lunar New Year on February 5th. Your Lucky Days are 1, 7, 13, 19 and 25.]*

This month welcomes in the energy of Earth Pig. This is a somewhat contentious energy. In the natural world, a pig can't do much to a tiger but a tiger can make a meal out of a pig. This means there's a world of opportunities for you this year, but there's also a lot of ways to anger people around you. As a rule, you shouldn't snack on people who are trying to help you. So look at what you can do for them as well as what they can do for you.

Your talents and abilities shine brightly this month. You'll have opportunities to excel at work and at home. You might be the hero parent to your child, or be honored by family members for your dedication and love. You may receive some recognition at work and even a raise. Accept the honors with your usual modesty. Share the awards with others and you'll make lots of friends for the future.

An overheard conversation in a public place gives you an idea for a new venture.

Education is highlighted. Look at the knowledge you've accumulated in your life. It's possible you have expertise in one or more areas. On the other hand, you may be lacking in some tech skills that are important these days. Take a class or find a tutor and get up to speed.

March: *[note: Mercury is retrograde from March 6th to March 29th. See the section on Mercury retrograde for more information. Uranus moves into Taurus on March 6th—it's time for change. Your Lucky Days are 3, 9, 15, 21, and 27.]*

You are very visible to the world this month. This means you will be recognized for what you have done or noticed by others for some reason. Don't worry all of this will be too much. You can handle it.

You are money hungry this month. This could mean that you have been a little too free with your spending in the last month or two, or that some large purchase or debt is looming. Either way, you're focused on bringing in the bucks. Set your goal and take action. Remember Tigers get what they're after.

Your energy comes and goes. If you're tired, take a nap! Not only will you feel better, the Universe will send you answers while you rest.

Love is running to catch up with you but you're paying it no heed. While you may be thinking you want a relationship, or about improving your existing relationship, your actions are not showing this. Pause for a moment. Sit still for an hour and think about what you want in your love relationship. Then you can be on the move again and love will meet you half way.

April: *[note: Jupiter goes retrograde on April 10th, Pluto goes retrograde on April 24th and Saturn goes retrograde on April 29th. Your Lucky Days are 1, 7, 13, 19, and 25.]*

There's no hiding this month. You are noticed by all, sometimes for things you want to be recognized for and sometimes for things you don't. This is an excellent month to take a moment before pushing the "send" or "post" button. Really think about the implications and long-term consequences.

You seem to be stalled in the area of finances. Time to get your creative mind working again. This is a good month to activate the energy of the Universe through positive visualization and clear concepts about your goals. Create a vision board or write in your journal. Then take a step on the path to what you want to accomplish.

Inspiration and an answer come from a movie you see. Make a note of it.

When it comes to love you are in pursuit (as a Tiger should be). You have spotted what you want and are moving in. Remember, some can be skittish when they see a tiger charging towards them so understand they may be hesitant at first.

If you're already in a love relationship, you find yourself planning things to do with your partner. They may decline because they're overwhelmed with their work or obligations. Instead of giving them advice try to provide them with some practical help, or just be there to listen. This will bring you closer.

May: *[note: Your Lucky Days are 2, 8, 14, 20, and 26.]*

This is a challenging month where you feel restricted by other people's rules and expectations. Even if what they are saying is valid you still don't necessarily want to do it their way.

There can be some restrictions on resources as well. This is to let you know you don't have endless energy. You must pick and choose what's important to you and focus your time, energy and financial resources in that direction to really make progress.

A rather tall man seems to block your way but is actually trying to guide you in the right direction.

When it comes to your finances, you should keep a close eye on your spending this month. Examine your bills and see if some, especially subscriptions and recurring charges, can be eliminated. Review credit cards and see if interest rates can be lowered, or see if some debt can be consolidated.

You find joy in love this month. If you're looking for love, you are particularly magnetic at this time, so it's beneficial to be out and about in the world. Consider attending MeetUp groups, social dinners or simply a hiking group. Any new people you meet could lead you to the "one."

June: *[note: Neptune goes retrograde on June 21st. Your Lucky Days are 1, 7, 13, 19, and 25.]*

Home is the focus this month. There could be energy around moving, renovating or perhaps someone is moving in or moving out. Tiger natives are always up for adventure but there's little feeling of excitement over doing a bunch of tasks at home. Try to find some help. Enlist friends and family, or if no one is available, hire some help.

When it comes to money matters, your head seems to be in the clouds. You are spending without consideration and wishing it was this way all the time. A change of mindset to, "I am solving the money puzzle." or "I create opportunities for prosperity." would help at this time. Prayer, meditation, or simply lighting a candle for additional money energy is also helpful this month.

For your love life, you have the opportunity to have someone new this month. They are standing at the door, waiting to be invited in. Why do you hesitate? Yes, you're picky. Yes, you don't trust people. But you're also the fearless Tiger. Leap and then look and you'll find someone of value in the process.

If you're already in a committed relationship, you find a need to discuss and compromise in some areas. This could be in relation to household duties, outside friendships and how you are taking care of yourself. Listen before you start suggesting. This is a relationship that can get better as a result of open communication.

July: *[note: Mercury is retrograde from July 8th to August 1st. See the section on Mercury retrograde for more information. There's a Solar Eclipse on July 2nd and a Lunar Eclipse on July 16th. Check out the section on Eclipses for more details. Your Lucky Days are 1, 7, 13, 19, and 25.]*

Tigers are known to be restless and hotheaded. This month you are living up to your reputation by clearing out what's not serving you. But be careful not to pick quarrels with people you care about. Just because they move slower doesn't mean they aren't supporting your goals.

There's a lot of activity around money this month. You have opportunities related to career, as well as money likely coming from other sources. But you are also feeling very impatient about larger sums owed to you. These will come to you later in the year. If you were counting on that money this month, you might want to look elsewhere to fill those obligations.

Love isn't on your radar at this time. Sure, you want to have a great relationship but you're not feeling motivated to put in the work. Though ferocious on the outside you're quite emotionally sensitive on the inside, and this month you're feeling like a kitten who can't take the rough stuff.

This applies to those Tigers who are already in a love relationship. You feel like you've been beaten up just a little bit and you want some gentle cuddling instead.

August: *[note: Mercury moves forward again on August 2nd. Both Jupiter and Uranus move forward again August 11th. Your Lucky Days are 6, 12, 18, 24, and 30.]*

Communication is highlighted this month. You need to have a heart-to-heart with someone in your life, most likely a relative. This person has overstepped their bounds and put you in an awkward situation. While there's no trouble you can't handle, you still feel annoyed that they brought this to your doorstep.

Transportation is also on your mind. Now that Mercury is direct, you can get your vehicle repaired or you can get a new one entirely.

You can consider selling some things you no longer use. Tigers aren't usually great at budgeting. Their impulsive nature and their love of risk typically cause money to be here one day and gone the next.

In love, it seems like the wires are crossed somewhere. Your attempt to communicate what you need has backfired or perhaps you have been told, and yet you have misunderstood. Either way, you won't get anywhere obstinately thinking you're correct. Tigers don't hold grudges. They're too busy moving forward. So let this go; no matter who's in the right.

If you're looking for love, consider looking in new places. These hunting grounds you've been busy hunting in aren't yielding any results.

September: *[note: Saturn moves forward again on September 18th. Your Lucky Days are 5, 11, 17, 23, and 29.]*

As you "invest" in yourself sometimes your bank account feels the pressure. This is one of those months. It's important to look at where your money is going and make sure you're getting a return on your investment. If you're spending on education, that's great, but make sure the classes or school leads to career advancement. Avoid frivolous spending this month. If you have extra put it in a savings account and let it work for you.

This is your most significant month of the year. Projects will come to a completion point. Calls you made weeks ago are finally returned with satisfying results. Take risks and contact people who have the power to help you with your goals.

Your aspirations come from the core of you. The Universe is helping you by making you uncomfortable until you're on the right path. If you don't feel right then change direction.

When it comes to your relationship, there are lots of projects that can keep the two of you busy. Some involve the home itself (you can move this month or do a serious declutter) and other projects include the extended family.

If you're looking for love, you need to get out of the house this month. Get out and be seen. Go dancing, hiking or just sit in a coffee shop. Be where love can find you.

October: *[note: Pluto moves forward again on October 3rd. Your Lucky Days are 5, 11, 17, 23, and 29.]*

Your brain is buzzing with ideas. This could be from a lecture you attended, a TED talk you saw or a book you read. This is one of those times when you can leap and get amazing results.

Dreaming lotto numbers is possible but takes practice. Keep a dream journal by the bed.

Money is really stored energy which you can exchange for goods or services. You can also use that stored energy to make you more money. This is what investing is and where your opportunities lie now.

A woman with long hair and a lovely face pays you a compliment and she means it.

Also, look at what you're spending your hard earned dollars on and where you can cut back. Reduce subscription spending on websites or services unless you really use them.

Love opportunities abound this month. You receive affection and admiration. This can come from your committed relationship—or if you're looking for love, you find an admirer in someone you've known for a while. What you need in your love life is the typical Tiger daring where you go for what you want. If you frighten away the prospect, no worries. Another will come along soon.

November: *[note: Mercury goes retrograde from November 1st to November 21st. See the section on Mercury retrograde for more information. Neptune moves forward again on November 27th. Your Lucky Days are 4, 10, 16, 22, and 28.]*

Tigers don't often have to worry about their health. They are born under one of the healthiest signs of the Chinese zodiac. But this month you're feeling run down and need a break. Or you may be recovering from a recent injury or surgery. Your impatience to heal is not helping you here. If you're ordered to stay in bed, you would be wise to do so. You would also benefit by sticking to a healthy diet at least for the first three weeks of the month (during the retrograde Mercury). You will feel so much better because of it.

With your usual Tiger luck, you have money opportunities knocking at your door. People come to you for your ideas and energy. Make sure you negotiate for what you want before handing over the goods. Gather some friends or supporters to help you capitalize on what could bring you a lot of money in the next year or so.

When it comes to love this month, you seem to be in a cycle of quarrel and make up and then quarrel again. It's a good idea to look at the root causes of these disagreements. Is it your hothead or is there something really wrong with your partnership? You are feeling more restless than usual. Maybe a break would be best (separate holidays perhaps).

December: *[note: There is a Solar Eclipse on December 26th. Check out the section on Eclipses for more details. Your Lucky Days are 4, 10, 16, 22, and 28.]*

You end the year on a high note. Your health is back to its usual vibrant self. You wake with energy and bursting with new ideas. This month you're focused on routines, how to streamline them and mostly how to rid yourself of them. Then open yourself up to inspiration. The answers will flow in.

Positive money month is ahead for you. You may find an end-of-the-year bonus or other windfalls this month. Risks you took earlier in the year now pay off. There may be a rebate check or cash from a return that also fattens the wallet. The desire to shop will be strong but consider holding some money back for next year when you may want to invest in some education or travel.

Your partner appreciates you and tells you so. It would be good to reciprocate with not just a gift but the words as well.

If you're looking for love, it can be found connected to parties, religious events, and charity work. Put yourself out in the world with a smile and love will find you.

January 2020: *[note: There is a Lunar Eclipse on January 10th. Check out the section on Eclipses for more details. Uranus moves forward again on January 11th. Your Lucky Days are 3, 9, 15, 21, and 27.]*

This is the last month of this cycle, and your focus is on your resources. You have learned new skills and sharpened your abilities. You have met some good people who are able and willing to help you. You have a list of innovative ideas to implement. Now it's time to put it all together. The future may feel uncertain but that's what Tigers love, a sense of liberation and running towards the goal. Don't let the hesitation and caution of others hold you back. Move forward.

The song that keeps playing over and over in your head is a message. Time to decipher it.

If you're in a long-term relationship, you feel intimately connected to that person more than you have in many months. Take hold of the person's hand. This relationship is improving.

If you're looking for love, you need to consider what's been blocking you. There are no obstacles but the ones you keep constructing. The love you want is waiting on the other side of the wall you've built. Tear down that wall. Be your rebellious, captivating self and accept love into your life.

Attract New Love

This is a highly romantic year for Tiger natives. You are much more easily able to find the physically-compatible relationship you've been looking for. Your magnetism is strong, and it's up to the other person to capture your attention and your heart.

It's possible you've already met this person by the time the year is underway but there's no need whatsoever to chase that person. The energies will shift and change throughout the year, and if this is the right choice, they will make their intentions clearly known to you. You can be stubborn and contentious wondering why it took them so long to come around. Try to relax and trust in the timing of the Universe.

You can also meet someone brand new by attending classes, doing things associated with religion or spirituality, traveling or visiting places in your town where tourists hang out. Place yourself in a position where you can be seen. Choose a table in the middle of the restaurant or attend "happy hour" at a bar and make conversation with those around you. There are likely several who will try to get your attention.

Double Happiness is represented by a pair of Chinese characters. The single character translates as "joy." When two of these characters are written together, it is associated with love unions and weddings. It's called "Double Happiness." This motif dates back to the Song dynasty (960-1279 AD). This pair of symbols can be found in artwork, on vases, rugs, or brass sculptures like the one shown here.

Hang a Double Happiness symbol in your bedroom to attract a love relationship. If you prefer to move slowly into a new relationship such as meeting a friend who, over time, grows into a romantic relationship, then hang this symbol in your living room. Hang it where it can be seen from the door. This will attract the energy of a person who is like you in many ways and desires to unite with you.

Enhance Existing Love

You may have been voted by your friends, "Least Likely to Settle Down" but you have every reason to feel happy and content in your love relationship this year. You have opportunities to see how great things can be when one is committed to the happiness of another and vise versa.

At times you are still reckless, sometimes putting your foot in your mouth. It would be wise to apologize quickly and avoid a row. Tiger natives are capable of great acts of love and devotion. Make a show of how happy you are to have found this soul to spend your days with. If your partner is Tiger also then recognize the ups will be higher and the downs will be lower all year long.

At the mid-year point, there may be a third person, friend or foe, who creates some issues in your relationship. They are able to do this because you're sometimes impulsive in what you say or do. As July approaches keep partner's goals and well-being in mind and you will do just fine. Then later in the year, you will see your relationship is stronger than ever.

To create more harmonious feelings and happier times spray orange scent in the bedroom. You can also put out potpourri made with dried orange peels. If you prefer not to have the scent in the house, have pictures of orange blossoms in the bedroom. Orange blossoms not only help relationships but it can also attract prosperity energy, which certainly doesn't hurt.

Looking to Conceive?

Find a necklace made of cowrie shells. Cowrie shells have long been associated with pregnancy, due to the shape of the shell being very like the shape of a uterus. Small cowrie shells, usually white, are made into necklaces and bracelets.

You can also find larger cowrie shells; these may be striped or spotted brown and white. Place one or more of these larger shells on your bedside table. Cowrie shells are not only reputed as fertility cures but also have been used as currency in some cultures; so the shell will attract good money energy, too.

(From Donna Stellhorn's book, A Path to Pregnancy: Ancient Secrets for the Modern Woman)

Family and Kids

You have options this year. You can stay in your home or you can leave. You can get a larger place, maybe one with land attached. You can downsize even to the point of living in a caravan or motorhome. What's important is to start to consider all the different lives you could lead and what they might mean for you and your family. Tiger natives are natural risk takers, and this is what brings you success when you leap into something that feels right.

If you have kids, you will see them going in all different directions. Some may be going off to school, others starting businesses or finding new career opportunities. They find you encouraging the chances their taking, and they love the support you provide. But be careful about handing over all your cash. Your children will do better if they bootstrap their own ventures.

Travel is strongly featured, especially when it involves going with relatives or visiting relatives. You can also see historic family sites and find your roots. Consider reaching out to distant relatives and making a connection, you might get a free place to stay. Explore your family tree this year.

To help you feel more safe and secure for wherever you land, use the representation of the turtle to bring protection energy to you. In fact, three turtles would be even better. Find a figurine of three turtles stacked one on top of another. This represents protection, friendships, and security through community. Each turtle has everything they need with them to protect them no matter what comes. Place the figurine on your nightstand or in your family room.

Money

You have one of the best charts this year for making money. In fact, any action you take can lead to a profit. The only wrong move you may make is to do nothing. Don't let indecision or procrastination hold you back. If you've been thinking about asking for a raise or starting a business, this is the time to take action.

While you do have good energy for investing, Tiger natives tend towards riskier investments and this might not pan out as well as you hoped. If you're investing money you can afford to lose, it's okay to do a little gambling but keep your main funds in regular, insured securities or in real estate.

This year more than one person will ask you for a loan. Their circumstances might be real, but it may not be the best thing for you to give to them. You must weight the circumstances and what the person's financial history has been. In some cases, you might be better off just giving them a gift of the money and that way the friendship or relationship can be preserved.

To increase your money opportunities this year place stacks of coins on the windowsills in your home office, kitchen, and entryway. Coins represent a universal symbol of money. It's especially beneficial to have at least one stack of coins on your kitchen windowsill to ensure the house never lacks for money.

You can use Chinese coins or coins of your country. Stacks of odd numbers are best, three, five and nine coin stacks are the most beneficial. You can start out with a stack of just three coins and then add a couple of coins each week to increase the energy.

Job or Career

Your job is a little irritating this year but not so much you're climbing the walls looking for a way out. This is an opportunity for you to hone your skills at manifesting. Give the Universe a list of what you want to have change. Don't like your boss? Create a list of the qualities you would like to see in a manager. Don't like the commute? Visualize the option of working from home. Don't like some of the tasks? Outline how you do want to spend your day.

As the months go by there may be changes in your job title or some of the duties. There are people around you leaving for other jobs. This gives you some routes to follow in the future. There may be new people coming in which changes the team dynamics. New technology will be introduced in the middle of the year that will first not work then will work better than what you had before.

There are possibilities for travel for business. You may attend a convention or conference. Consider taking a leadership role and speaking at an event. Also, it's beneficial for you to speak up at meetings. This will give you favorable notice and possible project opportunities in the future.

To welcome new opportunities in your career, get a new welcome mat for your front door. Choose a simple mat. It can be black and made of rubber (representing the water element and flow of opportunity), or it can be made of natural grass (representing the wood element and growth). It can say the word, "Welcome" or it can say "Home" but it shouldn't have any pictures on it (no pictures of kittens, flags, or clever sayings that could have negative connotations).

About once a month, weather permitting, take the time to clean up the porch to welcome in new positive energy. Shake out the mat to stimulate the energy flow. If the mat becomes worn, then replace it.

Education

Education is one of your highlighted areas this year. You have more luck and support in this area than you've had in some time. This means you can go back to school or finish a degree program if you just set your mind to it. You may also consider studying abroad. There will be opportunities from some surprising places, you just have to knock on the door.

While there is financial support for education this year, there's a fair bit of work involved. Tiger natives will have to put themselves on notice to get all the paperwork gathered, completed and sent out. Remember, if possible, don't submit important papers during Mercury retrograde (or if you do, make sure you have a backup copy).

You may be graduating this year and tempted to sign up for the next degree. This should be fine if your goals are clear.

Legal Matters

There's a good chance you will be signing an agreement having to do with employment or contract work this year. This is not a matter to rush through. Even though you may be excited about this opportunity, you still have the power to negotiate the terms you want.

Terms and conditions on loan agreements may also be important, especially around the middle of the year. Keep paperwork orderly so you can find it when you need it. You can keep copies of relevant contracts (such as residential leases) on your phone so they are handy.

Health and Well-Being

This is a more stressful year for you in the area of health. In Earth Pig years the eating habits of Tiger natives, which served you well for many years, now don't seem to work. It could be you're consuming too much food or the quality of food in your area has changed. It will take some research, plus trial and error, to find out what your body needs. By February you will already have some idea of what needs to change.

Tiger natives can be a balance of high-intensity movement and perfect stillness. This year, good forms of exercise will include dance, swimming or diving, and weight training. Also, consider energy moving exercises like Qi Gong.

Stress for you this year is centered around secrets. You have a suspicious nature and can sense when people are keeping things from you. But this year it's better to focus on trusting yourself rather than trying to figure out if you can trust other people. Put your faith in yourself that you can handle whatever happens and you won't need to rely on someone else. Most of the secrets will be revealed around mid-year. By the end of the year, you'll have the full story.

Turquoise, a beautiful blue-green stone, is often made into jewelry. It's long been known for its healing qualities. Find either a piece of turquoise jewelry or a tumbled stone you can carry with you. The turquoise will remind you to stick with positive health changes. Once your new habits are established, you can keep the stone in your kitchen or in the bedroom on your bedside table.

Rabbit

January 29, 1903–February 15, 1904: Yin Water Rabbit

February 14, 1915–February 2, 1916: Yin Wood Rabbit

February 2, 1927–January 22, 1928: Yin Fire Rabbit

February 19, 1939–February 7, 1940: Yin Earth Rabbit

February 6, 1951–January 26, 1952: Yin Metal Rabbit

January 25, 1963–February 12, 1964: Yin Water Rabbit

February 11, 1975–January 30, 1976: Yin Wood Rabbit

January 29, 1987–February 16, 1988: Yin Fire Rabbit

February 16, 1999–February 4, 2000: Yin Earth Rabbit

February 3, 2011–January 22, 2012: Yin Metal Rabbit

January 22, 2023–February 9, 2024: Yin Water Rabbit

Rabbit Personality

It may surprise many to know I consider Rabbit to be one of the strongest signs of the Chinese Zodiac. Most imagine him as a fluffy bunny, an animal who cannot speak, has no claws, and short little legs to hop away with. But the Rabbit sits between the Chinese Signs of the Tiger and the Dragon in the wheel of the Chinese Zodiac, and he alone keeps these two powerful forces apart.

Rabbit (also called Hare in some translations) generally serves as the sign of kindness and sensitivity. People born under this sign have good manners, common sense, and ability to soothe and comfort others in any situation. For this reason, Rabbit often finds him- or herself in a leadership position.

The Rabbit personality is neither forceful nor rash, and they do have a way of bringing people together. Rabbit is the perfect arbitrator, networking expert, negotiator, or diplomat. They always have something positive to say about and to everyone.

Because of Rabbit's love of peace, they are sometimes seen as weak, or even self-indulgent. A Rabbit prefers to apply brain over brawn and will avoid a confrontation whenever possible. They may be perceived to be thin-skinned, but in actuality, Rabbit is merely cautious; after all, they don't want to be on anyone's menu. Rabbit can be a treasured friend, as he or she is good at keeping secrets, and offers very sensible advice.

Rabbit people tend to run in the best circles. They enjoy the finer things in life—everything from the best table in the restaurant to the best parking space at the mall. Those born in the Year the Rabbit look for the easy way to do things, and more often than not, this way leads to the best side of town. They tend to be a little flashy at times, which helps them fit in perfectly with their A-list friends.

Rabbit is realistic, yet sympathetic. They will listen to your troubles, and while they offer great advice, they never push an agenda. As a parent, they are neither the disciplinarian nor are they given to criticism. They are positive and rarely embarrass their children in public.

In business Rabbit's quiet, unassuming air can cause others to think they are not paying attention. But there's more to Rabbit than meets the eye. Before you know it, you have been encouraged to sign the contract or seal the deal—with Rabbit taking the lion's share of the rewards. In spite of this (and possibly because of Rabbit's impeccable manners), you come away feeling grateful Rabbit was even willing to do business with you.

How to use your Lucky Days: *On these days plan to take important actions, make vital phone calls, send emails. These are days when your energy and luck are high.*

Rabbit: Predictions for 2019

January: *[note: This month there is a Solar Eclipse on January 5th and a Lunar Eclipse on January 21st. Check out the section on Eclipses for more details. Your Lucky Days are 3, 9, 15, and 27.]*

The year starts off great. The changes you made to your finances are paying off big. You likely have more income opportunities, and others are offering you products and/or services that save you even more money.

You are comfortable at home and you're getting along with your family members. Life is going great. Count your blessings and let go of worry. Things can get better this year, and you can enjoy an even more harmonious life.

Spiritual wounds take time to heal, just like wounds to the body. This month you are healing from what happened in the past. It's been a slow process, but you will soon feel stronger and more resilient.

Next thing to work on is your schedule. How are you prioritizing, taking care of yourself, your body, and your mind? Where are you Number One, at the top of your own priority list? Your natural compassion for others often winds up making you "last" on your own To-Do List. Start this project by imagining how your day could be. Schedule times for favorite activities, exercise, and meditation or prayer. Give yourself a few minutes each evening to write a sentence or two in your Gratitude Journal.

February: *[note: Happy Lunar New Year on February 5th! Your Lucky Days this month are 2, 8, 14, 20, and 26.]*

This month we enter into the Year of the Earth Pig. This energy is naturally beneficial to you. You are highly intuitive and this skill will be beneficial this year.

This month your focus is on communication. Right now it seems you're having trouble connecting with people. They're not answering your emails, not picking up the phone, not responding to texts. This is simply a sign you need to chill. Set aside some quiet time, and listen to your inner voice and your sense of Spirit instead. Once you do this exercise for a day or so, the phone will start ringing; people will be reaching back to you, seeking connection.

Some changes in the area of friendships can be expected this month. You may find yourself growing closer to a new friend. You're finding connections with this person you didn't realize before. They reciprocate your caring energy with invitations, phone calls and texts. This month join with this person and gather a group of friends together for a celebration or impromptu party.

You may wish for an easier life now. Take a moment and envision how your life could change to make things easier for you. Would you have less stuff? Ask for more help? Remove/release some old obligations? It's time to plant a seed with the Universe, stand back and let it grow.

March: *[note: Mercury is retrograde from March 6th to March 29th. See the section on Mercury retrograde for more information. Uranus moves into Taurus on March 6th—Time for change. Your Lucky Days this month are 4, 10, 16, 22, and 28.]*

You are really drawn to personal betterment this month. You're doing so much without feeling the support from friends and family. They want you to give them your attention. The particular issues surrounding your family members are many and varied this month. Your phone is buzzing with requests for your help. However, this is the time for you to examine your own life and do something for yourself for a change.

You may be thinking it wouldn't hurt to have some extra money right now. Consider trading for services (or things you need) rather than spending money on them. This is a good month to call money to you during meditation, or by offering spiritual prosperity prayers.

There is more friction than usual between you and your beloved. There's a coolness/coldness between the two of you that wasn't there before. This could be because you've been feeling hurt and lonely while trying to make the other person feel fulfilled and happy.

Your relationship is out of balance. The awareness you've recently acknowledged in connection with your partner may be something your partner hasn't even noticed. You may need to sit down and have a talk with each other. This isn't something Rabbit likes to hear, but it will help to resolve the problem.

If you are looking for love, consider asking your friends for help. Have them steer suitable people to you.

April: *[note: Jupiter goes retrograde on April 10th, Pluto goes retrograde on April 24th, and Saturn goes retrograde on April 29th. Your Lucky Days are 3, 9, 15, 21, and 27.]*

This month you're feeling less than powerful and a little off center, off your path. This will lead to a wonderful (and much needed) course correction, one which will help you out enormously later in the year. Don't fight it. This is a good month to sit and ponder your feelings. Make changes as opportunities present themselves.

There's a little more energy around finances this month indicating you feel a need to watch your spending. This opportunity may mean some money goes out before a larger amount comes in later. It also could mean your current accounts are vulnerable at this time. Change your passwords and check your accounts for any suspicious activity.

There are investment opportunities you can tap into. Move money to where it will work for you.

In your love life, there are more irritations than harmony. You are a peace-loving Rabbit and even these slight annoyances feel like nails on a chalkboard to you. Speak up and let your partner know things are bothering you. This brings harmony towards the end of the month.

If you're looking for love, you find the whole process to be quite irritating. You're looking for an intelligent, sophisticated individual with good manners. But you won't find this person where you've been looking in the past. Try a new venue.

May: *[note: Your Lucky Days this month are 3, 9, 15, 21, and 27.]*

They say you can read a person's life by studying the five people they hang out with the most. What do your five people indicate about your life? Sometimes your warm and friendly nature attracts people who want you to carry them. Stick to friends who support you as much as you support them.

You are easily noticed this month. Reach out to people you're interested in being with, and you will get a response.

Money and communication are linked this month. You can make more money by asking for more. Don't sell yourself short, and certainly don't wait for others to bestow it on you. First, tell the Universe what you want through prayer or affirmation. Then share your thoughts with a friend or supportive family member. Finally, tell a business associate, or put your thoughts out into the world via social media. Ask and the opportunity comes. ("Ask and you shall receive!")

Most of your focus this month is on love relationships. You will benefit now by feeling grateful for your past experiemces. Find wonderful shared memories to talk about with your partner— even if you simply mention them in passing.

If you're looking for love, you'll find multiple choices this month if you will just put yourself out in the world, or post on an online dating site.

June: *[note: Neptune goes retrograde on June 21st. Your Lucky Days are 2, 8, 14, 20, and 26.]*

Your friendships are important this month. One of your good friends or your best friend may have been drifting away. Both of you are definitely busier than you used to be. It's time to reconnect.

You also show a need to look at organizations—either for your profession or a hobby—and see if you need to take on a greater leadership role. The organization would benefit greatly from your good judgment and even-temper. You may as well volunteer, because even if you don't, you may find yourself in the position anyway.

Financial matters are a little rocky this month, but nothing you can't handle. There have been some issues with accounts, or income in general, has been diminishing for a while, This situation needs to be addressed. Time to use your diplomatic skills to negotiate for more.

Also, consider setting up automatic savings/payments/withdrawals to allow your accounts to grow organically.

Your partnership improves. The work you've done has paid off—though you may still be hurting from some things said last month. Don't let these sad thoughts fester and become a bigger wound. Gently point out where you feel things were unfair and see what changes the other person is willing to make.

If you're looking for love, you may be feeling more pushed towards something you don't want to do this month. Maybe online dating doesn't appeal to you, or you may be pursued by someone you don't find all that interesting. No reason to hurry here. Move at your own pace. Love is out there when you're ready.

July: *[note: Mercury is retrograde from July 8th to August 1st. See the section on Mercury retrograde for more information. There's a Solar Eclipse on July 2nd and a Lunar Eclipse on July 16th. Check out the section on Eclipses for more details. Your Lucky Days are 14, 20, and 26.]*

You watch from the sidelines as several friends or family members start to go through major changes in their lives. You are steady and strong in a crisis while others feel uneasy with their changes happening. You see what should be done but others aren't listening to you now. Be patient. They will approach you for your good counsel when they are ready. In the meantime, make an assessment of changes you could make in your own life.

In money matters, it seems you are waiting for others to bring you what you need. Time to be proactive. This may mean you need to send an email reminder, make a phone call or have a conversation to get the money flowing. The good news is once you start this process money will flow freely in your direction.

When it comes to your personal relationship this month, you feel a little under the gun. Your lover is making demands on you. Rabbit natives don't like to feel cornered. You have a desire to run, to hide, or at the very least, avoid. But things are not as dire as they first may seem to be. The issue has been blown out of proportion and things will soon calm down again.

If you're looking for love, you may be feeling a little wounded from past encounters. This is causing you to want a break from the whole dating thing. But love is waiting to find you. Try to get out there again.

August: *[note: Mercury moves forward again on August 2. Both Jupiter and Uranus move forward again August 11. Your Lucky Days are 1, 7, 13, 19, 25, and 31.]*

There is a strong new beginning possible this month. You can let go of the past and move forward with confidence. There will be decisions about possessions. This is a good month to let go of what you're not using.

This is a perfect time to reinforce good health habits such as eating your veggies and exercising regularly.

If you operate a service business, expect increasing numbers of referrals. If you need funding, this is a good month to ask people for money or to ask through an online platform like GoFundMe. com

This month you streamline your routines, making them more effective, and efficient and you get more done in less time.

In your love life, there are still some blocks you're working your way through. You are a sensitive soul, and the hurts you've endured in the past take time to heal. It would be good to clear the pain of the past through some techniques like tapping, meditation or therapy. Once the block is removed, love comes in.

September: *[note: Saturn moves forward again on September 18th. Your Lucky Days are 6, 12, 24, and 30.]*

This month focus on what you say to yourself. How you treat yourself directly mirrors how you're treated by others. If you're constantly nagging yourself or putting yourself down, you'll find others aren't treating you with love and respect. Do take whatever time is needed to treat yourself with love and kindness.

Money matters are better this month. You may be putting your bills in order and sticking to your budget. Late in the month, a friend or sibling will ask you for a loan. If it's a first time you may say "Yes," but if this is a habit, consider saying "No" for a change.

If you're looking for love, you have reason to celebrate. You have worked on blocks and torn down barriers to what you want. No one is in your way anymore. Now state to the Universe what you want in a partner and step out into the world. This month consider going out with a person who may not be exactly what you have thought you might like, just to get the energy flowing. If they're not a match, then kindly tell them, "Thank you, but no thank you." and move on. Saying "No" to the wrong relationship will help you to be able to say "Yes" when you find Mr./Ms. Right.

October: *[note: Pluto moves forward again on October 3rd. Your Lucky Days are 6, 12, 18, 24, and 30.]*

The need for balance is highlighted this month. As you seek to balance your life, don't be surprised if your family tells you how much they need you. When you step out of your normal role as caregiver, people are quick to remind you of what they need. But balance requires you take time for you and your wellbeing.

Your finances are stable (of course you can always wish for more). The house needs some repairs or updates, and that can bite into the budget. Even if you're feeling frugal, the rest of the household members are not. If you're not firm with them now, this could throw off the positive financial energy of the month.

A small windfall is possible from a risk you take this month.

You and your partner feel united to stand up to opposition in your life. Any arguments at home are started by extended family members (who don't live with you). Everyone has an opinion but the problem comes when an opinion is stated as if it were a fact. Remind people they are entitled to their opinion and leave it at that. You won't be changing anyone's mind this month.

You can expect better things this month. Trust in your ability to make correct decisions and to create what you want. Your inner voice is correct now.

November: *[note: Mercury goes retrograde from November 1st to November 21st. See the section on Mercury retrograde for more information. Neptune moves forward again on November 27th. Your Lucky Days are 5, 11, 17, 23 and 29.]*

Rabbit natives prefer a flexible, almost eccentric schedule. This month take some personal days to enjoy the weather, your family, and your home. Decorate and, if you feel inclined, bake. Let the scents of the season be around you.

There is positive energy for putting your wishes out to the Universe and seeing tangible results. Review your vision board (or, if you don't have one, create one).

A family friend gives you investment advice (or a warning of what not to do) and paying attention to this will help you now and in the next few years.

Your job has been rather taxing the last few weeks. This could be due to a boss who is less than understanding. However, things at work improve this month and you receive some well-earned recognition from a surprising source.

Something happens this month to let you know that your partner really does care. It's not just lip service. Your beloved steps up when needed and comes through for you.

If you're looking for love, you can find it while helping others or being around people you have already met. Just don't hide in the corner. Get out and mingle.

December: *[note: There is a Solar Eclipse on December 26th. Check out the section on Eclipses for more details. Your Lucky Days are 5, 11, 17, 23 and 29.]*

There is change energy around relationships of all types: friendships, workmates, or neighbors. You may have to shift a relationship with one or more of these people or end the relationship entirely. Identify who is supporting you in your life and who is draining you.

This is a positive money month. Money opportunities are around you, waiting for you to take even the smallest step before activating. Yes, some of the actions needed may be ones you find uncomfortable. This could be phone calls, public speaking or asking for the sale. Rabbits are not known for being pushy salespeople, so it might feel quite challenging to activate these money opportunities. But Rabbits are adept at telling stories. Use the story as your sales pitch.

As mentioned before, relationships are a significant factor this month. But your main squeeze may be just fine this month. In fact, because of the work you have done this year, your love relationship is a source of support for you as you remove yourself from other unhealthy relationships.

It's a different matter if you're single and looking for a partner. You must look at what is blocking you from the love of your life. Rabbit natives are sensitive and can hold on to past pain for longer than others. Try not to let past pain keep you from present and future joy.

January 2020: *[note: There is a Lunar Eclipse on January 10th. Check out the section on Eclipses for more details. Uranus moves forward again on January 11th. Your Lucky Days are 4, 10, 16, 22, and 28.]*

The new year begins with a focus on your role in the world. This could be related to your career, but it can also be your reputation (how you are seen at your church, in your neighborhood, by your friends?). Also, consider your online reputation based on your past social media posts. This would be a good time to remove posts which may no longer represent you as you wish. Avoid posting in anger or when under the influence. Rabbit natives are generally prudent about these things, but this month be extra careful.

Money opportunities continue to flow in. Now you see a direct relationship between your state of mine and the financial support you receive. This doesn't necessarily mean you need to be positive all the time. Instead, it's a time to activate your creative self. See problems for what they are, a challenge; then look for a creative solution. There are possibly as many as six sources of income or chunks of money available for you this month. Start every morning with the thought, "What can I do to solve the money question today?"

If you're already in a love relationship, you may feel others are trying to keep you apart. This could be quite innocent—because a friend needs you, or work is hectic for your partner. Sensitive Rabbit natives will pick up if whether there's anything suspicious going on. This is mostly just external circumstances, so be patient.

Attract New Love

This is an excellent year for you in the area of love. You may have several opportunities presented to you quite early in the year. Your luck continues throughout the year, though there may be a dry spell in July and August, where love seems to be courting everyone but you. Soon you are the life of the party again, and your friendly manner is charming one and all.

You may have someone specific in mind that you've been patiently waiting for. This year it's a good idea to consider someone new. This person may have been in a serious relationship before, and they may bring children into the mix. You may need to blend your family with theirs. All this will take a bit of effort but the rewards are great.

Rabbit natives are known for their eloquence and can be quite entertaining, but you can find online dating limiting. Consider joining dating groups where you can meet people in person. Look at social clubs, dinner clubs, and hiking groups. The more new people you are around, the faster you will find the right person.

We are more sensitive to scent than any of our other senses. Odors are known to influence our emotions and behaviors. Scent triggers memories in our brains and associations with those memories, and then we take actions even if we're not fully conscious of the reasons. Those small actions add up, bringing us closer to our goals.

The scent of vanilla is wonderful for attracting new love. Vanilla extract can be found in most grocery stores. Place a drop or two on cotton balls and place these in your bedroom. These can be placed behind a picture or on a small dish on your bedside table. You can also spray vanilla-scented air fresheners, however, the more natural the scent, the better. Or place a small amount of vanilla in a pot of boiling water on the stove and allow the aroma of vanilla to fill the house. At the same time visualize the love relationship you want easily coming to you.

Enhance Existing Love

You prefer moving through the world based on your feelings rather than your logical brain, but sometimes you forget that you may not exactly know how other people feel. This is a year when communicating openly with your sweetheart will help you create a better, stronger relationship. It can help them see what an amazing person you truly are.

You love peace and harmony. This can cause you to run away from confrontation, even in a situation at home. This year you may be asked to choose between your love relationship and a family relationship. Perhaps your partner is asking you to set some boundaries when it comes to a sibling or younger family member. It's better to adjust than to stand your ground on this point. Your love relationship is more important at this time.

Other times this year you may feel like the romance has drained out of the relationship. You're stuck in a routine of chores, work, and TV in the evening. Break the routine. Yes, you're both tired, but an occasional change of scene will do amazing things for your love life. This will get you back on track.

Not all Feng Shui cures have to be traditionally Chinese in origin. There are many symbols broadly used in many cultures. The wedding ring quilt is a such a symbol, in this case of love and fidelity. To enhance your existing love relationship place a wedding ring quilt on your bed. You can also hang a small lap quilt or quilted wall hanging in the same design on your bedroom wall to help enhance the energy of your partnership.

Looking to Conceive?

Display a peacock feather to increase your fertility energy. In Indian folklore, the peacock dances to attract a mate, and so its feathers are associated with abundance and fertility. Place your

peacock feather on the wall at the head of your bed. You can attach it to the wall or the headboard. Use more than one peacock feather if you really want to make a statement. The more feathers, the more positive energy.

Stellhorn's eBook, A Path to Pregnancy: Ancient Secrets for the Modern Woman)

Family and Kids

While most of the year is quite pleasant with regards to home and family, you seem to be worried about one member in particular. This person's wellbeing may keep you up at night (there may be an issue with an addiction or debt). You can send this person positive energy through prayer and meditation and watch them get better in months to come.

Your home life seems dependent on a family member's situation. This could mean your partner gets a job and the family needs to move, or that an older family member needs to come to stay with you for a while. Rabbit natives are compassionate and are able to assess people and their situations. You are reading this assessment correctly, and you will take the right action.

If you have children, you may be seeing one or more enter into serious relationships. If they are young, these could be pivotal friendships for them. If they are older, they could be choosing life partners. A celebration could be happening this year or early next year.

For a little extra protection energy for the family this year, plant lilac in your garden, or get some dried lilac buds and mix with some potpourri in a bowl. Place the bowl by your front door (inside or out). Ancient stories tell of lilac driving away evil. It helps attract positive energy and keeps negativity away. In Winter you can sprinkle a little dried lilac on your doorstep. When Spring comes, plant this beautiful flower.

Money

This is a good year for focusing on creating passive income. Even if it's just a dollar a month, it's a start towards something you can grow into a secure income for yourself and your family. It begins with the mindset that it's possible. Look for information on investments you're comfortable with and interested in. Consider putting some funds into this early in the year and then adding a little each month.

There is money to be gained through a spouse or family member. Or, if you're in business, money could be coming from a partnership. In either case, this means working one-on-one with another individual, finding things you agree on and moving forward. If this is with family, there may be wills and trusts involved. In a business partnership, get advice from a lawyer if drawing up a contract. Do it right and you'll be happy in the long run.

It's also important to look over your insurance. Make sure you have enough coverage for home and other valuable things you own. If you're unhappy with your insurance provider, plan to make a change after July.

To help attract money this year, consider placing a Lucky Money Frog by your front door. The Lucky Money Frog sits on a pile of coins and has a coin in his mouth. If you place him by your front door, he will collect money as a result of the energy that comes in. Place him on the floor by the front door or on a table nearby. If he's sitting inside the house, (most people do place him inside the house) he should be facing the door, like your personal butler. If he's sitting outside the door, his back should be to the door, like your personal bouncer.

Job or Career

This year your career isn't your main focus. Perhaps you're just not being challenged, or you're stuck in a rut. You go to work, attend meetings, see clients or customers but your heart's just not in it. This may signal a time for a change, but this can be a time when you don't have a expend a lot of energy at work so you can focus put your attention on other aspects of your life. Since work is less important this year, you can have more work/life balance.

What is important to you in your career right now is the people. You have good relationships with many you work with as well as with the people you serve in your job capacity. You may have had some trouble with a few managers in past years, but there is a healing this year (this could mean some managers are leaving) and you are getting along better with bosses.

You may consider gathering some favorite people and starting a side business. Get together some talented, energetic friends who have skills you don't have, and see what you can build in your spare time. Again, career isn't the big focus, so it's okay if this is just a drawing on a napkin for now. There will be time in the future to make this a real thing.

One Feng Shui cure to attract positive career energy is the gemstone citrine. Citrine is a form of quartz with a gold or yellow color. Find one in its natural form or polished smooth, either will be a good choice for this purpose.

Display your citrine on a table near your front door or choose several tumbled citrine gemstones and place them in a basket near the front door. As long as you can see the basket or the gemstone when you walk in the front door, your remedy is in the right place. Clear your citrine about once a month to re-energize it. (Note: See the section at the end of this book on clearing stones for how to do this.)

Education

Short classes or accelerated programs are good for you this year. You may want to look into classes on technology—everything from computer repair and hardware maintenance to coding apps and network security. If this is in line with your profession, all the better. But even if you work outside the technology industry it's beneficial at this time to know how to build a website, create a powerpoint, or network a printer.

You may look outside the standard University system to find the education you need. You might discover classes online or a private tutor (doing classes by video conference, perhaps). Avoid private institutions that promise jobs but only leave you with high tuition costs and student debt. If you are already saddled with student loan debt, look at government programs designed to aid students and see what assistance you may qualify for.

Legal Matters

A business partnership or employment opportunity will likely bring a contract to your attention. This agreement may have been signed a while ago but it's become relevant now. Even though there's some expense involved, you may want to get help from a lawyer if this contract is being challenged or if the other party is in breach of the terms. While you're not in any legal jeopardy over these matters, they can be a source of irritation and disruption if you don't get it handled properly.

Health and Well-Being

2019 is an excellent year for Rabbit natives in the area of physical and mental health. For a few years now you've been focused on yourself, and this year there are opportunities to show a great deal of improvement. You do need to stick to your positive routines, however. There will be those who tell you to lighten up on your diet or to stop working out—mostly because they don't want to do it themselves. Tell them you are happy sticking with your good health routines.

As mentioned before, your eating habits may be challenged by friends and family. You may be cajoled into an extra drink or a larger piece of pie (when you've sworn off sugar and wheat, and don't want pie at all.) Rabbit natives are sensitive to the feelings of others but it doesn't mean you have to change your behavior to suit everyone else. Instead, give them "permission" to have what they want while you stick to your routine.

That said, you won't be surprised to find your relationships with friends and family is the source of your stress this year. Whether this is negative is all in how you think about it. Everyone wants to see you and you feel pulled in different directions. You can only be in one place at a time. So enjoy the popularity but decline invitations that don't fit into your schedule. Balance the time you spend with others with pleasant, peaceful alone time, too.

Many cultures know about the mystic knot. The knot is known throughout Asia, the British Isles, and are even mentioned in Greek mythology. The mystic knot is a decorative knot is tied in such a way it seems to go in an endless loop. It represents eternity or longevity.

Mystic knots come in various colors and in a variety of materials, such as rope, wire or yarn; but the best for our purposes is bright red. Hang your mystic knot in the kitchen, bedroom, or family room to bring positive health energy to everyone in the home.

Dragon

February 16, 1904–February 3, 1905: Yang Wood Dragon

February 3, 1916–January 22, 1917: Yang Fire Dragon

January 23, 1928–February 9, 1929: Yang Earth Dragon

February 8, 1940–January 26, 1941: Yang Metal Dragon

January 27, 1952–February 13, 1953: Yang Water Dragon

February 13, 1964–February 1, 1965: Yang Wood Dragon

January 31, 1976–February 17, 1977: Yang Fire Dragon

February 17, 1988–February 5, 1989: Yang Earth Dragon

February 5, 2000–January 23, 2001: Yang Metal Dragon

January 23, 2012–February 9, 2013: Yang Water Dragon

February 10, 2024–January 28, 2025: Yang Wood Dragon

Dragon Personality

When considering the qualities of a Chinese Zodiac animal, it's a good idea to examine the traits, behaviors, and personality of the animal—except, we don't have any dragons to study (at least anymore). In the Shuo Wen dictionary (200 A.D.) dragons are listed; so we can read a description of this creature: The dragon has ." the will and power of transformation and the gift of rendering itself visible or invisible at pleasure."

It is said there are three types of Dragon: one, the most powerful, inhabits the sky; the second lives in the ocean, and the third resides in dens (or caves) in the mountains. There are some who say a dragon can shrink to the size of the silkworm, or expand in size, lie down and fill up an entire lake! All of these powers are described as the traits belonging to this creature, the Dragon. This explains why so many people envy those born in the Year of the Dragon.

The Dragon seems not to be of this world, and likewise, Dragon natives are seen to exist "above it all." They have big ideas and the power to make them happen. Even when young in years, Dragon will take on and carry enormous burdens and responsibilities.

Dragon can tap into a seemingly endless supply of energy, and they are eager to talk about their ideas. The Dragon has the potential to accomplish great things—or to simply fly around in the heavens, never allowing his or her feet to touch the ground.

Despite all of this magical power, people born in the Year the Dragon can have violent tempers (and explosive temper tantrums) when things don't go their way. Sometimes a Dragon is not diplomatic. They would much rather say what they want to say, rather than tell others what these people might want to hear and when a Dragon breathes fire everyone in the vicinity gets singed!

It's imperative for the Dragon native to have a very clear purpose in life. They must always have a cause to champion, a wrong to right. No matter what Dragon does for a living, he/she will have their pet projects and their dreams. Without these, Dragon becomes listless and depressed.

The Dragon is known to be very skillful in finance and management. Dragon very sensibly looks at long-term investing as a way to protect their assets. They are good at spending money and is always on the lookout for some innovation to adopt. Dragons rise to the top of whatever field they choose. They are often chosen to be the leader, even if they're new to the organization.

Dragons hate to be trapped, to see no options for change. If stuck behind a desk or saddled with a long list of rules, Dragons will revolt. For all their seeming confidence, the Dragon can feel quite insecure on the inside. There is a constant struggle going on there between the desire for success and the fear of success. They're status conscious and don't like to fail, especially in the eyes of others. This causes them sometimes to shoot for small goals, rather than pursue the big dreams.

Dragon is by far the largest personality of the Chinese zodiac. As the only mythical animal of the twelve, a Dragon can take on many forms. In the tradition of the past, a dragon can manifest as a creature the size of a gigantic cloud formation to one as small as a butterfly. Because of this remarkable ability, Dragon holds the vision for our future in this world; he or she can see where we are heading, and also is aware of where we should be going.

Dragon's confidence is as big as their personality. They easily motivate everyone around them. They will undertake the greatest adventures, eager to experience wild success—or willing to endure crushing failure. There is no stopping a Dragon once their mind is made up. They will go right to the edge to see if they can make something happen. If things go wrong, well, that's when Dragon truly shines as a leader, the one to lead everyone else out of danger.

Dragons have nothing to hide (Why should they? They have nothing to fear!). Their feelings are always out in the open for everyone to see. Dragons do not keep secrets. After they share the news, the Dragon will tell you he or she was absolutely right to reveal everything. So, if you keep a Dragon as your confidant, do be aware that whatever you have told them will come out sooner or later.

Dragons are sensitive to the climate. In pleasant weather, they are calm and levelheaded, but when a storm comes, they become easily rattled or irritated. When a storm is on its way, it's time to steer clear of Dragon! Dragon doesn't mind either way—although he or she is nearly always surrounded by friends, they are perfectly happy spending time alone.

Those born in the Year of the Dragon need a mission or a life purpose. When their life purpose is clear, Dragon is capable of soaring to heights other animals couldn't even dream of reaching. Dragon is very decisive, once they've chosen a path is very hard to dissuade them from continuing along it.

However, sometimes Dragon is not particularly smart in the realm of business. They don't pick up on the cunning of others. Dragon natives are often unaware of the plots and schemes surrounding them. Dragon is more concerned about reaching their goal, and not at all willing to play the petty games of others.

The most challenging thing for a Dragon is the stubborn desire to do everything on their own! They never call for help, never ask for support. Dragon is powerful and can even be intimidating; natives have a strong temper and a very fixed idea of the ways things should be. Dragon often speaks without editing, letting people know exactly what they think.

How to use your Lucky Days: *On these days plan to take important actions, make vital phone calls, send emails. These are days when your energy and luck are high.*

Dragon: Predictions for 2019

January: *[note: This month there is a Solar Eclipse on January 5th and a Lunar Eclipse on January 21st. Check out the section on Eclipses for more details. Your Lucky Days this month are 4, 10, 16, 22, and 28.]*

The New Year finds you sober and serious. After assessing the last year, you realize you are on the path to your goals, but you want to speed up the progress. Outline a plan of attack. Define your distractions and eliminate them. Consider where you need help and enlist those helpers. This year you want to make real progress, and everything starts with you creating a visionary campaign.

You are brimming with ideas. You are joyful and filled with the energy of possibilities. Create a vision board for the new year. Post it where you can see it at least once a day, or take a picture and make it a screen saver on your favorite device.

Some changes could be made at home. You may want to make some repairs or renovations. Decluttering is a possibility. These are all excellent activities to start out this New Year.

Be extra kind to your neighbors. Sometimes they may be irritating, but it would be good to avoid any out and out conflicts at this time. Keep things on a happy note or you'll be breathing fire later in the year.

February: *[note: Happy Lunar New Year on February 5th! Your Lucky Days this month are 3, 9, 15, 21, and 27.]*

This month we enter the Year of the Earth Pig. This is a challenging animal for Dragon natives. At first sight, you have nothing in common with his highly intuitive, gentle animal. But as the world enters into this energy remember that you always move to your own beat anyway. Let the world say or do what they will. Your creative energy is flowing. You can create the life you want.

You may be picturing what you want, but it's time to think bigger. Imagine something even better than your best scenario. Envision the resources you need, the happy home you'll enjoy, the travel and adventure that awaits. As you picture this, you draw in creative energy from the Universe to help you manifest everything you want.

You are lucky with money this month. Most Dragon natives thrive on a bit of risk taking. Keep it in moderation, and you could manifest a small windfall.

This is also an excellent time to ask for a raise or inspire a loved one to do so. You can coach others as they negotiate what they want and they will pay you in favors and adoration.

As money rolls in, take some of the extra and put it in your piggy bank. There will be some fun thing you want to spend it on later in the year.

March: *[note: Mercury is retrograde from March 6th to March 29th. See the section on Mercury retrograde for more information.*

Uranus moves into Taurus on March 6th – Time for change. Your Lucky Days are 5, 11, 17, 23, and 29.]

You are one busy Dragon this month. You have work and health stuff going on. This could mean you're feeling run down or you are healing from a past injury. Dragons are known for their amazing vitality so if you're feeling tired all the time it's probably a signal you need a break. Examine your daily routines to see what needs to be recreated into something offering you greater support. You have the potential to accomplish great things, but often visionary Dragons have trouble putting in the daily, mundane effort to get something big going.

You tend to be lucky but this month focus less on risks and more on coming in prepared. Try to get some of the extra money into a savings account or investment as you'll want it later. Consider setting up an automatic deposit to a retirement account or upping the percentages. A discussion with a boss now could increase your income down the road.

You are not giving much time to your relationships this month. Your laser focus on finances is causing you to ignore your partner and your other admirers. A smile and a compliment from you smooths everything over.

If you're looking for a love relationship, this is a good month to attend group events. Look for parties or social dinners to go to. Once there you will draw people to you like a magnet.

April: *[note: Jupiter goes retrograde on April 10th, Pluto goes retrograde on April 24th and Saturn goes retrograde on April 29th. Your Lucky Days are 4, 14, 22, and 28.]*

You may not have the funds or time for a big trip but even a day trip will be mentally and spirituality refreshing. You are feeling a little alone this month. Friends and family members are caught up in their own stuff, so you don't have many social engagements on the calendar.

Some of your daily habits aren't supporting the wealthy lifestyle you want. This could mean you're spending too much on non-essentials or that you're not taking care of your most important asset—you. Time for self-discipline especially in the areas of diet and sleep.

The greatest gift you can give others is your example of how to do things right. Show rather than tell.

You are lucky in love this month. If you're already in a love relationship, you are on the same wavelength now, and things are going quite smoothly. You are practically finishing each other's sentences. Time for a little romance. Plan a romantic evening of dinner and maybe dancing.

If you're looking for love, you are in luck as there is a love opportunity on your doorstep. This could be someone you met recently or just met today. Time for a first date.

May: *[note: Your Lucky Days are 4, 10, 14, 22, and 28.]*

You're in the spotlight this month. While you are very able to handle whatever is thrown at you, you don't always want to be the center of attention. Compliment and support others, and you will be celebrated.

You have manifestation energy around you now. Walk around your home and look at all you've been able to attract and collect. Everything you have was at one time something you wanted, and it came to you. Reaffirm your power to bring what you want into your life.

You're a little short on cash this month. Perhaps a large bill was due, or you were just too generous for your own good. Others will gladly give you their time and energy for the privilege of being in your company for a few hours. For this month, keep your hand out of your own pocket and save a few dollars.

Relationships can be sometimes great and then hit a short but rocky patch. This month there's some irritation around relationships. What you may not have recognized is that you are at the center of the issue. Sometimes your requests come off as orders, and your suggestions sound like pronouncements. A quick apology will smooth things over, but Dragons are loath to say they're sorry. Just this once, give it a try.

June: *[note: Neptune goes retrograde on June 21st. Your Lucky Days this month are 3. 9, 15, and 27.]*

As the year approaches its halfway mark, you find yourself thinking about the past and the future. Let go of your irritation in the lack of vision in others. Let go of any fears others have instilled in you about failure. Win or lose, the projects you have in mind are worth trying. Time for action.

Your finances are improving, but still need your attention in order to continue increasing at a good rate. You seem distracted by other things in your life and so making money isn't as high on your list as it could (or should) be.

This is a good time to cast a wider net. Look at finding support from strangers with a GoFundMe or Patreon campaign. Consider a partnership with a past coworker or schoolmate. Be creative when it comes to financing business ideas or side projects.

If you're looking for love, check out your friends and the friends of your friends. There is a connection here that can spark your interest. Consider what qualities you seek in your love partner, the ones you feel are truly desirable. Don't wait until everything lines up, or you may be waiting all year.

If you're already in a committed relationship, you may find yourself in an argument over something petty. Only get into a fight when it's something important, otherwise just walk away (from the fight, not the relationship).

When trying to be helpful, focus on small acts of kindness. You will be overwhelmed by the positive results you receive in return.

July: *[note: Mercury is retrograde from July 8th to August 1st. See the section on Mercury retrograde for more information. There's a Solar Eclipse on July 2nd and a Lunar Eclipse on July 16th. Check out the section on Eclipses for more details. Your Lucky Days are 3, 9, 15, 21, and 27.]*

Change is happening around you. Perhaps your company is being bought or taken over, or your managers are changing. Either way, change is good—that is if you're prepared. Have your resume updated and make a list of what you want in your ideal job. You can manifest a better situation in just a few weeks, even if you end up staying where you are.

Your overconfidence in money matters or investing may have put you into a tight place this month. If you're making investments find a way to protect yourself from the downside.

If you're investing in a business, then you are the asset. Use your power of persuasion to let others know about your mission. Try not to borrow from yourself. Instead, find loyal investors who believe in you. Don't procrastinate or get distracted. Stay on task.

Your romantic nature is coming through, and it's likely you will make a deal this month, showing someone you care. All the thought you put into this will be appreciated. This will win you a lot of points.

If you're looking for love, you need to get out of the shadows and into the light. Give the bar-scene a rest. Consider hiking groups, seaside sports or swimming at the Y to meet new people and expand your circle of friends.

August: *[note: Mercury moves forward again on August 2nd. Both Jupiter and Uranus move forward again August 11th. Your Lucky Days are 8, 14, 20, and 26.]*

You are a very loyal friend, but sometimes you can't help being the center of attention. This can make others feel a little left out. This isn't your fault, this is just what being a Dragon is. When you notice these feelings in others, try to turn the spotlight back to them.

A word of caution: make sure you take extra good care of your health this month. You may be working or living around people who are not feeling well. Eat right, exercise and get some fresh air and you'll have a good month.

This month, don't sit on a great idea. Copyright it or patent it if need be and then start telling people about it. See who is excited by this concept and wants to help you.

This is one of your best relationship months of the year. You and your partner are in sync. The love between you is apparent to everyone. You feel quite at peace.

If you want a relationship, there's no better time than now to get out there. Put yourself online, tell your friends, light candles, say prayers. Don't miss an opportunity to attend a party or meetup group. Fortune (in this case relationship opportunities) comes from action.

September: *[note: Saturn moves forward again on September 18th. Your Lucky Days are 1, 7, 13, 19, and 25.]*

Another month where change is the focus. Whatever has been boring you, displeasing you, or just plain irritating you can leave your life now! You have permission from the Universe to fill your life with what you enjoy. But for some reason change has you a little apprehensive this time. You're not sure what you want, or you're not slowing down long enough to really get a sense of what is and what could be. Try meditation or journaling. Sit down to coffee with a close friend. Hash out what it is you want, and the world will offer it up to you.

This is a fine time to negotiate a higher salary or to find a company to pay you what you're worth. The only thing holding you back is your own habit of procrastination. Visualize the conversation beginning to end and then go find the person and talk.

Create new love energy by changing things up. Shop in different stores, take a different route to work, visit new malls. The more new things you do, the easier it will be to find the love that's waiting for you.

If you're already in a happy relationship, you'll want to plan some surprise for the two of you. Make it something you both like to do and you'll be showered with admiration for your thoughtfulness.

October: *[note: Pluto moves forward again on October 3rd. Your Lucky Days this month are 1, 7, 13, 19, 25 and 31.]*

In every relationship, there's a point when you find you both want a change, but you also don't want to change. It's when there are pros and cons to each option. Here's where a lot of people could get stuck—but not the mighty, magnificent Dragon. You don't fear discomfort if it's for a lofty goal. You don't shy away from change if there's potential to accomplish something better. Here you are faced with a choice. Leave the familiar or strike out into new territory. Need I say more?

You're busy now. You're likely making phone calls, sending emails, basically knocking on the door of opportunity. Even then things take a while to manifest. You may not see the signature on the contract until the end of the month. Still, it's worth your time and effort.

Lessons are going on right now to help you learn to love and accept yourself for who you are. Of course, you're improving, growing and expanding your potential. Loving who you are at this moment helps you become a magnet for good things you want to manifest.

Good communication is key this month as you find your beloved in a combative mood. The same goes for those Dragons who are dating. Don't be quick to unload your feelings until you know their side of the story. Do less talking and more listening and you'll move from the first date to something more serious.

November: *[note: Mercury goes retrograde from November 1st to November 21st. See the section on Mercury retrograde for more information. Neptune moves forward again on November 27th. Your Lucky Days are 6, 12, 18, 24, and 30.]*

Home and family is the focus this month. You are a very loyal person and when someone in the family calls for help, you are there in a flash. This month you may have to find some patience as one who is often in hot water is back in trouble. You can fly to the rescue, and you will be rewarded with love and praise even though you may have to say, "This is the last time!"

You're clear about your path right now. There will always be problems at home. You don't need to use all your time and energy solving the same issues over and over.

Your finances are good this month. There are lots of work opportunities and sales possibilities to keep you very busy.

There's peace in your love relationship this month. You and your partner are both working together to help other members of the family. This united front gives you a sense of closeness that feels wonderful. No matter what, try to stay on the same side of the issue throughout the trouble. Arguments between the two of you could snowball into real fights.

If you're looking for love, stay close to home. Meet the neighbors, talk to family and let close friends know you are in the market for someone new.

December: *[note: There is a Solar Eclipse on December 26th. Check out the section on Eclipses for more details. Your Lucky Days are 6, 12, 18, 24, and 30.]*

When faced with challenges in life Dragon natives grow personally and spiritually. Keep that in mind as you enter this quite irritating month. Everything you want seems countered by others. No matter who you talk to you they give you a reason why you can't get what you desire. Just bite your tongue for now and look for the common theme. Is the Universe trying to dissuade you from this line of thinking? Is this a block to overcome or a sign to turn and take another direction? These questions are answered through meditation, journaling, and prayer. Take a moment and hear the answers in the music of the Universe.

You have the potential to have more money coming in than going out. Be open to all sources of income this month.

This month spend some time getting your finances back on track. This may require bookkeeping, finding a new accountant, or just getting your files in order. This is a task you can't put off any longer. By mid-month you may have taken on this project with almost religious zeal. You find many places where you could be saving money and a few where you are owed money. This month could turn out to be quite profitable.

Communication in your relationships is highlighted. Have a clear conversation with loved ones, be open and complimentary and you will get good results.

If you're looking for love, it's found this month through your work or health routines. Join a new gym and meet people there.

January 2020: *[note: There is a Lunar Eclipse on January 10th. Check out the section on Eclipses for more details. Uranus moves forward again on January 11th. Your Lucky Days are 5, 11, 17, 23, and 29.]*

The year starts off with intense energy around your job. You may find one or more of your coworkers quite irritating at this time. It also can be a change of procedures or rules that put you off. You're starting to wonder if this is the place for you to be. Be at peace. There's no forced move yet but it's good to be prepared. Dust off your resume and look around a bit on the job-hunting sites. Things may calm down on their own by month's end, but it's good to be ready in case they don't.

Money is neither good nor bad, it's just energy. Looking back over the last year you see money opportunities that didn't happen—or didn't pay out as much as you had hoped. You may have been out of sync or in some way didn't feel ready for the opportunity. All these options are still open to you. Go back and see what you want to try again.

You are the focus of someone else's attention. If you're already in a love relationship,, take their interest as a compliment but do no more with it. If you go down this path, you are more likely to stir up trouble.

If you are looking for love, then this month could bring success. Your charisma is high. Allow yourself to be admired and found by love.

Attract New Love

While Earth Pig years can be challenging for Dragon natives, this year you have a lot of luck and opportunity when it comes to dating. You can find an interesting person who thinks the world of you, and you can begin to build lives together. The luck for this year is activated by you taking action.

If you're looking for a long-term relationship or even marriage all the better. Dragon natives are romantic and love the big gesture, but this year consider that many people are cautiously looking for love and a big performance can scare off some good potentials. Instead be direct and honest, share your feelings and be open to what you get in return.

While luck is on your side this year, it doesn't mean you need to accept the first person who comes along. There will be several opportunities this year and possibly even several at once, so don't think you need to settle. Have a clear vision of what a happy life would be when you're in a healthy, loving relationship and you will be able to read the signs about the person in front of you.

If you are looking for a serious relationship with a person to settle down with, then consider using the Wedding Ring cure. Find a replica wedding ring (you can often find these at party stores in the bridal section), and place the ring under the mattress on the unoccupied side of the bed. Just lift the mattress up and slide the ring underneath.

If you're not ready to settle down but you still want a romantic new love in your life then instead of the ring put a copy of your house key under the mattress. Put it under the side of the mattress where your new lover will rest their head. If you decide later you want to make the relationship more permanent and official, change out the house key for the replica wedding ring.

Enhance Existing Love

While you may not feel it every day, your love relationship is actually growing into one to be envied by the people you know. This is because you have kept it fun by doing creative things. You have shared the duties at home (or hired some help). Every single hour may not be a song and dance but there are many days when you fall asleep with a smile on your face.

This is a year when you need to blend energies. This could be about bringing family members together or helping children from different marriages get along. You may need to find a way to deal with different schedules, or one of you may take a job at some distance. You have the creative skill to work this out. You may have to break some rules (something a Dragon native is up for at any time) but you will find a way.

It's a good year to find new things you like to do together. Write a list, each of you, of things you want to try. These could range from bungee jumping to a quiet walk on the beach. Make the list and then start checking things off. The new experiences will breath new life into your love. This will pay off in greater intimacy between you.

This year consider getting a moonstone to increase love energy. It can be part of jewelry or a loose, polished stone. Reasonably priced moonstones are available in mineral shops and online. It's said if you light a red candle on the night of the full moon and place the moonstone by the candle so that the moonstone will gather the energy of the moon and bring you luck with love.

There are also stories of how the energy of moonstone can smooth out trouble in a relationship. Give a moonstone piece of jewelry or a tumbled stone to your beloved and let the moonstone's loving vibrations bring peace to the relationship.

Looking to Conceive?

Don't clean under the bed! According to traditional Feng Shui, to attract a pregnancy, I would suggest that the couple do a deep cleaning under their bed, removing any items stored there. Then I would suggest they leave the space under the bed undisturbed, "Do not clean under the bed, nor put any other items there."

If a pet goes under the bed or sleeps under the bed, it's actually a positive sign. This has been effective for quite a few couples I have worked with.

(From Donna Stellhorn's book, A Path to Pregnancy: Ancient Secrets for the Modern Woman)

Family and Kids

You may be faced with a choice this year, renovate or move. You are not that happy keeping things as they are so you want either a little change or a lot. Even though it's quite a bit of work, you are up for the creative challenge. Note: moving in July may not bring you the peace and happiness you're looking for.

New health routines for you and the family are making a marked difference in the quality of your life. Perhaps it's the purchase of a blender for smoothies or you've discovered yoga - whatever it is, keep doing it. It's fantastic. Dragon natives can be known for going overboard, but this is a change for the better.

There's a lot of activity around kids. They may be needing your help to excel in school or to find a college to attend. If you don't have kids, you may be receiving visits from nieces and nephews. There's also a lot of activity around animals. You may be getting more pets or having animal activity around your property.

To protect your property—including things like your car—use the symbol of the firecracker. The firecracker is used in many countries to scare away evil beings or negative energy. I don't mean live firecrackers, instead, use symbols of firecrackers.

Firecracker symbols look like red tubes and are usually decorated with Chinese characters. It might be as small as your little finger or stand a foot tall. Often times you can find them strung together along with other Feng Shui charms. Hang your firecrackers by both the front and back door. You can also hang a string of small firecracker symbols in the car to protect your vehicle.

Money

For the Dragon native who's willing to work hard, there's quite a pile of money waiting for you this year. This is not a vacation year, nor is it a cruising year. This is one where rewards come after effort. You can think big, but you need to put in the hours in order to create success.

It's essential that you are well insured this year. Beyond the usual health and life insurance, consider looking at the downside of your investments and find a way to cover losses if they occur. This is how the wealthy make their investments. Dragon natives are known as the Guardians of Wealth and Power, so it's good to know how to guard your own wealth too.

Your block to money shows up when you're not thinking clearly about money. Sometimes you have such big ideas you don't consider asking for or requiring remuneration for your services. Don't wait until you make it big to get paid. It would be better to be paid all along the way.

If you have a business, are you training the business not to pay you? Or are you taking a salary, albeit a small one, right from the beginning?

A good Feng Shui cure for attracting new prosperity energy (and attracting more money in general) is to get yourself a golden piggy bank. Choose a style which appeals to you, perhaps a classic western-style piggy bank in metallic gold, or the traditional Feng Shui piggy bank decorated with the Chinese characters for wealth and good fortune.

Place your bank in near your front door or in the home office, and feed it coins at least once a week (no pennies please). Place a list of your money wishes inside the bank along with the coins to bring in opportunities and positive career energy.

Job or Career

You are busy, busy this year. If you have your own practice (like a lawyer, coach, or healing practitioner) you may develop a waiting list of patients/clients to see you. Your reputation is improving, and people will be sending their friends and family to you. This is, for the most part, work you enjoy and things are really feeling good in this area.

There are a few aspects of your current career you're not happy with. In your own business, it may be the bookkeeping. If you're employed by a company, it may be the meetings. In both cases see if you can do less of what you don't like so you can focus on using your talents doing things you enjoy. This may mean having some conversations with people to ask for their help.

You are having a little trouble keeping yourself on a schedule. This is very important if you have more than one job, are freelance, or you have a side business you're trying to get off the ground. Look into scheduling methods and apps to help reduce distractions. Study how you can be more productive, doing more in less time.

Dragon's Blood incense sounds as magical as it is. It's made from the blood-red sap of a particular tree. The resin, when burned, has a woodsy, spicy aroma. It has been used in many cultures to increase power and confidence.

Burn Dragon's Blood incense about once a month especially when there's a lot of career activity in your life. Burn it by the front door to increase positive career energy. If you don't feel comfortable burning the incense look for Dragon's Blood oil. Put some drops on cotton balls and place them in a bowl near the front door.

Education

One of the projects in your life making you so busy is your education. You may be taking more classes than previous years or the classes themselves may be more challenging. You are wearing yourself thin rushing from work to school to do homework, and then rushing some more on your way back to work. You must find a way to delegate at least some of your chores at home. Consider working part-time for a while if that's possible. Or cut back on a class, especially towards the end of the year.

You do very well to study subjects directly related to your career or that help you with technology. Also consider classes in accounting, finance or investing. You may want to get a certification or licensing rather than a formal degree. Stay with the practical, these will be the most useful for you at this time.

Legal Matters

A legal matter that's been hanging over your head for a while comes to a quick and surprising result. You may be tempted to continue the fight if you feel justice hasn't been served, but this is not a good year to initiate new legal proceedings. If you're signing purchase agreements or service contracts, do your homework and ask for changes in the contract to suit you. You have more power in this matter than may first appear and the other side is more agreeable than you expect.

Health and Well-Being

It is an excellent idea this year to make your health a priority. This could mean shifting or adjusting your eating plan or exercise routines. It would be good to find the balance in these things, so you're not utterly obsessed with your health but also not ignoring your personal well-being.

This year, some restrictions in the area of diet come up for you. This could mean having to give up some favorite foods because you know they're not helping you in the long run. This is a good chance to look for substitutions like fruit for candy or a salad with a protein instead of a burger.

It's also important this year to take care of your body's flexibility and range of motion. This means stretching and perhaps massage for your muscles. Care like this now may keep you from getting injured in the course of daily life. Consider adding meditation to your day. There are a lot of popular apps that teach meditation.

Most of the stress in your life seems to be from your job. It could be you just have too much to do at your job and less and less help to support you. You also show some unhappiness around your routines, ones which no longer benefit you. Maybe you want to get a side business going but when you get home from work you're too tired. Or you want to investigate your creative side, but at home, everyone is asking you for help with their stuff. Creating time for yourself is important and will take saying "No" to some people, but it will benefit you this year.

Consider adding the fragrant flower, jasmine, to your front yard or, if this is not possible, place a picture of jasmine in your bedroom. You can also have cut jasmine flowers in the bedroom about once a month. Artificial or silk flowers will work energetically for a few months but will need to be cleaned or replaced to renew the energy. This pretty, night-blooming flower is said to bring sound sleep and prophetic dreams. In the morning you will feel both rested and have an inner knowledge of what the day will hold.

Snake

February 4, 1905–January 24, 1906: Yin Wood Snake

January 23, 1917–February 10, 1918: Yin Fire Snake

February 10, 1929–January 29, 1930: Yin Earth Snake

January 27, 1941–February 14, 1942: Yin Metal Snake

February 14, 1953–February 2, 1954: Yin Water Snake

February 2, 1965–January 20, 1966: Yin Wood Snake

February 18, 1977–February 6, 1978: Yin Fire Snake

February 6, 1989–January 26, 1990: Yin Earth Snake

January 24, 2001–February 11, 2002: Yin Metal Snake

February 10, 2013–January 30, 2014: Yin Water Snake

January 29, 2025–February 16, 2026: Yin Wood Snake

Snake Personality

When considering the qualities of a Chinese Zodiac animal, it's a good idea to examine the traits, behaviors, and personality of the animal, well, Snake in this instance. At first glance it may seem Snake is at a disadvantage, having no hands or feet. But Snakes use their sense of smell to track their prey. Their sense of smell comes from using their forked tongue to collect airborne particles. You may already be aware your sense of smell is more acute than the average person. This is one of your advantages.

The scales covering a snake's body allow them to grip things tightly and to move swiftly along the ground. These scales are shed off periodically, revealing new skin beneath as the snake literally crawls out of its old skin. This means you can reinvent yourself whenever you want. When your life needs to change, you can change it in a big way.

People born in the Year of the Snake rely on their intelligence and wisdom to make their way through the world. They have a very keen intuitive sense about other people. They easily attract people and keep them near for as long as they need. Snakes can also enjoy spending time alone when they wish.

Snakes cope well with making significant life changes. It seems they can renew themselves at will. They may change careers or move to a new city, leaving everything behind. They are reborn. Snakes admire power and look to gain power for themselves. When Snake realizes they're stuck in a situation, or they feel limited in their choices, they will move on.

Snake is the wisest of the zodiac signs and can rely on their own judgment. They're excellent with money and have a good sense for investments. They have a computer-like brain which never stops calculating. They are incredibly tenacious when they want to achieve something. They never forget a broken promise. Some say the Snake is paranoid, but that doesn't mean people are not plotting against him/her.

While Snake natives always have money in the bank, they are cautious about speculating and should avoid gambling. If they do gamble, they need to make safe bets.

Snakes are passionate lovers (not necessarily limited to one person). Snakes are loyal, but they will wander if they suspect the other person is not entirely devoted. When they've been wronged, they like to crush their enemies completely. Snake will strike without warning, although he or she can be patient until the time for revenge is right.

People born in the Year of the Snake keep their feelings a well-guarded secret. They're often seen as detached and cool, but in reality, they feel things very deeply. If surrounded by negative people it breaks their concentration and Snake becomes suspicious and wary. But Snake has the power to win people over, and many fall into line with whatever Snake wishes.

How to use your Lucky Days: *On these days plan to take essential actions, make vital phone calls, send emails. These are days when your energy and luck are high.*

Snake: Predictions for 2019

January: *[note: This month there is a Solar Eclipse on January 5th and a Lunar Eclipse on January 21st. Check out the section on Eclipses for more details. Your Lucky Days this month are 11, 17, 23, and 29.]*

You feel free this year. You've realized you're the captain of your ship. You may not be able to control the seas, but you can steer your ship in whatever direction you want.

Travel is highlighted this month. It would be good to take a trip, even if it's just for a day or so, as a reminder that you can point your life in any direction you want and go. Sometimes you are challenged by indecision, not sure what you really want from life. That's okay. You'll find it on the way. Just pack and go.

A brief encounter with an intriguing stranger gives you an affirmation that speaks to your heart.

You have many answers this month. When you ask the question and then are silent for a while, the information will come to you. Some people are afraid to ask, fearing they won't like the answer, but Snake natives never shy away from useful information.

There are a few changes you can make in your relationship or your search for a relationship that will aid you greatly. You already know what to do, you just need to settle on doing it.

A special friend will come back into your life to share some beautiful memories of the past.

February: *[note: Happy Lunar New Year on February 5th! Your Lucky Days this month are 4, 10, 16, 22, and 28.]*

Now we enter the year of the Earth Pig. This sign is directly opposite your own sign. This 'opposite' energy means the world is not paying attention to you. This can feel like people are turning away from you—just as you thought your relationships and friendships were making progress. It's a time when you need to speak up for yourself. Use your natural humor to get people back in your corner. Don't overdramatize their absence, it only appears they are unsupportive because of the shift of energy in the New Year.

Snake natives are known for their ability to make quick, firm decisions. This is a gift in a world where you are often surrounded by indecisive people. This month a choice leads you to add another layer to the foundation of your life's work. You are on your path. Move forward confidently.

Your luck with money matters is high this month. You may have a small windfall or receive some bonus from a job. You have opportunities to make money on the side. If you want to sell some large item like a car or a house, this is an excellent time to get it ready and list it. This is a good month to ask for a raise or if you're in business for yourself, to raise your prices. You will get a little pushback, but once you're past the usual objections, they will see it your way.

March: *[note: Mercury is retrograde from March 6th to March 29th. See the section on Mercury retrograde for more information. Uranus moves into Taurus on March 6th—Time for change. Your Lucky Days this month are 12, 18, 24, and 30.]*

Consider taking a day trip to an interesting part of town or to a neighboring community you've wanted to check out. Take in a concert, a comedy show or go see a ball game. The more you unplug, the better able you will be to access your inner creative mind and come up with ideas that will serve you all year.

Snake is known for their business acumen and wisdom. Look for ways for your money to work for you. Do you have equipment you could rent out? A room to let? Or can you find a partnership you'd like to support? Investments this month could pay big later. Take steps towards your eventual financial freedom.

Your love relationship is okay, not at it's best, but certainly not anything to kick up a fuss about. You are tempted to spend some time alone, but it's not healthy for your relationship to be apart too long. Your partner looks like they want to have a "talk," and you seem to be avoiding it. That's not the best idea. Just hear them out and acknowledge them and things will be better.

If you're looking for a relationship, you are in luck. There's a lot of energy bringing you several potential candidates. No need to sit on the sidelines. Set a date and find out right away if this is going to go anywhere.

April: *[note: Jupiter goes retrograde on April 10th, Pluto goes retrograde on April 24th and Saturn goes retrograde on April 29th. Your Lucky Days this month are 5, 11, 17, 23, and 29.]*

Your reputation in the world is highlighted this month. If you have a business, you can expand your presence on social media to bring customers your way. This isn't really what you like to do. Snakes prefer just to be their charming selves and have people flock to them. But to stand out in the crowd, you must first be seen.

The key, this month, is reaching out to helpful others and seeing who is willing to create a partnership with you. First, envision what you want and how the conversation will go. Then connect through a phone call or email. Set up a meeting and talk about your vision. If they're smart, they will see the value right away and sign up to do business with you.

A day spent in quiet reflection this month pays itself 10 fold with insights and information. Take a personal day.

Love is in the air. If you're already in a love relationship, you find a new spark bringing romance back in. You're in the bedroom more than the living room. Joy is back and you couldn't be happier.

If you're looking for love, know that someone is trying to catch your eye. Little do they know, Snakes are good at hiding how they feel. Show you're interested and you will get good results.

May: *[note: Your Lucky Days are 5, 11, 17, 23, and 29.]*

Education is the focus this month. You could be traveling to a conference or taking an online class. It's also possible for you to teach a class or put up a video on YouTube demonstrating something you know how to do. Snake natives love information, and you may be a perpetual student. But you know enough to teach a variety of classes. Set yourself up as the authority by teaching and you will find it helps you in many areas of your life.

All this hard work and discipline is great for your pocketbook, but it's not renewing your spirit. You feel blocked and put upon by others. Consider keeping your focus on work this month. There will be months in the future that will give you "me" time.

Your relationship energy is, but your partner is quite demanding right now. You're getting the romance you want but there's also an unpleasant surprise or two as your lover corners you and makes demands (like helping more with the kids or taking vacation time to see the in-laws). It's all part of being in a committed relationship. Best to nod and go along.

June: *[note: Neptune goes retrograde on June 21st. Your Lucky Days this month are 4, 10, 16, 22, and 28.]*

This month, the theme is relationships of all kinds. This includes partnerships for business and how you get along with co-workers. If there has been trouble in this area and it hasn't been solved with a conversation or two, you may have to consider removing your self from the equation by looking for another position.

Over the past few months you have been able to take action on money matters, but now it appears you're just waiting. This month you are challenged not just to retain the power you have but instead, to make what you want happen. This may not be clear to you at first. Snake natives know how to focus on a goal—but don't allow yourself to be the blocked by waiting for the other party to take action.

There are many roads to get to your destination. If the road ahead seems blocked, it's time to brainstorm new ways to achieve your goals. Snake natives are excellent thinkers and great at researching options.

More attention is coming your way from a source outside your love relationship. This could make your life very complicated and so only proceed after careful thought. But if you want to get into a relationship, this is an excellent month to proceed. Be impulsive and suggest a trip together.

July: *[note: Mercury is retrograde from July 8th to August 1st. See the section on Mercury retrograde for more information. There's a Solar Eclipse on July 2nd and a Lunar Eclipse on July 16th. Check out the section on Eclipses for more details. Your Lucky Days are 4, 10, 22, and 28.]*

One of the reasons Snake natives are so intuitive is because a snake lives on the ground where he can feel even the slightest vibration, the softest footstep. What you feel now is the vibration of change. Many of these changes are happening to people you care about rather than directly happening to you. That doesn't mean, however, you won't be materially affected.

When change happens some Snakes wrap themselves tightly around what they want and don't let go. But the Universe will have its way this time. Holding on may be more painful than just allowing the change to happen.

Money is a little more challenging this month, as you're trying to do too much on your own and not finding others to help you. Some of the reason is these people are going through changes in their lives, so they are distracted and unresponsive. You don't need to do everything alone, but you may also not be able to rely on those you thought you could.

Your love relationship has that hazy, romantic filter on it giving you the idea everything is okay. But your partner may be feeling very different than you are at this time. Watch your partner and look for signs of what they want.

If you ready to get into a relationship know that you're taking the "watching" part a little too literally. Now is the time for an approach. If you are rejected, move on quickly and don't wait around even one minute for a person who's doesn't recognize your value.

August: *[note: Mercury moves forward again on August 2nd. Both Jupiter and Uranus move forward again August 11th. Your Lucky Days are 3, 9, 15, 21, and 27.]*

Snake natives possess the gift of communication. You are able to sway others to your cause. But, at times, you must be cautious with this gift. Someone could hear your words and make a huge deal out of something you don't want to be known generally. Stick to the truth in conversations and confessions this month. If you're going to keep a secret, tell no one.

You know how to hold onto a dollar. This month shows you are counting pennies feeling as if your pockets are empty. Your money is there, it's just hidden from you right now. There could be delays around getting paid. There could be issues at your bank. Keep your eyes open and be ready to make phone calls if you sense any signs of trouble.

Your love life seems to have faded into the background. You're more interested in hanging out with friends in the basement or playing video games on your phone rather than working on a relationship. Escaping every once in a while is okay, but not every weekend. Time to put a toe outside the comfort zone by doing something different for a change.

September: *[note: Saturn moves forward again on September 18th. Your Lucky Days are 2, 8, 14, 20, and 26.]*

You are full of energy and enthusiasm. You can't wait to take action on a project. You feel inspired. But you're not sure what action to take (besides buying equipment or signing up for an online course). This is your perfectionist side coming out. You want to do it right. You don't want to repeat any steps. So you sit and wait rather than taking action. This is the best time to jump in. Yes, you might be making a mistake. The result will be growth which is the result you really want to achieve.

You are still feeling the financial pinch from last month, but now you are more determined than ever to make sure there's enough money in the bank. You are looking around at what you can sell or how you can create more income. This is beneficial to you in the long run. Snake natives have a talent for attracting money opportunities.

Your love life improves considerably. The small steps you took last month got you out the door, and now there are opportunities for a relationship to come into your life (or if you're already in a relationship, improved relations with that person). Keep up the momentum. Attend a party. Join a workout group. Find a meetup group that goes hiking. Love can be found at any one of these.

October: *[note: Pluto moves forward again on October 3rd. Your Lucky Days are 2, 8, 14, 20, and 26.]*

Have you noticed how you feel about yourself directly impacts what the Universe brings you by way of opportunities? You understand this principle on a conceptual level, but it's been difficult to put it into practice. You may be running the same depressing tape over and over. You say things to yourself you would never say to a friend. Time for a change. Erase the old tape and install a new, positive one.

Money energy is much improved this month. Opportunities are coming in. However, not all of these opening doors are ones you're thrilled about. That's okay. If something doesn't meet your high standards, just wait for the next one. You're very good at finding solutions. You just need to ask yourself the right question, and the answer will come. Money comes this month from two or three new sources. Keep your eyes open.

Romance is all around you but you're not sure if this is something you want for yourself. Your friends and family all seem to be paired up. Everywhere you go it seems as if everyone seems to have someone. It's not true of course. There are more single people (happily single) than ever in history. If you're not already in a relationship, you may want to remain unattached this month to keep your options open.

If you're already in a love partnership, everything seems to be going well, —though the timing in the bedroom may be just a little off. Maybe you're tired or your partner has a headache, but it feels like the romance just isn't there right now. No worries. It will be back soon.

November: *[note: Mercury goes retrograde from November 1st to November 21st. See the section on Mercury retrograde for more information. Neptune moves forward again on November 27th. Your Lucky Days are 7, 13, 19, and 25.]*

There is a lot of energy around neighbors and siblings this month. You may be called on to help with a situation involving one or both. One of the people involved needs to let go and move on. If not, there could be talk of legal consequences, though a savvy Snake native like yourself isn't afraid of standing up for what is right.

There are vehicle or commute issues this month. This could be around parking, or your regular route for getting to work is perhaps blocked for repairs. If this is about a vehicle, try waiting until after Mercury goes direct later in the month to have repairs done.

Money opportunities abound for the industrious Snake native. You have no shortage of ideas, and these days there are many sources of information through online platforms to help you achieve your goals.

If you're are on a set income, this is a good time to find ways to spend less time making at least the same money (more money would be ideal.) Focus on figuring out how you can become more efficient and effective.

This is a good month to check in with your boss about work-at-home opportunities for the future.

When it comes to love your feelings are running away with you. Romance is in the air and you can sweep your lover right off their feet.

If you're looking for love, you may be too focused on some imagined ideal and not seeing the love opportunity right in front of you.

December: *[note: There is a Solar Eclipse on December 26th. Check out the section on Eclipses for more details. Your Lucky Days are 1, 7, 13, 19, 25, and 31.]*

This is an important month for you. Many of the projects you have been working on come to fruition at this time. Declutter old papers and clear some space in your home (especially your home office). Bring some color into your life with fresh flowers or by hanging new artwork in your workspace. This will add positive energy to your workday.

When it comes to your finances, you usually follow the conventional, practical routes. But this month it's time to activate money energy on a different level. Send out your "all" to money via meditation, chanting, candle lighting or even dance. Money is just another form of energy. When you are in harmony with that energy, money simply flows into your life. Welcome this energy this month.

Your loved one could be taking you for a ride with their new idea or scheme. The best advice is to stay seated while the "car" is in motion. Ride this one out. You'll be glad you did.

If you're looking for love, jump on in! Ask someone out, or accept the invitation to date. See what happens.

January 2020: *[note: There is a Lunar Eclipse on January 10th. Check out the section on Eclipses for more details. Uranus moves forward again on January 11th. Your Lucky Days are 6, 12, 18, 24 and 30.]*

Risks take the form of contact with strangers this month. Reach out to people you want to know. Send an email or make a phone call. Make a connection even if you feel you're not ready to move forward. You are more prepared than you think.

Positive energy shows up in the form of an opportunity for a nice windfall this month. Remember, you can't win if you don't buy a ticket. In this case, your ticket is a job application, freelance proposal or an ad campaign for your small business.

Imaginary blocks are impenetrable, but real blocks have solutions. Use your cunning mind to see where you have obstacles and where you have excuses.

There is massive support for you this month in the area of love. Usually, when this much help from the Universe is available, it means you're in a growth period (i.e., life feels highly challenging). You are protected now and so what happens is for the best. If this means you are airing your grievances in an argument, you'll discover that in the long run great benefits derive from it.

If you're dating and you get stood up, thank the Universe; you have been protected. If you don't get a call back when you were expecting one, you've been protected again. Look at what happens this month as beneficial, and let go of whatever you think "should" happen.

Attract New Love

There are some challenges for you this year in the area of love. These are not blocks, just some hurdles you need to overcome. Chief of these is time. You are very busy this year. Your job and personal obligations have you running from one thing to another. This leaves you little time and mental space to even think about love. Yet, if love is what you want, you need only make time for it to find success.

It's entirely possible you still feel the pain of a previous encounter. Snake natives can be jealous lovers, and a past partner who strayed could once again be bringing you sadness. It's time to clear this energy by reviewing which signs you missed in the past. Know that whatever happened before doesn't have to happen again, especially if you choose a new person (rather than going back to the old one).

You can bring yourself much more luck in love by being very honest with yourself about the blocks you have to love. Snake natives can be more observant than the other signs, and you notice opportunities for love in many directions. You may have to choose to be faithful to one and miss a chance somewhere else.

A good Feng Shui cure this year for Snake natives is a gemstone. Gemstones have powerful energy. To attract a new love into your life use the gemstone: Garnet. For centuries, this deep red gemstone has been used to attract worthy partners. You can carry a polished stone with you, or choose to wear garnet jewelry—perhaps earrings or a pendant.

If you already have the garnets and you want to use them now to attract a new love, it's a good idea to clear the stone. See the section in this book for instructions on clearing stones and crystals.

Enhance Existing Love

Earth Pig years are challenging years for you personally, but it doesn't have to mean difficulties in your relationship. In fact, your partner could provide the support you need to help you through some of the changes in other areas of your life. But you do let others know when you need help. Even when in a relationship, Snake natives can find it hard to focus on one person. Don't take your relationship problems outside the relationship, unless it's to see a relationship counselor.

You are naturally good at the long game. You don't do things for a quick payoff now that may come back to haunt you later. This process will serve you well this year. Your psychic sense will warn you in advance if something in your plans needs to be adjusted. At this time, it would benefit you a great deal to let your partner in on your long-term plans. They can help and support you if you let them.

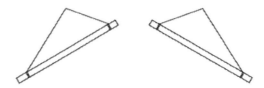

No matter your age, Snake natives are attractive and alluring. This fact could cause a little trouble for your relationship around July when someone pays you more attention than usual. If your partner is the non-jealous type, then this will come and go with no issue. But know that your behavior here will indicate how the rest of the year will go in the context of your love life.

The sweet, soft sounds of a flute have been used in Feng Shui for ages to bring harmony to the energy in a home. This year create harmony in your existing love relationship by hanging flutes. Simply take a pair of wooden flutes and hang them in the bedroom. Use a piece of red ribbon or string and tie the ends around each end of the flute. This will give you an easy way to hang the flute. See the diagram for hanging flutes below.

Looking to Conceive?

Olives and olive oil have long been a symbol of fertility. Eating olives was said to increase sexual potency in men. Consider adding extra olives to your lover's salad or chop up some olives and sprinkle them over a savory dish.

In the past, women would wear wreaths of olive leaves on their wedding day to increase fertility. If you have olive trees nearby, you can cut some small branches and put these in your bedroom. Extra light olive oil (which has no scent) can be used for a massage before and during love-making.

(From Donna Stellhorn's eBook, A Path to Pregnancy: Ancient Secrets for the Modern Woman)

Family and Kids

You have positive energy this year around home and family. There's peace and a feeling of contentment where you live. At this time you most likely benefit from staying where you are for a while longer (though you could redecorate if you want a little change in your environment). You could even add a media room or playroom. Or, consider updating the backyard for entertaining.

There is a lot of energy around children this year. This could mean you're deciding to homeschool younger children, or that older children are returning home for a little while. (If this is the case, you may want to set some boundaries with them before they arrive).

If you don't have kids now, you may be involved with children in the neighborhood, perhaps little league coaching, or babysitting. You may be introduced to neighbor children. You may also receive visits from out of state relatives and their kids.

It's good to do creative projects in the home this year. If you've considered taking up a hobby like painting or pottery, this is a good year to start. You might want to make jewelry or fix up an old car in the garage. Get yourself the tools you need and set up a place at home to explore this new passion.

An excellent Feng Shui cure to add some additional positive energy to the home is to place houseplants in clay pots in or around your home. Clay pots which commonly hold the houseplants are made from the Earth element and have a very grounding energy. The plants themselves symbolize growth, health, and prosperity.

The brick red, terra-cotta color is the most grounding of the colors you can choose, but ceramic pots in various colors will work as well. Place several in the living room or home office. Also, place a couple of small ones in the kitchen.

Money

You have several great creative ideas in mind, but these may take some serious work before they start to pay off in hard cash. If you're determined to go for this, start early in the year so you can be making money before the change energy of the mid-year hits. Take time in the second half of the year to make adjustments from the lessons learned, and you will most likely enjoy good profits by the end of the of the year.

You are possibly working more hours this year. For some, this is a welcome change as you've been under-employed for a while. But for some Snake natives, this is more work piled on more work. If you're going to do all this work, make sure you're charging a reasonable amount per hour— or you risk burning yourself out.

Money is possibly going out to pay for a real estate purchase for you or your children. Be very cautious! If the market you're buying into is overinflated, be prepared to hold on to this piece of property for a long, long time. Home improvements, on the other hand, look like they will help increase the value of your home.

When you wish to find or bring new money into your life, imagine you are unlocking a magic door. Behind this door are all the opportunities for money you could imagine. What better symbol could there be than a key to unlock the magic door? Indeed, the perfect Feng Shui cure to attract more money into your life this year will be a symbolic key!

Find an old-fashioned key. It can be large or small; it can be a replica key – even a key on a necklace, or a key chain. You might find your key made into a piece of jewelry, or you might find an old key at a swap meet or in an antique shop—any store where you buy things for your home may have decorative keys you can use as your Feng Shui cure to attract wealth and money.

Once you have found your key, either hang it by your front door, or on the wall in your home office area; or place the key on the desk or table where you work (or pay your bills). Having the key there will constantly remind you to keep looking for the magic door to wealth and abundance. (You'll know as soon as you find the door, you already have the key to unlock it!)

Job or Career

This year you find yourself working more behind the scenes than in previous years. It could be you're busy on a large project, or you are getting ready to launch a business. You might be writing a book or producing a series of videos. Whatever you are working on, remember to give yourself a firm deadline. Snake natives can get bogged down in the details. Remember, it doesn't need to be perfect to launch. The ability to make changes along the way is helpful.

You have the opportunity to inject some creativity into your career. Consider what direction you need to start heading in to achieve more enjoyment in your daily life. This may mean a bigger change down the road, but for now, make some small steps in the right direction. Make this a puzzle you want to solve.

If you're looking for something new you have luck in the areas of real estate, businesses related to children, "sin" businesses (for example alcohol) and office support like social media manager or personal assistant to the CEO. You are lucky this year when you take calculated risks.

In the West, when we think of gold, we think of a gold bar, but in the East, a gold ingot is shaped like a little boat. This is called the yuan bao. These ingots were used as a form of currency. Now you can find replica gold ingots in painted metal to be used as a symbol of wealth. They often have embossed Chinese characters of "wealth" and "fortune." Place your ingot on your desk or in your family room on a shelf near a picture of your family to attract a great job opportunity or a raise from your current employer.

Education

Going back to school or continuing studies this year offers a few challenges but overall is beneficial. The struggles you encounter are with your own ability to concentrate and time management skills more than anything else. You're quite busy now, and it's hard to fit in the time or find the energy to get the homework and school projects done. Look for time management tools and distraction removing apps to help you focus and get the job done.

Use caution when borrowing money for education. It's not a good idea to put these types of expenses on a credit card (nor should you co-sign on someone else's education loan this year). If there's no way to continue education without financing, then consider taking a break until more funding options are readily available.

Legal Matters

This is a good year to avoid lawsuits and disagreements that could turn into legal matters—especially ones involving employers, health care facilities and your own children. Look at the possibility of arbitration or settling outside of court. It is, however, a fine year to get end-of-life matters taken care of either for yourself or for older relatives. Look at trusts or asset transfer to help you and future generations.

Health and Well-Being

You are generally pretty health conscious, and this year you can feel confident you will stay at your usual level of good health. Snake natives usually take more time to care for their physical bodies than other signs, but you can sometimes struggle with allergies or slow healing from injuries. This year you are likely to avoid major health concerns.

This year it's a good idea to change up your exercise routine. Look to vary the schedule or change the intensity of your workouts. You may find a new class or trainer. You may try a new program, a different type of yoga or perhaps take up an active sport like cycling. This will help you release stress.

You seem concerned this year about your children, pets or some creative project you've been working on for some time. But overall this is nothing more than you're used to. The problems people bring to you are easy to handle when the action is broken down into easy steps. So while you may be tired of dealing with the same issues over and over, there is no more stress than usual.

A good cure for clearing negative energy from a space is to use salt. Salt is a potent substance. It takes all forms of energy and returns them to a neutral state. This means salt removes negative energy—and it also removes positive energy—bringing everything back into balance, to neutral. Once energy is neutral, you can then add positive energy very easily by focusing on happy thoughts, playing happy music or infusing the air with a floral scent.

To clear a house using salt, dissolve a half teaspoon of salt in warm water; pour the liquid into a spray bottle. Spritz the salty water around the house (taking care to avoid delicate fabrics). Once the entire house is clear, you can add back in the positive energy by burning a scented candle, burning incense, burning sage, or by playing uplifting music. When clearing a house of health issues, pay particular attention to the bedrooms and bathrooms, spray liberally with the salt water solution.

It is also possible to clear yourself and remove residual energy from a stressful or negative experience by using salt. Just add a teaspoon of sea salt to your warm bath; soak for a few minutes and think about the good things that will happen in the future.

If you prefer to shower, soak a washcloth in a basin or bowl in which you have combined warm water and a teaspoon of salt. Place the bowl and washcloth in the shower, and lift the wet washcloth to squeeze the salty water over your shoulders and body as you stand in the spray from the shower head. Repeat several times until the bowl is empty. This will cleanse you of any negative energy, and help you feel more balanced and peaceful.

Horse

January 25, 1906–February 12, 1907: Yang Fire Horse

February 11, 1918–January 31, 1919: Yang Earth Horse

January 30, 1930–February 16, 1931: Yang Metal Horse

February 15, 1942–February 4, 1943: Yang Water Horse

February 3, 1954–January 23, 1955: Yang Wood Horse

January 21, 1966–February 8, 1967: Yang Fire Horse

February 7, 1978–January 27, 1979: Yang Earth Horse

January 27, 1990–February 14, 1991: Yang Metal Horse

February 12, 2002–January 31, 2003: Yang Water Horse

January 31, 2014–February 18, 2015: Yang Wood Horse

Horse Personality

When considering the qualities of a Chinese Zodiac animal, it's a good idea to examine the traits, behaviors, and personality of the animal. There are many myths and legends about horses in our culture. Humans began to domesticate horses around 3000 B.C., so many cultures have traditions and stories about horses, which help us identify specific traits and behaviors of these beautiful animals.

Horses are extremely sensitive creatures; they can sense danger and know how to flee. They can sleep standing up, giving them the ability to start running at a moment's notice. Even baby horses, foals, can run very shortly after birth. Horses have enormous endurance and are highly intelligent.

Those born in the Year of the Horse are highly sensitive to the moods and motivations of others. They are quick to take offense and can explode with anger. But once Horse feels safe again, he/she quickly forgets their rage. Horses like to move things forward, sometimes rushing others. They become impatient when results manifest too slowly.

They like things done their way. While they believe in the pursuit of happiness for everyone, their way is the best way, and they will become aggressive if you try to block them, or pull them off their chosen direction.

Horse natives are great at business—especially from the perspective of sales and promotion. They are sociable beings, eager to connect people together for the benefit of all. However, they're not good at sticking to a schedule, nor do they like adhering to procedures. The more stimulating the job, the better! Once involved in their tasks, Horse would much prefer to keep working on a project until it's done, and then take time off to play.

Horse natives are better at short-term projects; they may not have the staying power to tackle lengthy processes. Goals should be broken down into quick steps. Horses are great at solving problems, and they love to get things done, no endless projects, please! Horses are curious and enthusiastically interested, or they're not interested at all. Once they lose interest, they're out the door. (This goes for love as well as business.)

Horses need both mental and physical exercise. They are graceful and elegant in their movements (and in their decision-making). They can be defiant nonconformists. When you try to put them in a box, they become a hot-tempered and headstrong.

Their biggest problem is their lack of focus and their readiness to jump to another project when something seems to be moving too slowly. They will abandon the original goal, and then wonder why they are not making much progress.

Horse natives excel at making money. They are strong leaders, who allow people the freedom to work on their own thing. They can be extremely generous with their time and energy, but if Horse doesn't like what you're saying (or doing), he won't think twice about trampling you.

How to use your Lucky Days: *On these days, plan to take important action, make vital phone calls, send emails. These are days when your energy and luck are high.*

Horse: Predictions for 2019

January: *[note: This month there is a Solar Eclipse on January 5th and a Lunar Eclipse on January 21st. Check out the section on Eclipses for more details. Your Lucky Days this month are 6, 12, 18, 24, and 30.]*

The New Year begins, and the dust is starting to settle after two months of really intense activity. Now you can do an accounting of what worked and what didn't. Do this with everything in your life, your finances as well as your relationships.

Be honest as you carry out your accounting and notice if you try to make something rosier than it is just to give yourself permission to hold on to it. You will receive support from your family for this process. They are more than eager to tell you what you need to change.

Horse natives live their lives in integrity. You are honest with yourself when you feel you're not ready to move forward. But finishing school or an online course doesn't automatically make a person feel "ready." You must feel your way at a slower pace until you do feel confident to gallop.

There's a lot of activity around home and family this month. You may be moving, or someone could be moving into or out of your house. The house will at times feel very crowded and stuffed and other times feel lonely and quiet.

It would be a good idea to do a space clearing a couple of times this month just to balance the energy. Horse natives don't like to feel alone, this can make them quite nervous. Ask for your spiritual family to be with you in the home, and the house will never feel empty of love.

February: *[note: Happy Lunar New Year on February 5th! Your Lucky Days this month are 11, 17, and 23.]*

This month brings a new year: the Year of the Earth Pig. This is challenging energy for Horse natives. While both Pig and Horse live in the farmyard, they don't really interact, so the energy feels a bit uncomfortable and unfamiliar.

You'll feel good about the positive social energy this year, but you can also encounter considerable boredom when many people in your circle want to stay home rather than go out to socialize. This is a good month to take a short trip. You could do a weekend away or even just an afternoon if that's all the time you have. Try inviting a sibling, neighbor or close friend to go with you. Explore a museum, a national monument or a visit to a specialty mall.

Your genius is strong this month. Any question you put to the Universe will be answered (sometimes in the oddest fashion, like coming across a billboard with a message for you during a drive through the desert). Remember to ask the questions otherwise the messages you receive may not be for you but for someone you know.

Speaking of driving through the desert, give your vehicle a little TLC this month. If you don't have a car, then look at your own mode of transportation and see if a change is needed.

March: *[note: Mercury is retrograde from March 6th to March 29th. See the section on Mercury retrograde for more information. Uranus moves into Taurus on March 6th—Time for change. Your Lucky Days this month are 1, 7, 13, 19, 25, and 31.]*

This month communication is highlighted. You may feel that no one is really listening to you, not taking your concerns seriously.

There may be a heated argument with a family member or neighbor, and your inclination is just to walk away from the relationship entirely. This is easier said than done. There is responsibility on both sides. Look at where you are wrong or possibly mistaken, and see if you can mend your side of the fence at least (and this could be a literal fence between you and a neighbor). Avoid escalating things to a legal matter if possible.

As a project comes to an end, you reap the rewards. If you have planted good strong seeds, the harvest will be good. You may have to let someone know it's time to pay you. Once past that chore, money rolls in.

Progress in your finances is slow this month. A lost or stolen credit card can cause you lots of headaches this month. Keep your cards and passwords secure.

You are lucky in the area of friendships. A bright-eyed person with curly hair brings you information that helps you on your path.

Sometimes love comes in inviting packages. For those already in a love relationship, there are some rocky times this month. There's a desire for freedom and autonomy on one or both sides. You may need some time apart (even if it's just spending time on opposite sides of the house). Horse natives don't like to stay alone for long. Soon you will be playing and laughing together again.

April: *[note: Jupiter goes retrograde on April 10th, Pluto goes retrograde on April 24th and Saturn goes retrograde on April 29th. Your Lucky Days this month are 6, 12, 18, and 30.]*

This month finds you a bit frustrated with all the things you have to do. Your schedule is not to your liking right now—too many obligations and not enough fun! You are usually both optimistic and generous, but this month you're looking for some "me" time. If you don't get a break, consider giving yourself a "personal day" (or a full weekend) to have some fun. Also, consider delegating some of the tasks on your plate. This may involve springing for a cleaning service, or hiring someone to run some errands for you.

You have good financial energy in your life this month. You've been working hard, and this may mean more money as a result of overtime at work, or because you are expanding your business. You have positive energy around starting a side project that will add another source of income in the future.

Things are much more settled in the love arena this month. You and your partner are working hand-in-hand together. Whatever was bothering them is now in the past, and they are more committed to making things work.

If you're looking for love, consider checking out business networking groups, health clubs, and juice bars.

May: *[note: Your Lucky Days are 6, 12, 18, and 30.]*

Your reputation is the focus this month. How do you want to be seen in the world? Most Horse natives are active on social media, and you probably have lots of followers and friends. Social media can help you achieve your goals or hinder your progress in key areas of your life, depending on how you use it. This month be strategic in your postings and in your dealings with others. Don't just try to entertain but instead make connections that matter.

There may be an unexpected expense this month. This could be related to travel, education or a legal matter/contract. Keep this in mind early in the month and put some extra aside. Avoid payday loan borrowing if at all possible.

Also, you may have to put a check on your generous nature if a friend asks to borrow money this month. If it's the same friend as before and a similar issue as last time, you need to find a way to say: "No."

You are lucky in relationships this month. If you're looking for love, you will have an opportunity coming to you through a friend. Be your naturally cheerful self, and you will have no problem attracting positive attention.

If you're already in a love relationship, try to avoid fights or squabbles at the end of the month over matters pertaining to in-laws or extended family. This could lead to long-term resentments. Try to be united as a couple.

June: *[note: Neptune goes retrograde on June 21st. Your Lucky Days are 5, 11, 17, 23, and 29.]*

This month you're feeling uncharacteristically insecure. This is not like you. Horse natives usually have confidence to spare. But this month you are in a scarcity mindset and having trouble shaking yourself out of it. Look at what media you're consuming lately and see if this is contributing to your fears and making the problem worse. Notice who you're hanging out with and how the conversations are going. You might have to remove yourself from a group of people who are inadvertently bringing you down.

That said, you are financially supported this month by the Universe. You can readily get loans, increase credit limits, dispute incorrect credit reports and expand financial opportunities. You may be in line for a windfall toward the end of the month. Your money mindset, though, does need a reboot. You are focused on lack rather than abundance, more on problems than solutions. Look at how your thinking may differ to that of financially successful people you know or have read about. Create a new vision for yourself and envision the steps to get there.

For those Horse natives who are looking for love, the conversation you need to have is with yourself. What are you not facing about relationships? You can have quite a temper, and if that anger is turned inwards, it may be blocking you from meeting the right person.

For those already in a relationship, cuddle up together in bed on an early Sunday morning and enjoy the sunrise together.

July: *[note: Mercury is retrograde from July 8th to August 1st. See the section on Mercury retrograde for more information. There's a Solar Eclipse on July 2nd and a Lunar Eclipse on July 16th. Check out the section on Eclipses for more details. Your Lucky Days are 5, 11, 17, 23, and 29.]*

The eclipses are bringing much-needed change into your life. Horses can turn on a dime when the winds of change blow, but like anyone else you would rather make the changes you want to make than the ones suggested by the Universe. So consider what you can change about your home, career, relationships and start working on them early in the month.

Financially there's a work/career or insurance related expense this month. Otherwise, money is flowing in as usual.

You are noticed at your job for good performance. You are well liked and are being considered for a better position, if you're interested.

At home, there are many things you would like to fix or change. The cost of doing so could wipe out any gains pretty quickly. Notice whether this represents a desire to keep up with the Joneses, or if repairs are truly needed right now. Don't spend where you don't need to this month.

A trip with your beloved is an excellent idea this month. You can visit relatives of course, but it would be better to travel to see some entertaining friends. Your work obligations may make things difficult, but even a Sunday afternoon spent at a potluck or barbeque would be the highlight of the month.

If you're looking for love this month, you want to accept every party invitation you can. This is not usually an issue for Horse natives. You could find a great match this month through an introduction by a friend.

August: *[note: Mercury moves forward again on August 2nd. Both Jupiter and Uranus move forward again August 11th. Your Lucky Days are 4, 10, 16, 22, and 28.]*

Your heart of gold is showing, and your stable of real friends is expanding. You are meeting new people and finding some great connections. These people will be helpful to you in the future.

Yes, it's more fun to be out of the house this month than at home. At home, there are chores and grumpy faces. You want everyone there to feel as good as you do, but if they won't follow you to the party, you can't drag them with you. Don't get angry, just go to the festivities by yourself.

Money energy around your career is powerful this month. You could be receiving a bonus or award (though this may be expected money, it's still a welcomed addition to your bank account). You can negotiate a new salary or find a job that pays more (and even get a signing bonus).

If you're attempting to borrow money, this could be a challenge. It would be better to look for additional sources of income rather than to take out a home equity line or another form of debt.

Some people might describe you as aloof. This month your partner is not feeling you are present in the relationship and they are trying to get your attention. Horse natives are faithful lovers, but they often have so many friends they can spend a considerable amount of time away from the relationship. Circle back home a little earlier this month and spend some time reconnecting with your lover.

For those who are dating, you will fall in love easily this month. This can lead you to think the other feels the same way. But don't jump in until you have evidence of their true feelings.

September: *[note: Saturn moves forward again on September 18th. Your Lucky Days this month are 3, 9, 15, 21, and 27.]*

After so much social activity last month you almost seem like a hermit this month. You are glued to the TV or your video game, and you don't let even friends or family in. This isolation isn't good for you. You may find yourself avoiding people—possibly because you've been hurt. On the other hand, you may just find your new video game really compelling. Figure out why you're isolating yourself, and treat yourself with kindness and compassion. Then check your schedule. You have places to be and people who want to see you.

Your personal money magnet needs a clearing this month. Every once in a while, it's a valuable idea to re-energize your ability to attract the resources you need. You can do this through prayer, meditation, candle burning (or lighting) or Feng Shui. Find a modality that works for you. Meditate on how valuable you are to your family and to the world. Picture the resources you need and send the message out as though you're making a "call" to the Universe. In a few weeks, you will see the results in your bank account.

You have guilt, and it's showing on your face (even if you haven't put a toe out of line). You are a loyal and faithful lover, but you have noticed someone, and they have caught your eye. First, tell yourself it's okay to have feelings. Feelings aren't something you can control. Once acknowledged, get yourself back on the straight and narrow. Indulge in an affair at this time, and you will pay a heavy price.

If you're looking for love, consider taking an acting class, going to see a play or getting involved in a charity. You will meet interesting people in the process.

October: *[note: Pluto moves forward again on October 3rd. Your Lucky Days are 9, 15, 21, and 27.]*

This is a month you can feel an urge to change almost everything in your life. You want to transform, to become the butterfly after spending such a long time as a caterpillar. You have particularly targeted family patterns as things to change.

You may have you noticed yourself repeating things your parents or siblings do, things you've pointed out to them. Now you see the mirror. You may be feeling estranged from relatives because of this. It may feel awkward, as there's likely a lot of contact with family members this month. But that's okay, give yourself permission to be a butterfly and transform.

You're feeling a pinch in the pocketbook this month. Some unexpected bill is draining the extra cash. Luxuries you have waited a long while to acquire are costing more than you thought. There are those annoying annual bills that are so easy to forget. The tightness in finances does bring your attention to your record keeping methods.

Horse natives are naturally good with money and enjoy the ability to attract more than they need, but record keeping is not your favorite thing. This month look for a better way to keep track of your money.

You can sometimes lose your temper and then be over it while others are still smarting from the blow. You may have been a little too blunt recently. Time for a heart-to-heart with your love partner to clear the air.

If you're looking for true love, first be kind to yourself. If you attract people who are emotionally unavailable, see whether you're giving off that vibe yourself.

November: *[note: Mercury goes retrograde from November 1st to November 21st. See the section on Mercury retrograde for more information. Neptune moves forward again on November 27th. Your Lucky Days are 2, 8, 14, 20, and 26.]*

This month is intense for more reasons than just Mercury being retrograde. You have a strong desire to complete something. In fact, you are so done with this project, person or situation you are ready to walk away no matter the cost. The trouble is it's challenging to really finalize something on Mercury retrograde as the retrograde energy is asking us to reconsider, to take a second look at things, to revisit past decisions. Check twice before sending off a note to your boss to let them know you've completed the work. If you have school work, double check it as well before you submit it. Triple check before ending a relationship.

Your finances are positive for most of the month. However, a spending spree at the end of the month does throw your budget into some chaos. This could be connected to holiday giving as Horse natives are known for their generosity. You may be traveling, and that's taking a bite out of the budget.

There's a lot of activity at home. You might be expecting guests, and you have a lot of projects you want to complete before they get there. You may be doing this all alone or receiving very little support for your projects as everyone else seems busy. Remember people are coming to see you and so let go of insecurities you have about how your house looks.

Plan to cook with others (even if you don't cook, you can spend time in the kitchen with those who do). You will find joy in the experience. If you are looking for love, attend a holiday cooking class or spend some time at a local diner. You are lucky in finding love in these types of places.

December: *[note: There is a Solar Eclipse on December 26th. Check out the section on Eclipses for more details. Your Lucky Days are 2, 8, 14, and 20.]*

You are busy this month. You might be organizing paperwork to get ready for the new year. Changes and tasks like these don't have to take up all your time. Just a few minutes here and there will shift the energy in your favor. You are likely to get lucky in the process (perhaps you'll find an uncashed check or a much needed receipt).

You are quite busy this month juggling multiple money opportunities. Your job is keeping you hopping but that's okay. They take the time to are express admiration for the work you've been doing. There may be a work-at-home opportunity for you or another job opening within the company coming in the new year.

Look at your investments and make some adjustments based on the shifting energies. When this month comes to a close, there will be a surprise announcement from a loved one that could mean changes in your life.

Your relationships are going well, most especially the peripheral ones like with neighbors and business colleagues.

At home, things are moving along well until after Christmas, and then suddenly things get bumpy. Someone's feelings are hurt, and though you may not be directly involved, they may turn to you for a solution. Your wisdom and good sense is a healing balm.

If you're looking for love, it's good to get out of the house. Online dating is useful at times, but you need face-to-face meetings to suss out the right person for you.

January 2020: *[note: There is a Lunar Eclipse on January 10th. Check out the section on Eclipses for more details. Uranus moves forward again on January 11th. Your Lucky Days are 1, 7, 13, 19, 25, and 31.]*

There's a great deal of activity going on at home. You may be considering moving or doing a major renovation. Someone else may be moving into the house, or a child may be leaving home. This will mark a turning point in your family (and perhaps give you reasons to celebrate). Even if someone is leaving this month, you see the benefits for you and your family in the future.

You are bringing in money and feeling opportunities to expand your income this month. You will encounter some obstacles to this expansion, and may need to put some effort into this endeavor if you want it to succeed. There may be no signs of growth or success until early next month. This has you irritated and doubtful. But it is quite reasonable to take risks this month. Even if your efforts don't pay off, you will still learn valuable lessons which will help bring profits in the future.

Family happiness is the focus of love relationships now. You want to see and be involved with members of your extended family, too. But don't neglect your beloved or there will be hard feelings towards the end of the month. Plan a trip (even if it's to see family). A change of scene will bring a fresh spark to your love life.

Attract New Love

Lucky, lucky year for Horse natives looking for love but it will come from very unexpected places. You may have your eyes and heart fixated on a person and be getting little in return. Consider socializing in new circles and meeting new people. Greet each opportunity with your usual eager enthusiasm, and you will attract love right to you.

In the past, you may have stayed in a difficult relationship or clung to the hope of reviving one just to avoid being alone. Horse natives thrive in healthy relationships where they can love and be loved. Don't waste time this year trying to resuscitate a half-hearted relationship. When thoughts of the past come up, replace them with a happy vision of the future.

You can speed up the love-finding process by being of service in your community. Look at where you can volunteer for a group or a charity where you are working side-by-side with others. Groups involving homes, the environment, music, and the arts, and also children are outstanding this year. By December, you are most likely one of the happiest people you know.

To attract the right person into your life use a treasure bowl— this is a covered bowl made from a natural material such as metal, wood, or stone. Write three wishes for your new relation-ship on a piece of paper. Make the wishes specific, describing something you could easily see in the other person. For example, "He cares for my well-being and shows me by taking my hand when we're going down steep stairs.," or, "When she sees me, she lights up with a smile.." Then place your wishes in your trea-sure bowl and set the bowl on a table or shelf by the front door. This will call the person's energy to you, attracting qualities you want to find in a partner.

Enhance Existing Love

Horse natives are probably the least judgmental of all the signs, and this year you use this accepting nature of yours to your advantage. Your partner isn't always a saint, but you love them just the same. This year you have the opportunity to fall more in love than before because you are able to overlook any irritating habits and find the joy. This is a gift you have and one that you can share.

The troubles of the past year with your family which put a strain on your love life seem to have faded away. Perhaps there were objections to your choice in a partner or just the way the two of you were doing things, but suddenly the limitations your family was putting on you no longer have any weight in your decisions. You are free to be in your love relationship. True, there may not be a lot of support from family, but at least they are not trying to pull you apart.

Your relationship is improved when the two of you socialize with other couples. Find some new people to dine with, see concerts or maybe invite to come to your place for a game night. Broaden your circle of mutual friends, and you will increase the enjoyment you have in each other. Watch your friends come to you for relationship advice as your partnership is admired and talked about.

For those born in the year of the Horse, it's a year to deepen your existing love relationship. You are independent, but everything is easier with someone who cares about you. This year find some pearls to bring into the bedroom. It can be a strand of pearls or a single pearl. Pearls have been worn by people in many countries to increase happiness in marriage. Pearls are said to increase loving vibrations in the people around them.

Looking to Conceive?

As well as being a symbol of money and abundance, fish are a Feng Shui symbol of fertility because fish have been so abundant in our waterways, lakes, and the sea. You could choose to have a fish tank in the bedroom (keep brightly-colored fish, or a school of fish, not fighting fish). Or, if live fish sounds like too much work, consider hanging pictures of fish (such as koi or goldfish in a pond), or brightly colored fish swimming through a clear sea. You could also place colorful glass fish figurines in a group on a surface in the room, or find some cute fish-motif pillows to put on the bed.

(From Donna Stellhorn's book, A Path to Pregnancy: Ancient Secrets for the Modern Woman)

Family and Kids

You begin the year feeling your home is peaceful and comfortable. Sure, there are some cosmetic changes you'd like to make, painting here and new windows there, that sort of thing, but overall you're quite satisfied with the home. Somehow though by the end of the year, the house doesn't feel like it's the right size any more. It may feel too big or too small, and next year you may even move.

Changes in the home may be due to the arrival of a new little person in the family, or of an older child moving back home; you may simply feel you no longer need so much space. You and your family may opt for a more minimalist lifestyle, and you start to think of downsizing. You may begin to dream of a whole different lifestyle—like moving to the mountains or living abroad. It's good to start to have a vision now.

There's a lot of activity at home. There are many visits from family members and friends. You may have parties or just discover your home is the go-to location for the book club or soccer team. This can bring a lot of mess into the home which could be one of the reasons you feel like you want a change.

Gain additional protection energy for your home by placing a pair of Foo Dogs (also spelled Fu Dogs) by your front door. These "guard dogs" come in pairs; one male with his paw on the world and one female with her paw gently on the baby. There are some Foo Dog pairs where all four of their paws are on the ground. This is fine. In this case, there may be no visible male or female dog.

Place one dog on either side of the door. This can be inside the house or outside the house depending on the size and material the Foo Dogs are made of. Some pairs are so large, they must be outside. Or you can find decorated and painted Foo Dogs of the most delicate porcelain and these should be placed inside.

Display the dogs with their raised foot closest to the door. So the male dog who often has his left paw on the world would have the door to his left. The female dog, who holds the baby with her right paw, would have the door to her right.

Money

There are some choice money opportunities for you this year. You may need to make some effort—perhaps even moving outside your comfort zone to ask for an increase or to raise your prices. But this will directly bring benefit to you and make it easier in the future to add to your income.

A financial gain is also possibly connected with real estate. You can invest, or you may be selling raw land or some developed property. This energy can also mean you are making money through your home. You might have an opportunity to rent it out or perhaps add a business at home. Home is your most robust center of financial success this year.

Horse natives would do well to remove blocks to money flow this year. You can do this by looking at the patterns of earning, spending and investing you may have picked up from your parents. What did they do right and can you copy that? What could they have done better and how can you improve on what you're doing?

This year consider displaying an abacus. This device was used for thousands of years to calculate money and do accounting. Displaying a beautiful abacus helps you attract so much money, you'll need help counting it.

Place the abacus in your home office or where you pay bills and work on your finances. You can display it on the wall, or place it on a desk or table. You can also learn how to use it. People who are adept at using an abacus can calculate sums as quickly as a person with a state of the art calculator.

Job or Career

You may want to make a sizable change in your daily routine, like going from an office job to working at home. This could be because you want to or need to be home more, perhaps for your family, or because the commute is becoming longer and longer. It is possible with some creative thinking and help from friends, to make a move from a conventional job to one of your own design.

There's a lot of energy and focus on home. This may mean you do something in the area of construction, real estate, moving and storage, or decorating. You may consider child care in the home or become a tutor using an online platform. While there's not a lot of job change energy at the beginning of the year, if you start building a side business now, you may be able to slide into it full-time next year.

Horse natives love to be of service to others so if you find working at home too isolating, consider moving your "office" to a local coffee shop or take a shared space in an office co-op.

If you work for a company, you may find yourself moved to a more open office plan. You can shift positions within your company, especially during the second half of the year. A transfer to out-of-state offices is also possible if you want to make a more substantial change this year.

When considering a new career or new job, you sometimes want to draw the energy in quickly. The traditional cure for this is to take ground cinnamon (the kind in your spice cabinet,) and sprinkle a bit on your porch—especially on top of your welcome mat. A single teaspoon of cinnamon should do for the whole porch. This will attract positive career and financial energy. Repeat every couple of days until you have the job you want.

Education

You may be at the tail end of an educational project, or you may be just a few credits short of a degree you should have gotten years ago. Now is the time to finish it up! This year you have a lot of support around education from your family and employers. However, you're not so excited about it. You may be tired of the classroom, the homework or the seemingly endless submission of prerequisites. You may not want to complete your studies, but you do want that degree.

While you may not be in the mood for long study sessions and pop quizzes, the Universe is opening doors for you in the area of education. This means you can find not only the classes you want to take but get help paying for them as well. Look for relatives or friends who want to support your goals.

Legal Matters

There is a lot of energy around contracts involving career and/ or real estate this year. You may be purchasing rental property or leasing a property you own. Some of the contractual dealings feel out of your league, and this would be an excellent time to find some help, either a professional or a family member who has direct experience with this type of agreement.

Around December there may be an upset, so include a breach of contract or a clause to cover any interruption when signing a new agreement. This irritating development will smooth over in a few weeks. Be patient.

Health and Well-Being

You have real opportunities to improve your health this year. Perhaps you finally find the right doctor or the proper treatment for something you've been struggling with for a while. It could be an inspiration or breakthrough or something you can do to make improvements.

It's good to add meditation to your day, a period of time where you sit, empty your mind and allow the Universe to send you messages. It takes some practice but it will help you gain remarkable insights.

Exercise looks like it's returning home. If you work out in a gym now, you might consider putting together a home gym. You might decide to have a personal trainer come to the house. If you like to walk, you might set up a time with a neighbor to walk the neighborhood. Also, consider getting family members involved. After all, you could do yoga in the living room with the kids.

You may experience some allergies or sensitivities to things this year that you haven't in the past. This could be due to changes in the ingredients of things you've been using. Or it could be environmental. Or maybe your body just can't tolerate the same substances anymore. You can speed healing by identifying whatever is causing the allergic reaction, and then avoiding it—at least for a while. You'll see positive results too, with help from alternative practitioners.

To protect your health this year consider getting a piece of petrified wood. It can be part of jewelry you wear or a piece of polished stone that you display in the home. Petrified wood is from ancient trees and represents a long life filled with joy and peace. It's been used for centuries as a barrier to protect against negative energy.

If you find a piece of petrified wood, you can display it in your kitchen or family room. If it's a small, smooth stone, you can keep it in the dirt of a houseplant. If it's large and flat, you can use it as a coaster. Or you can display it near family photos to protect everyone in the house.

Sheep/Goat

February 13, 2007–February 1, 2008: Yin Fire Sheep/Goat

February 1, 1919–February 19, 1920: Yin Earth Sheep/Goat

February 17, 1931–February 5, 1932: Yin Metal Sheep/Goat

February 5, 1943–January 24, 1944: Yin Water Sheep/Goat

January 24, 1955–February 11, 1956: Yin Wood Sheep/Goat

February 9, 1967–January 29, 1968: Yin Fire Sheep/Goat

January 28, 1979–February 15, 1980: Yin Earth Sheep/Goat

February 15, 1991–February 3, 1992: Yin Metal Sheep/Goat

February 1, 2003–January 21, 2004: Yin Water Sheep/Goat

February 19, 2015–February 7, 2016: Yin Wood Sheep/Goat

Sheep/Goat Personality

When considering the qualities of a Chinese Zodiac animal, it's a good idea to examine the traits, behaviors, and personality of the animal. There are two animals we need to consider this year, Sheep and Goat. They both have very distinctive qualities. We'll start with Sheep.

There are many traditions and stories about Sheep. (A ram is a male sheep, and a ewe is a female sheep, and lambs are both the male and female young.) Sheep are gregarious creatures who enjoy living in a flock. They can become stressed when separated from others in their flock. They have a natural inclination to follow a leader. Sheep are not territorial, but they do like to stay in familiar spaces. They flee speedily from danger, but when cornered they will charge and "ram" you.

Even though the traits of Ram represent the masculine expression of the energy of the sheep family, people born under the Zodiac sign of Sheep tend to also appreciate the more "feminine" expression of their essence. By this, I mean qualities such as shyness, sensitivity, tolerance, and compassion. These attributes are strongly represented among Sheep natives.

While Sheep can come across as thin-skinned, they will willingly forgive when they sense the honesty in an apology. Sheep do not like to be hemmed in, preferring not to be under someone else's rule or schedule. Neither do they like to rule—often opting for the supporting role.

Sheep is a very generous sign; he/she is known for their kind heart. Despite their generosity—or perhaps because of it—they always have a good home, plenty of food, and money in the bank. He or she spends his or her life helping others, and they are generously reciprocated.

When Sheep make a list of their material goals and share it with others, people step up to help Sheep make these goals a reality. Sheep often receive legacies from people not related to them.

The only time a Sheep is straightforward in word and deed is when they are angry. Most of the time, they will take a very circuitous route to tell you what they want or think. They may tell you their story in the most expressive and creative of terms, yet never come right out to say what they need or expect of you.

Sheep are devoted to their families and their friends. They remember birthdays, celebrate occasions, and are quick to send help when they sense trouble for the people they care about. This is often not reciprocated, their birthdays or their special events are often forgotten by those around them, and this hurts the kindly Sheep very profoundly.

Sheep natives tend to worry and perceive future events as being dark and potentially disastrous. They can spend many hours—even days—stuck in a dark depression. They benefit greatly by talking over their difficulties with others, but many Sheep try to hold everything inside, and this can cause physical issues such as fatigue and low energy.

Sheep can receive money, but they often spread it around quickly, leaving themselves with just the minimum to meet their requirements. They often attract money in the first place because of someone else, someone they love, needs it. It's imperative for Sheep to plan for their financial security in the future, although they rarely do so.

They are astute in business and are masters of the soft sell. They're able to get past objections and help others come to a decision.

People born under the sign of the Sheep spend time waiting for the right moment to take action on their goals. This means they can wait for quite some time to get what they want. They are so committed to doing things the "right way,." things often do not get done.

Sheep tend to be hypercritical about their own actions (and sometimes the actions of others), and this leaves them feeling vulnerable, as well as causing them a great deal of suffering. They need to take chances more often. They are more sure-footed than they realize.

In some parts of the world, the creature symbolizing this section of the Chinese Zodiac is considered to be the Goat—not Sheep or Ram. While many of the qualities ascribed to Goat are similar to those of Sheep or Ram, the energy of Goat has somewhat different qualities overall. A person born in the year of the Sheep/Goat can access the attributes of the Goat as well as the Sheep.

While Goat is a different animal than a Sheep, they are a sub-family of sheep. A simple way to tell the difference is by noting a goat's tail points to heaven, and a sheep's tail points to earth. When you are acting more like a goat, you are focused on climbing to new heights; you seek to get to the top and see the view below. When you're feeling more Sheep-like, you tend to want to stay home and stay in your comfort zone, your routine.

Goat forages for its meal, sheep graze on grass. People born in this year may find they spend time investigating lots of new things, new foods, new places, and new people. Then they might spend months at a time doing the opposite—sticking to a routine and the places and people they know well.

One of the valuable qualities of Goat we see in people born in Goat (or Sheep) year is curiosity. This quality allows you to explore and examine opportunities all around and to find out whether or not they may be viable for you to pursue. Curiosity keeps you interested in the motivations of the people all around. Your life is enriched as you find yourself entranced by new topics and ideas. This keeps life very interesting.

How to use your Lucky Days: *On these days, plan to take necessary actions, make vital phone calls, send emails. These are days when your energy and luck are high.*

Goat/Sheep: Predictions for 2019

January: *[note: This month there is a Solar Eclipse on January 5th and a Lunar Eclipse on January 21st. Check out the section on Eclipses for more details. Your Lucky Days this month are 1, 7, 13, 19, 25, and 31.]*

The year begins with fresh hope. You see opportunities on the horizon for your career and the careers of those you love. Changes are coming but you see what they are and you're getting ready. You know you have nothing to fear.

The house is coming along. You are clearing out more clutter, and it's starting to feel like the open, peaceful place you want to live in.

You are slightly irritated by a neighbor or someone close by. This could be a minor thing, like where they leave their trash cans. Don't let something petty stress you out. Definitely, do not allow it to lead to something legal. You are not lucky in lawsuits right now. A kind word and a smile from you can work everything out.

For those Sheep natives in an existing love relationship, it feels fresh and alive this month. Your love for each other can be more profound than it's ever been. Let past hurts wash away. This is a superb time to start again.

If you're looking for love, seek it in places where people want to get healthy—such as gyms and juice bars.

February: *[note: Happy Lunar New Year on February 5th! Your Lucky Days this month are 6, 12, 18, and 24.]*

This month we enter the Year of the Earth Pig. This is harmonious energy for Sheep natives. Intuition and sensitivity will be prized this year, and you have ample abilities in these areas. Where you need to police yourself is in your thoughts about yourself. You need to watch out for negative thinking and spiraling into depression (often this feeling comes from thoughts you pick up from other people). Keep yourself positive and clear your energy often.

You have some surprise opportunities for income this month. You can receive a small windfall or a new job position. You can negotiate for more money at your current job as well. It's all a matter of preparing what you will say ahead of time. Sheep natives don't like pressure, and you can take the pressure off by knowing what you want and feeling determined to get it. When you're prepared, you have fantastic luck.

In matters of the heart, this is one of your best months of the year. Others hear you and are sympathetic to your concerns. You finally get your message across.

If you're looking for love, you can find it in places where people make transitions, such as railway stations, airports and also spas and resorts.

March: *[note: Mercury is retrograde from March 6th to March 29th. See the section on Mercury retrograde for more information. Uranus moves into Taurus on March 6th—Time for change. Your Lucky Days this month are 2, 8, 14, 20, and 26.]*

You're lucky, You get a second significant month this year. During this month you will have more opportunities and luck especially connected to the seeds you planted in the past few months. You may be asking for something very specific, or you may just be sending out good wishes. As new contacts begin, positive things will start to happen for you in all areas of your life.

You are lucky with finances this month too. You may receive a windfall or at least a superb deal on a necessary purchase.

Guard your cell phone as an accident or loss can occur this month. That said, luck is with you, and you will find good deals on new phones and devices.

You continue to experience very positive energy in the area of love in your life now. You look forward to spending some time with your beloved, and perhaps it's time again to plan a quick trip, just the two of you to a favorite destination.

If you're looking for love, you're in luck, someone is very close, ready to make your acquaintance. You just need to find the courage to say "Yes" to a date. You tend to focus on tasks rather than the people around you. Time to smile at the world and see who's smiling back.

April: *[note: Jupiter goes retrograde n April 10th, Pluto goes retrograde on April 24th and Saturn goes retrograde on April 29th. Your Lucky Days are 1, 7, 13, 19, and 25.]*

This month marks a new beginning in several areas of your life. You feel you are getting support (especially emotional support) where you haven't received it before. It's a little overwhelming at first. You're not used to getting so much unsolicited attention. Sheep natives tend to shy away from asking for support for fear of receiving similar criticism to the kind they have received in the past. However, this is not the case now; it's is a good month to make a list of how others could help you and when you are ready, the help will appear.

This is a good month for investing. You may be ready to start an investment program, perhaps opening a brokerage account for the first time, or setting up automatic deposits. You might need to change your investment plan at work. It might be time to give your current investment adviser a call and schedule a check-up. You can also consider diversifying your investments into something more unusual or exotic that suits your interest.

There's a little shake-up in your love life. Your partner drops a surprise announcement they thought would make you happy, but you're just irritated they have sprung this on you. Sheep natives never like to fight so you're biting your tongue right now. This will work out to benefit both of you in the long run, it's just hard to see anything positive from this vantage point.

May: *[note: Your Lucky Days are 1, 7, 13, 19, and 25.]*

Your finances need some attention. This could be a change of health insurance provider, taxes that need to be completed or perhaps rolling over a 401k. None of this is stuff you want to do. In fact, the idea is quite irritating; but you would benefit greatly this year by handling these tasks this month.

While you explore your money situation, you find some blocks this month. You'll be surprised when you realize that you are the impediment. You clearly understand how to stretch a dollar, but you may hesitate when it comes to getting those dollars to work for you by creating passive income. This month is a marvelous time to learn.

Consider a trip late in the month.

The things that need to or could change in your relationship are highlighted this month—highlighted with a spotlight. It will be hard to miss what needs to change. You hate a fight, so you often find yourself giving in quickly, but this time you may want to stand your ground on a few points. You are generous but there is a point where things are no longer fair.

If you're looking for love, the thoughts and feelings causing you to procrastinate become quite apparent to you. You see what you need to do and how to get what you want.

June: *[note: Neptune goes retrograde on June 21st. Your Lucky Days this month are 6, 12, 18, 24, and 30.]*

This month you feel a desire to learn new things. You may want to take a class or attend a lecture. Go explore the local college (though classes may not start for a few months). Join a group, specifically one that focuses on writing, teaching, travel or world affairs. During this exploration, you will be meeting some new people, some of whom can become friends. Sheep natives generally hate being tied to a schedule (work is bad enough) but this is worth putting on the calendar.

You tend to have a fine home, a car that's paid for and all the necessities. But when it comes to accumulating money you are irritated with your investment performance. You would like it all to work automatically but the more you have, the more careful and protective you need to be. Check all your accounts this month, change passwords and balance checkbooks. If you find anything amiss report it immediately.

You feel a little stressed and moody, and you don't quite know why. You receive an invitation which is nice, you just wish it had happened a few weeks ago. Now your schedule doesn't really accommodate all this social activity.

Love is your solace this month. You come home and as soon as the door closes behind you, you feel better. Sit on the sofa and relax. Bask in the happiness of the moments with your family.

July: *[note: Mercury is retrograde from July 8th to August 1st. See the section on Mercury retrograde for more information. There's a Solar Eclipse on July 2nd and a Lunar Eclipse on July 16th. Check out the section on Eclipses for more details. Your Lucky Days are 6, 12, 18, 24, and 30.]*

Peace-loving Sheep wish for some new energy has come true. Change energy is straddling both your career and home areas. It could affect one or both. You may feel a bit concerned, but everything will work out so much better than you expect. The changes will bring you much more of what you've been looking for.

If you work a contract job and that contract is coming to an end, you may feel a little nervous about your finances. But this won't be for long. Another source of income will take its place very quickly. Sheep natives love to let go of worries. Meditate on what you want and send your message to the Universe.

You are very noticeable this month. While Sheep natives are generally faithful, they can also be well loved by others. An innocent encounter takes a dangerous (albeit sexy) turn this month. You could get caught.

If you're looking for love, you need to exercise some caution and not fall into bed with the first one who seems available. There could be some health consequences in the future for thoughtless acts today.

August: *[note: Mercury moves forward again on August 2nd. Both Jupiter and Uranus move forward again August 11th. Your Lucky Days are 5, 17, 23, and 29.]*

You draw a big sigh of relief as we enter this new month. Your life is going better. There are still some issues within the family, but nothing you haven't encountered before.

Children or someone younger than you brings their troubles to your door. They are looking for a handout rather than advice. You're great at problem-solving—it's just they don't want to hear your wisdom, they just want cash.

The check is in the mail, at least that's what they say. There are some delays in getting paid or disruptions in your usual income this month. You are always prepared, and you can cover the shortfall but it's annoying never the less. Despite this minor setback, you are doing well in your career, and at the end of the month you have some money left over.

This month you are flirting with your partner. This game is more fun than usual as you chase each other around the bed. You feel things are improving in many aspects of your love life as you and your beloved explore new aspects of your relationship.

If you're looking for a partner, this is one of the best months of the year to put yourself on the online dating site and make some dates. Don't waste the month just emailing back and forth. Set a time and place and meet for coffee.

September: *[note: Saturn moves forward again on September 18th. Your Lucky Days are 4, 10, 16, 22, and 28.]*

This month goes smoothly and easily. You can rest and catch your breath now. The work you've done on your finances and relationship pay off now. You sail through with a smile on your face. You have several invitations from friends. Consider joining a group or organization that interests you. Go hiking and be in nature, or sit at home and just enjoy your family.

You, of course, know that your wealth increases when you go out into the world and meet new people. You have such good luck when it comes to meeting the right person at the right time. Sheep natives are known for having celebrity friends. This is a splendid month to be seen, and some of the people you meet will be instrumental in your future.

Your relationships are going well. This includes the non-romantic ones. All the work you put into creating open dialogs has served you well. The people in your life are treating you fairly, with kindness and consideration. Your feelings matter to them. You're on top of the world. Yes, you know it won't stay like this, but the glimpse from this vantage point is terrific.

October: *[note: Pluto moves forward again on October 3rd. Your Lucky Days this month are 4, 10, 16, 22, and 28.]*

This month friends are pulling you in a million directions. If you don't turn down an invitation or two, you may find yourself in bed, too tired to see anyone. That might be an exaggeration—you just needed a reason to get out of an obligation you otherwise couldn't decline.

Your finances are fine this month. You have protection in this area right now. If you've been unhappy with any of your financial services providers, you could transfer your funds now.

If you own a business, this a good time to look into changing credit card processors or find a better bank for your business checking (and perhaps a line of credit).

You and your beloved are both lovers and friends. This month you are doing some fun/friendship things together. This is an excellent month to do some art or dancing or some other creative pursuit out of your usual comfort zone. Sheep natives are homebodies and often don't want to be bothered with all the effort and expense of going out, but this month it's beneficial for both of you.

If you're looking for someone special, this is a good time to attend work-related groups or professional organizations. You can meet someone who is doing as well as you or better.

November: *[note: Mercury goes retrograde from November 1st to November 21st. See the section on Mercury retrograde for more information. Neptune moves forward again on November 27th. Your Lucky Days are 3, 9, 15, and 27.]*

You are keeping a low profile this month, or you are spending more time at home. Your home is a very comfortable place. While you love nature, right now there's no place like home.

You may need to negotiate with some people in your business life for what you want. It's a good idea to know what you want before any meetings begin. These people's schedules will not be to your liking. By setting the meeting up yourself, you control the conversation and can achieve a happy outcome for both of you.

You're spending this month. You may say this is the last shopping spree of the year, but Sheep natives love quality items on sale, and there will always be more sales.

You can take some risks in business this month but do so only after meditating on the outcome you want. Put out a spiritual call to the Universe and be really clear about what your goals are. Then you can expect positive results (on the Universe's timetable, not necessarily yours).

Love relationships are going well except for some mix-ups on dates and times during the Mercury retrograde period at the beginning of the month.

If you're looking for love, you need to send a message to the Universe about what you're looking for. Perhaps you can consider writing what you want on a leaf, then letting it go in the breeze? Or maybe you can write your desires on a piece of paper and burning it in the evening fire, watching the smoke take your message with it up to heaven.

December: *[note: There is a Solar Eclipse on December 26th. Check out the section on Eclipses for more details. Your Lucky Days are 3, 9, 15, 21, and 27.]*

This is a high energy month where you have a lot of luck and opportunity—that is, if you can just keep your temper. In this case, you need to ask yourself if you want to be right, or do you want to be happy. Just when you think things are smoothed out, along comes the Solar Eclipse and trouble comes right along with it. Don't let this sudden attack from a person you've known for years throw you. Sheep can stay balanced no matter how narrow the ledge is.

While money matters continue to remain in your favor, you are irritated with a purchase you made. It may be not returnable, or it may just not be living up to your expectations. It may take considerable effort to make this right, but it's worth writing a letter or making a call or two in this case.

Look for places or venues where you can communicate your business message or showcase your abilities on this job this month.

In love relationships, your luck improves significantly. You are receiving a lot of positive attention and recognition for the love and consideration you've paid to others. Sheep natives are more in touch with their feelings than other signs, and it's beneficial for you to be open with your partner about how you feel regarding several things that have happened over the past few weeks.

If you're looking for love, don't be afraid to express what you want in a partner to friends, family and even on social media. Someone will step up to help you meet new people and find the one.

January 2020: *[note: There is a Lunar Eclipse on January 10th. Check out the section on Eclipses for more details. Uranus moves forward again on January 11th. Your Lucky Days this month are 2, 8, 14, 20 and 26.]*

The actions you're taking this month (ones you've been planning to take for a while) come at the right time. The results will be quite beneficial, so full steam ahead, Captain. Watch out for naysayers. You often go out of your way to avoid any sort of conflict, especially with loved ones. But this month, you have an opportunity to make real progress on your path.

There's the most energy in your area of money this month than any month in the previous 12. This means you can ask for the raise, promotion or transfer now, and get positive results. This is not a time for your usual Sheep peaceful nature. Action is key to getting what you want. Sometimes you hold yourself back, not willing to risk criticism or displeasure in others, but this month the summit is in sight. Climb, baby, climb.

You are at a bit of a loss why your partner is upset with you. This is because it all has nothing to do with you. There is a misunderstanding or someone is projecting their issues onto you. For kind-hearted Sheep, this is rather distressing until you realize it's not about you. Still, your feelings could be hurt—but before you fall into melancholy, recognize your partner is not perfect. You can struggle through this together.

If you're looking for love, you may feel the search is not yielding anyone even close to the type of person you want to spend time with. But the truth is you've been hiding at home or just taking the same path from work to home to the gym and back again. Break free of the pattern and love will be able to find you.

Attract New Love

Your vision is clear for what you want in a love relationship, but you may have been looking for a while. Sheep natives may say they're in no rush, but they are secretly longing to arrive at their destination. This year, take some time when you're looking for love. Sit in meditation and have a conversation with the Universe about the type of person you are longing to meet.

Sit quietly in a lovely spot, either at home or in a garden somewhere, and think about you being in a love relationship. Feel the happiness you will feel when you're sharing your life with some wonderful person. Then release the message into the Universe. Feel it flow upwards. Then go about your day.

If you feel you're not at your physical peak, no worries, who is these days? Remember, the connection you're looking for is a soul connection, and so you don't have to be in tip-top physical condition to attract the person who will make you happy. Sheep natives tend to do well in relationships in general, as they are sensitive, loving and kind. Be in the world, showing your loving nature, and you will attract those who want to connect with you.

Sheep natives can be afraid of hurting the other person as they are searching for the right one. It's tough to get into a relationship if you're afraid to have a first date with someone! You must know of a way to get out of something before you can comfortably get into it. So think of what you can say to suitors who are not suitable. Be ready to use gentle diplomacy to detach, and you will find someone to attach to.

To bring good luck in the area of love you can display the statue of an angel. Choose a depiction that is peaceful and sweet. Statues of angels with flaming swords are useful and powerful but not to maintain a love relationship. Display your angel figurine in the living room to promote the friendship and loving support you feel for each other.

Enhance Existing Love

In general, this is a lucky year for Sheep natives, but that still can mean your love relationship would benefit from working at it a bit. For the most part, things go well, but there are a few things your partner does that sometimes (not always, but sometimes), get on your nerves. You don't like to bring these up or even think about them. But this year it's time to say something. Confronting this could take your relationship from good to great.

This is a good year to travel together. You might be able to take a long trip you've been waiting to take for many years, or you may just gather up a few things and disappear for a long weekend. Spending time outside your daily routine is so helpful for bringing the love back into your relationship. Plan a few getaways this year.

You are generous and forgiving, but you can also occasionally be bossy (and usually when you're concerned with your partner's health or wellbeing). Keep in mind there is a time and place where your words of advice can be better heard. When your partner is tired or already irritated, they are not ready to hear your sage advice. Create opportunities to talk by first showing them love and support. You will strengthen your relationship in the process.

 When weather permits, plant gardenias in your yard this year or place a pot of gardenias on your balcony or patio. Gardenias have been used for centuries to raise the vibration of a place, to bring more loving feelings and to promote healing energy. Red Gardenias add passion, fuchsia (hot pink) will bring excitement and fun, and pale pink brings feelings of peace and rest. Try to keep the plant healthy during the warm months. If it's too cold for the plant outside, consider displaying a picture of gardenias in your bedroom. This will help boost the relationship energy.

Looking to Conceive?

For Sheep natives and any sign really, rabbits are a universal symbol of procreation, so using the image of a rabbit will help bring fertility energy. Choose a figurine, hanging artwork of rabbits, or place a couple of little, stuffed bunnies on the bed. But remember you need two rabbits to make things happen, so make sure there's more than one hare depicted in the bedroom.

What would be even better than a figurine of a pair of rabbits? Chocolate bunnies of course. Chocolate has long been known for its aphrodisiac qualities. These delicious rabbits will put you both in the mood.

(From Donna Stellhorn's book, A Path to Pregnancy: Ancient Secrets for the Modern Woman)

Family and Kids

There have been a lot of changes over the past few years. Change energy is dissipating now, and you are entering a period of calm. There is still some clean-up to do, perhaps you still have boxes to unpack and renovations to finish. But more peaceful times are coming. By year's end, things will feel a lot more settled.

It's beneficial to look at some of your home routines, and switch them out for more healthful methods. This might include changing cleaning products or reducing your carbon footprint by producing less waste. Get the family involved if possible, especially young children. Everyone can help.

There are changes in your neighborhood and in your local community. It's a good idea to meet new neighbors and make friends. Pay attention to what's happening in local parks and in the community in general. Make your voice heard in local elections. As you may be settled now for a while, you want the place you're in to be the best possible for you and your family.

For extra protection energy, those born in the year of the Sheep can carry a piece of hematite with them. Hematite is an unusual stone which looks like metal and feels like it weighs more than it should. You can carry this stone with you in your purse or pocket, or find a pendant or bracelet to wear made with hematite. Hematite is naturally magnetic and is made into lots of kinds of jewelry. Wear the piece anytime you want to feel a little extra courage.

Money

There's protection energy around your finances this year. This could mean you will keep a job even though others around you are laid off, or if you were to be laid off, you will quite quickly find a replacement job. Protection energy like this gives you more time to get ready for change, but doesn't completely prevent things from happening. So hope for the best and prepare for the worst and you will do fine.

You can make more money this year through writing and communication. This might mean blogging, writing a book, helping people with their social media or perhaps teaching/tutoring. If you've wanted to do something more creative, this is a good year to start to make that transition.

You have the opportunity to add to your investments this year. If you don't feel confident about investing it would be a good idea to take a class or read some books on the subject. Set up automatic savings programs through your bank so money can just flow right into your retirement savings account.

The Lucky Money Cat is an example of a cultural symbol that is very effective in shifting the energy of a home and bringing in prosperity opportunities. The story of the lucky cat is told of a poor priest whose job it was to maintain a temple in the woods far from the village. No one came to visit the temple, and so the priest had no income and yet he dutifully maintained the temple, keeping it clean, lighting the incense and praying.

One day a cat came to the temple and even though the priest had hardly enough food for himself he divided his dinner each night and fed the cat. So the cat stayed. What the priest didn't know was this was a magical cat.

Months later a nobleman was riding his horse through the forest to a neighboring town. There was a great storm and the nobleman got off his horse and took shelter under a tree. In the flashes of lightning, he could see the temple. On the temple steps sat a little cat. To his surprise, the cat sat up on his haunches and motioned for the nobleman to approach. Intrigued he left the shelter of the tree and went to the temple. At that moment lightning struck the tree. The nobleman recognized that he would have died if not for the little cat. So he spent his life and his fortune supporting the cat, the temple, and the priest.

To attract more income this year, place a Lucky Money Cat in your living room or home office. Place it in the far corner of the room and have him face the door. The Lucky Cat has his hand raised to call in money. Often these little statues are banks. Remember to feed him with coins and keep feeding him until the little bank is full. Then dust him regularly to re-energize him.

Job or Career

Many changes are happening around you at your company or with your particular team. Changes could include new offices or new office layout, new technology (and with it a need for more education) and new personnel. You may have the opportunity to lead a team though it's not your ideal job. All this change is just enough to alleviate some of the boredom you were starting to feel at your current position.

Towards the middle of the year, you will be offered one or perhaps more opportunities outside your current company. These may be jobs at competing companies or outside your current industry entirely (but still similar work as you're doing now). You may feel excited about the prospect of a change, but don't rush in without doing some serious negotiation about salary and benefits.

If one offer doesn't work out, then later in the year you will have a second offer, either from the same company or one that is similar. Don't worry that your resume is missing a key point the company is looking for. What they really want is someone easy to work with. Sheep native's social, generous nature will win people over immediately.

If you are looking to change positions, get a new job, to move up in the company you currently work for or expand your market share for your business, consider displaying a globe. The globe can be small-paper-weight size, or it can be a larger standing model (though it should be in keeping with your décor, so if a large globe looks out of place in your home choose a smaller version). The globe can be any color but should display the continents clearly. Place the globe in view of your front door. Once you have your new job, you can move the globe to your family room or home office to help maintain the positive energy.

Education

You may be feeling completely burned out with studying and school. Or you may find that returning to school is the last thing on your mind. But it is an option you really could consider. This foray into University won't be anything like the time before. This time it will be enjoyable, and the whole experience will help you grow.

It's possible to study abroad this year. Or you may travel across the country to your University of choice. Language studies are beneficial, as are classes on negotiation. At the beginning and end of each semester, the workload may get a little daunting but good time management and focused study time will solve the issue.

Legal Matters

There is strong energy around legal agreements and contracts for you this year. This could mean you get beneficial deals written and signed for things like employment, the sale of property, or perhaps the creative work you are doing. There is also the possibility of the purchase of a new vehicle.

Even though you are lucky in this area this year, it's a good idea to read contracts carefully and make changes where it would benefit you. Lawsuits, on the other hand, are not advised this year as they could bring you headaches and leave you with less money.

Health and Well-Being

Your own mind is one of the primary sources of your stress this year. How you speak to yourself and how you interpret the experiences in your life are actually having a physical effect on you. For example, some people view the stress of having to lead a meeting or perform on stage as exhilarating. Others, having the same exact experience, see it as crippling. How are you speaking to yourself about the experiences you're having?

You are probably making positive changes to your eating habits due to the advice of a friend or sibling. This may be the year when a sibling goes on a healthy eating plan, and you watch their life transforms. You will probably join them a few weeks or months after they get started and get the same remarkable results. This is good timing. You will benefit greatly from this change.

Exercise this year centers around walking, dancing, riding bikes or hiking. Look for things you can do outdoors or with other people. Be social and this will help lighten your mood and give you a sense of wellbeing.

For additional positive energy hang bamboo wind chimes out-side your home. If you have a front porch, hang the chimes there. Hang your chimes close to the door—but not where the chime will block someone from coming in the door. If you don't have a front porch or if your entry is in a hallway then hang the chimes on the back patio or balcony. Choose a bamboo wind chime; bamboo represents growth, protection, and longevity.

Monkey

February 2, 1908–January 21, 1909: Yang Earth Monkey

February 20, 1920–February 7, 1921: Yang Metal Monkey

February 6, 1932–January 25, 1933: Yang Water Monkey

January 25, 1944–February 12, 1945: Yang Wood Monkey

February 12, 1956–January 30, 1957: Yang Fire Monkey

January 30, 1968–February 16, 1969: Yang Earth Monkey

February 16, 1980–February 4, 1981: Yang Metal Monkey

February 4, 1992–January 22, 1993: Yang Water Monkey

January 22, 2004–February 8, 2005: Yang Wood Monkey

February 8, 2016–January 27, 2017: Yang Fire Monkey

Monkey Personality

When considering the qualities of a Chinese Zodiac animal, it's a good idea to examine the traits, behaviors, and personality of the animal. Of all of the animals of the Chinese Zodiac, the most agile and adaptable is the Monkey. Monkeys can live on the ground, or in the trees. They have dexterous hands and feet. Monkeys are also known for their ability to mimic behavior.

The Chinese Zodiac sign of Monkey is the sign of intelligence. This Zodiac animal rules the inventor—one who is intelligent enough and innovative enough to solve complex problems with ease. Monkeys have an excellent memory and proficiency in communication. They can give you an inspirational speech which motivates you, or they can give you are dressing down which leaves you feeling about two inches tall. Monkey is a problem solver. He or she is not going to provide you with sympathy but instead will offer you a solution.

Monkeys do well in business because they are connectors. They find people who can help them achieve their goals. In a sense they know how to play the system, trading favors as part of a strategy for success.

Monkey always has a plan, usually several plans. He or she wants to do more than merely survive, he or she wants to prosper! The Monkey native will avoid confrontation if there is a chance you can be of some assistance to them in the future. If they are wrong, they will exact revenge, but only when the time is right.

A Monkey is susceptible to incentives and bribes. To get them to work for you, you need to offer them something they want. You can criticize the Monkey, and they will not pay attention. They are incredibly confident in their talents and abilities.

Monkey can find ways to justify their actions to achieve or obtain what they want. For this reason, people find it hard to trust Monkey, and this can affect Monkey's career and personal life. They are rarely discouraged by failure or envious of the success of others.

Monkeys love a bargain. They're generally good with money and rather save it than spend it. They prefer to find their own solution to spending cash. This choice shows up in their home where innovative decorating ideas and creative uses for cast-offs abound. They do love a party at home (BYOB); if you're invited, you can expect an evening (or night) of stimulating conversation and lively music.

Monkeys are into self-preservation. This can give them a nervousness or hyperactivity, causing them to leap out of any situation they don't feel right about. They can get themselves in trouble by trying to avoid what they perceive is trouble.

But no matter what mistakes they may make, they are quick to rebound. Overall, the Monkey native gets what he or she wants without too much effort or struggle. If there's no benefit to be seen, they just lose interest.

Monkeys are at one moment a passionate lover, the next moment they've forgotten you entirely. When in a long-term, committed relationship, they can be a devoted partner; however, they like a lot of fun and attention, and they can get caught up in the moment. This can lead to some jealous feelings; Monkey doesn't notice, and in a moment he's back at your side as if nothing ever happened.

Monkey's love projects. They can continuously be renovating their home. They love to create new things or make improvements to old things. They also like sometimes just to move the furniture around to try to get a different look. Otherwise, the combination of half-finished projects and Monkey's love of new stuff can make for a very messy house.

How to use your Lucky Days: *On these days, plan to take essential actions, make vital phone calls, send emails. These are days when your energy and luck are high.*

Monkey: Predictions for 2019

January: *[note: This month there is a Solar Eclipse on January 5th and a Lunar Eclipse on January 21st. Check out the section on Eclipses for more details. Your Lucky Days this month are 2, 8, 14, 20 and 26.]*

You have lots of good ideas this month. Writing, speaking, and teaching is highlighted now. This can be done very informally by just teaching friends, or you can do this in a professional venue such as at a conference or at an important meeting at work. This is where you can show off your considerable skills. Don't shy away from any public speaking opportunities. Speak up in meetings. Give your opinions to anyone who's asking.

As you are lecturing and instructing others, make a mental note of changes you need to make in your own life. Go back to the helpful routines you had established over the past couple of months.

Exercise programs, healthy eating, work/life balance can all be revived now and bring great results. Turn off the TV and set aside the video game for a while. Listen to the music of the Universe by sitting quietly and hearing the sound of your breath.

February: *[note: Happy Lunar New Year on February 5th! Your Lucky Days this month are 1, 7, 13, 19, and 25.]*

This month welcomes the Earth Pig year. This is a somewhat challenging year for you, as Monkey natives have trouble relating to Pig's desire to stay home, covered in a soft blanket, watching the world go by. You crave adventure and social activities in town and places beyond. Travel gets shuffled around this month because of previous commitments and your ever-changing schedule. But it's possible you can clear stuff off your "to do" list and get out of town.

The number 11 is significant for you this month. When you see this number, it's a reminder for you to review your plans and make sure you're on track towards your goals.

You have a lot of luck around money this month. Your income is improving. The feeling of having a bit more cash in your pocket is making you want to go shopping. Make sure you set aside some of the extra money for the future. You have big goals that will need funding. Perhaps it's more travel or purchasing a home of your own?. No matter what it is, consider adding to that account rather than just blowing any extra amount on a grande latte.

March: *[note: Mercury is retrograde from March 6th to March 29th. See the section on Mercury retrograde for more information. Uranus moves into Taurus on March 6th—Time for change. Your Lucky Days are 3, 9, 15, 21, and 27.]*

Things are a little chaotic this month, no worries for Monkey natives, however, you can get above it all and observe the actions of others. Mercury retrograde has something to do with the chaos; you feel as if people are more unreliable and uninteresting than usual.

At home, there is a little unrest—though it may simply be the fun, playful kind with teasing and banter you do so well with. In the end, a person close to you may feel they want to go a different direction than you want. This sounds dramatic, but this is much more about expressing feelings than packing bags.

You're easy to talk to and have lots of advice for people who will listen. Now it's time for you to listen. The Universe is sending you omens to help you. Slow down long enough to read the signs in the words of other people and the things that are happening to you. Watch nature for clues.

If you're looking for love, (or sex) you need to rethink your strategy because what you're doing isn't bringing you the best results. You are charming and entertaining. Yet are you're still not attracting the match you want? Time to get help from those who care about you. A relative or friend keeps trying to give you advice. Now is a good time to hear them.

April: *[note: Jupiter goes retrograde on April 10th, Pluto goes retrograde on April 24th and Saturn goes retrograde on April 29th. Your Lucky Days are 2, 8, 14, 20, and 26.]*

This is probably the most significant month of the year for you. The changes you make this month will make a big difference by the end of the year. For quite a while you've been telling yourself what you need to do to make a positive difference in your life. This month someone will show you how beneficial it can be to make even some small changes to yield significant results.

Money is a little tighter this month than last. This is due to some investment spending on equipment or long-needed tech. Having the tools you need is paramount, and making yourself more efficient can pay off big in the future. But just buying the item isn't the solution, you must also sit down and learn how to best use it. If necessary, enroll in a class, find a tutor or at least check out some instructional YouTube videos. This is right up your alley. Monkey natives learn quickly.

This is one of the best months to find a love relationship, so if you're looking don't miss this opportunity. Enroll in an online dating site, try speed dating, attend social meetup groups, or just find a group to go hiking with.

If you put yourself out there this month, you may find you have more than one choice in love. That's okay, Monkey natives are good at decisions. Have fun on your dates together, trying new things like improv, indoor rock climbing, horseback riding or some crazy new restaurant.

May: *[note: Your Lucky Days this month are 2, 8, 14, 20, and 26.]*

People seem to want to get up in your face this month. Of course, they're no match for clever Monkey. The irritation you feel is a message for you from the Universe. Time to challenge yourself to do better. Some of this confrontation is your realization you've been leaving opportunities around for others to pick up. Instead of focusing on what should have been yours, calculate how you can get something better.

Money matters progress, but you are still only seeing the hints of improvement when you want to see bushels of it. Patience is needed now. The seeds are planted, and the best thing you can do to encourage growth is to connect with the Universe through meditation, prayer or candle lighting. When you do this money flows in. But Monkey natives can get distracted or try to be too clever, running after the latest marketing idea. Even 10 minutes of visualization a day would help more than investing in a marketing seminar with a guru.

Love relationships are going well. There is a lot of energy around a passionate time in the bedroom.

If you're looking for love, consider visiting places like amusement parks, shopping malls, carnivals, and arcades. Go to places where people have fun.

June: *[note: Neptune goes retrograde on June 21. Your Lucky Days are 1, 7, 13, 19, and 25.]*

Career and reputation are highlighted now. While Monkey natives are known for their skill and intelligence, this month something happens to shake your confidence. Just because someone tells you you're lacking in some area, there is no reason to think you are any less than amazing. By month's end, you are feeling yourself again, ready to compete in any arena you choose.

A younger person brings you a message that makes your day.

When it comes to finances, there's intense energy for change and improvement. You are naturally competitive, and yet you would rather be rewarded than ask for (i.e., demand) a well-deserved raise. If you don't receive an increase know the Universe is suggesting this current employer or business strategy needs to be changed out in the next few months or the next year.

If you're looking for love, it's a good idea to find the time to have a coffee date even though you're busy this month. Find someone (even if they're not your ideal match) and ask them out for coffee (or tea).

If you're already in a relationship, this is a great month for the two of you to go out with other couples. Not only is the social interaction good, but when you see how other couples are with each other, you will have insight into your own relationship. You will be able to use this valuable information to strengthen the love connection you have.

July: *[note: Mercury is retrograde from July 8th to August 1st. See the section on Mercury retrograde for more information. There's a Solar Eclipse on July 2nd and a Lunar Eclipse on July 16th. Check out the section on Eclipses for more details. Your Lucky Days are 1, 7, 13, 19, and 25.]*

This is an exciting month for those around you. Many people you know need to let go of something they've been holding on to (job, home, relationship, a chosen path, etc.) and the changes they make can directly impact your life. Nothing to worry about here. Monkey is the most flexible sign in the Chinese animal kingdom so you should have no trouble going with the flow.

You are likely receiving a gentle hint from the Universe regarding your finances (or, if you didn't take care to protect your finances last month you might be receiving a more forceful reminder). This will likely mean you need to make some phone calls or send emails to clear things up. At the very least, change your passwords and watch for suspicious emails requesting financial info.

This month let go of things that are not serving you to make way for new opportunities. You may need to let go of stuff around the house, or even a person who has outstayed their welcome.

Relationship energy is intense this month, and so you may want to tread lightly, especially at home. If you've fought over something in the past, bringing it up now may trigger WWIII. While this will clear the air, your quick wit and sharp tongue may do some long-term damage to your relationship. Of course, you'll win the argument but is it worth it?

If you're looking for a relationship, you are very noticeable this month, making it very easy for possible partners to find you. Many would like to be in your company, but not all are of interest to you. You want someone who is a partner, not a teacher or a parent. It's okay to be picky now.

August: *[note: Mercury moves forward again on August 2nd. Both Jupiter and Uranus move forward again August 11th. Your Lucky Days are 6, 12, 18, 24, and 30.]*

Education energy is all around you this month. You may be sending a child off to school or attending school yourself. This is a favorable month to give yourself a new skill, especially in some sort of technology or communication. You can get financial support for school for a future semester or receive monies for a current class.

There is also an opportunity to travel now, and it would be quite an enjoyable trip. Choose a warm place known for fun. Staying at home and doing the same old thing is too boring right now. Even if you're just traveling to the next town, try to get out of the house on your days off.

You have a lot of positive business energy around you. Take action like returning phone calls, sending in proposals, submitting your resume or trademarking/patenting ideas. Use various modes of communication to spread your message such as putting up a website, getting business cards, updating your LinkedIn profile. A windfall is possible this month and money owed to you can find it's way back to you now.

Things are going well at home—that is when the two of you are there. You have a lot of invitations and opportunities to be out of the house. A visit to a body of water is especially recommended (even if it's just a local swimming pool).

If you are looking for love, consider looking in "high places." This would include flying lessons, parasailing, rock climbing or dining on the top floor of a skyscraper.

September: *[note: Saturn moves forward again on September 18th. Your Lucky Days are 5, 11, 17, 23, and 29.]*

You have a performance opportunity this month. This may be related to a creative hobby you have, or be related to your career (leading a meeting, heading up a project, etc.). Taking risks in this area is advised. Aim high, make stretch goals, and you will stun others with how far you go. The advice to you this month is to prepare for the opportunity. Don't cut corners or try to wing it. Even a little prep will help you stand out and excel.

Your finances are bringing you a bit of a headache this month. You resent having an obligation someone else put on you. Perhaps you are handling the finances or a bill for someone else, or you just need to buckle down and try to make sense of your investment strategy going forward.

Insurance issues are also showing this month, and it may take several phone calls to get it all straight. You find this mundane stuff pretty irritating. Monkey natives often dream of a time when they can hire someone to do all this for them. But if that's not possible now, know you are actually quite good with money and can make it multiply when you put your attention on preserving and growing it.

You are mindful and enjoy living in the present. This month your love life would benefit by being fully present during the times you are together. Turn off the TV and spend some time talking. Take a walk, hand-in-hand, and just listen to your beloved.

If you're looking for love, you will need to enlist help from the Universe, since you're too busy to go out and look for yourself. Write down what you want in a partner, and burn a yellow or red candle next to to the list. Send your message through meditation or prayer, then keep your eyes and heart, open.

A career opportunity has come up unexpectedly for you or your partner. You're excited about change and ready to jump in despite fearful warnings from family members (when is Monkey ever afraid of anything?). You want to leap and there's no amount of talking that will reassure fearful others. Just jump.

Your cash flow is tight this month due to an extra expense, and you may be counting pennies by the end of the month to keep your hand out of your savings. But it's a good thing to invest in the tools you need daily. Monkey natives can be frugal, so wait for the sale or to get the best price.

This is a favorable time to activate your personal money magnetism through meditation or prayer. Set aside a few times this month (or daily if you really want to change your money situation) and visualize money flowing to you from many sources. It will take a few days but you will start to receive signs that it's working (like finding money on the street or receiving unexpected benefits at work).

Those of you in a relationship will have passionate and fun opportunities this month. Give yourselves a little time to spend together without the kids around or the TV on.

If you're looking for a relationship this month, you will be admired by someone now well-known to you. Accept the praise (or flowers, compliments or gifts) but only move forward with the relationship if you really like the person. There's no call for dating someone just because they think you are terrific. Of course they do! You are a Monkey, after all.

November: *[note: Mercury goes retrograde from November 1st to November 21st. See the section on Mercury retrograde for more information. Neptune moves forward again on November 27th. Your Lucky Days this month are 4, 10, 16, 22, and 28.]*

Mercury retrograde halts your forward motion this month. Everything was on track, and now it's stalled. This can include contracts for real estate or employment, elective medical procedures, trips, and transportation-related purchases. Somewhat irritating but your intuition tells you that things will move forward again soon. And they will.

You need to stay the course and focus on your goals. You'll hit the mother lode in the future if you stay on this path.

This is an excellent time to clean up your paperwork around finances. Doing financial paperwork is certainly not your favorite job, but this month it can be quite helpful to see how far you've come, if your money is well protected, and if you have it in places where it can work for you.

This is also a good time to check on financial backups, computer file storage systems or to switch to electronic storage from a paper system.

Monkey natives are often the life of the party. You have many friends and are well-loved. This month there's a chance a platonic relationship may cross the line into the romantic realm. This can be wonderful. What is better than having a lover also be a great friend. But if you're already in a love relationship, this could spell disaster for your current partnership. You must think carefully before venturing into the forbidden zone with this person. Even one kiss could lead to regrets.

If you're looking for love, you want to make sure the one you're considering is actually free of entanglements themselves before you go falling in love with them. This month, lies will be revealed and secrets will be discovered. To save your heart, don't fall for a person who's not available to love you back.

December: *[note: There is a Solar Eclipse on December 26th. Check out the section on Eclipses for more details. Your Lucky Days are 4, 10, 16, 22, and 28.]*

This month your powers of manifestation are strong. Visualize your home and the improvements you would make; or think about whether you want to move entirely. Picture the best job you could have or how to make your current job even better. Look at your relationships and think about what would make them more enjoyable and engaging. Then release these visions to the Universe—it's like dropping a letter in a mailbox and knowing it will be delivered.

You have the opportunity to recognize and remove blocks to money. It can be like a light-bulb moment where you have a flash of insight, or it can be the Universe knocking you over the head towards the end of the month by taking something away you had considered a near sure thing. To gain the insight you need before this happens, take time during the month to meditate or keep your mind clear.

If you always have the TV going or earbuds stuffed in your ears, it's hard to hear your higher self. Find moments of quiet. If you're not used to this, it may be uncomfortable for the first few minutes, but the insights you get are worth gold.

Something is ending in your relationship now. This doesn't mean the relationship itself will end. There will be an aspect that changes enough to cause you to move forward rather than clinging to any old behaviors. Monkey natives love to move forward and learn new things very quickly (being one of the smartest of the signs), so this is nothing to shy away from. Choose something you would like to end—maybe you want to stop arguing about a particular topic, perhaps you want to stop living like roommates and enjoy having more romance in your life. Any change will be beneficial now.

If you're looking for love and months have gone by with no new prospects, it's time to do an honest look at why you are "protecting" yourself from a relationship. Monkey natives have courage but they also love freedom. Are there too many benefits in staying single?

January 2020: *[note: There is a Lunar Eclipse on January 10th. Check out the section on Eclipses for more details. Uranus moves forward again on January 11th. Your Lucky Days this month are 3, 9, 15, 21 and 27.]*

The New Year begins with you feeling great about yourself and your future. The New Year energy is very harmonious with Monkey energy.

It's a great idea to do some decluttering of your space. Focus on getting rid of paper clutter first. Shred private information and toss the rest. See where you can go paperless. Then move on to household goods and consider selling things you're not using. The open space you create at home will bring positive opportunities during the year.

You may find that money seems to disappear: a check is late or a credit card is lost. Don't panic but take appropriate action to right whatever is going wrong. By the end of the month, you see how resourceful you can be and this adds to your confidence.

You share positive communication with your partner this month. This is a good thing because it's not always easy to connect with other members of the family. There is a lot of movement of people and things around your dwelling. Choices are being made, and you may not have a say in what is decided. Generally, Monkey natives don't need to feel in control. A little spontaneity can feel good.

You can create excitement at home by throwing a big party. Invite lots of friends and family. This activity could bring positive energy to the whole family.

If you're looking for a relationship, don't turn down any party invites this month. Seek out groups to join (or at least attend a meeting and check them out). Wear red to get positive attention.

Attract New Love

This is a very positive year for those looking for a new relationship. Your charm and magnetism is substantial this year. You can attract people who find you fascinating and fun. The trouble is, you tend not to trust other people, so you keep them at bay. You must remember it's not important whether the other person can be trusted, instead ask this question: "Do I trust myself?"

This year there are opportunities for short-term relationships, and one of these could turn into a long-term commitment. You often look for someone who has a sense of humor and is willing to take risks. You may search for signs to let you know "this person is the one..." But consider that all good relationships take some work. Allow yourself to enter into what may seem to be a short-term situation, and see if it grows into something more serious.

Monkey natives may be wondering if they have met the person already. One of the people from your past might be knocking on your door (virtual door, via email or text). This isn't necessarily a sign this person is the one you've been waiting for, or they would be the 'great relationship' you have been looking to attract. Use your good judgment to remind yourself why this person didn't work out before. Make a list of the pleasant qualities people in your relationships brought to the fore, and focus on attracting these qualities in your future relationship.

Make the act of finding new love easy and fun by displaying dolphins in your bedroom. You can have a painting, a photograph, a statue or even a couple of cute stuffed dolphins for your bed. If you choose a picture, hang it where you can see from your bed. Choose an image that has more than one dolphin. In fact, if you want a lot of love opportunities, choose a picture of a school of dolphins. But have at least two dolphins in the room to represent you in a relationship.

Enhance Existing Love

There's a lot of positive news for Monkey natives this year in the area of relationships. One of the aspects of your love relationship that's really improving is communication. Conversations are more candid and revealing, helping you both clear the air concerning past issues as well as come together to make plans for the future. Don't let a chance to talk at length pass you by.

Consider a weekend trip, or travel to a nearby place to put the spark back into your love life. Take a hotel room in the city center and go see a concert or play. Indulging in the arts or some creative activity usually puts a smile on your face, and this will be a reminder of why the two of you fell in love in the first place. Take turns making plans for nights out in the future.

If one or both of you have siblings, there could be an issue due to interference, or there may be too much concern for a relative outside the relationship. This could trigger an argument and some hurt feelings. This doesn't mean the relationship is over by any means, but it can be a stumbling block if you let the conflict go on too long. Everyone has expectations of what they "should" receive in a relationship—just make sure you're clear about what you want and what you expect.

If you are already in a relationship and you want to create more harmonious feelings and happier times hang a fan in your bedroom. It can be one of those large painted fans, one that depicts a landscape scene (make sure the scene is a prosperous and tranquil one, avoid pictures of people toiling in the fields or of wild animals with sharp teeth). Or it can be a small fan hanging from a hook that you grab and use on hot days. The fan is a symbol of peace and harmony, and this will help attract happy energy.

Looking to Conceive?

When you're hoping to conceive it's good Feng Shui to place a representation of what you want near where you sleep. This year place a figurine of a sleeping child (or children) playing on your nightstand or dresser. Choose a figurine you like, one that brings joy to your heart. Or ask a relative, one who has kids, if they have a favorite figurine you could borrow. A borrowed figurine would have phenomenal fertility energy.

Place the figurine in your bedroom where you can easily see it from the bed. Picture the energy of the symbol entering your body and your life. Wash or dust the figurine regularly to increase the energy of this classic Feng Shui remedy.

(From Donna Stellhorn's book, A Path to Pregnancy: Ancient Secrets for the Modern Woman)

Family and Kids

This year you have lucky energy around home and family, especially if you want to make changes. You might be moving or making renovations to the home. You can redecorate or do a major declutter. Any of these would help bring unexpected opportunities to your door.

A relative, perhaps a distant relative, will need your help this year. This is a time when you can show your devotion by giving advice, a place to stay or through financial support. Decide ahead of time what would be right for your family.

If you're on a budget, you may not have the means to give money right now. Decide how much support you can provide and then stick to your decision. Remember you can help by being an advocate for this person with others.

It's a good idea for you to hold parties at home. Bring friends and family together and make some wonderful memories. This is not a time to worry that your home is not in perfect order, or you're not fully settled in yet. Open your doors and let people you love come and share a meal with you.

Use a Feng Shui cure this year to add an extra layer of protection to your home. Choose a convex mirror. (A convex mirror is shaped like the back of a spoon.) Such a mirror can be used to reflect negative energy back to where it originated in a more forceful manner than a flat mirror can do. This adds additional protection for you and your family.

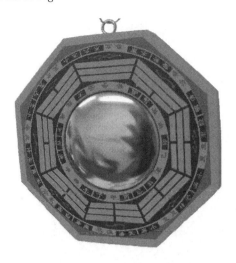

Hang your convex mirror in a window near the front door, in your bedroom window, or—if you have a particularly difficult neighbor—you can point it in the direction of their home. (This can result in them moving within a couple of months). Use only one of these mirrors at a time, as they are very powerful. Too many convex mirrors and you will block even positive energy from reaching you while simultaneously blocking the negative energy.

Money

You've been working hard on some big ideas. Maybe you're finishing your education and looking for it to lead to a better job. Or perhaps you've been building a side business and you're ready to launch. This year, you're starting to see some return on the investment of time and effort you've made. It's still slow going, but you will see progress this year.

Income from regular employment or contract work is robust this year. There's change energy in July, but you can prepare for it in June by letting superiors know how you help and support the company and its mission. Keep the lines of communication open with colleagues in your industry. When the changes come, you can move into a better position or negotiate an increase, rather than suffer the fate of some of your unprepared fellow workers.

This is also a good year to sell off excess stuff. Consider downsizing and really getting in touch with which items make you happy and which ones are part of your ability to collect a lot of stuff you really use. It takes time to sell things, but depending on the items, this effort could put some money in your pocket. Going through the hassle of selling stuff keeps you from mindlessly buying more.

Around the world, seaports are still the most popular places to live and work. Even though we no longer rely on ships for personal transportation, much of the goods we use come into the country via boat. For this reason, one Feng Shui cure is the 'Wealth Ship,' representing prosperity sailing into your life. This is one of the most potent symbols for attracting what you want.

When using the symbol, you can choose a model of a wealth ship or find a picture or painting you like of a ship. If you're feeling ambitious and craft-minded, you can build a model ship from a kit. Or if you have the inclination, you can paint a picture yourself of your own wealth ship. Any of these would make a fine Feng Shui cure.

Place your cure near your front door or in your home office. Position the ship or picture so it appears to be sailing into the room, not out the door. If the ship is sailing out the door, it will take a lot longer for it to return and for wealth to find its way to you.

Job or Career

This year, it's all about the money when it comes to whether you stay or leave a job. You're perfectly fine remaining where you are if the raise they have hinted at comes through (as well as that promised bonus). If you don't see better numbers in your paycheck by mid-year, you will be packing your bags and heading for more profitable opportunities in your own or related fields. You have a good sense of how the wind is blowing when it comes to your job and jobs like yours. You have ideas of when you will need to move out of the position you hold because of technological advances and automation. It's good to meditate on where you would like to be this time next year. This will help open some doors for you.

There are opportunities for you around communication, transportation, teaching, writing, advertising, marketing, and also in land management and the sale of luxury items. But even if you already work in one of these industries notice where jobs are opening up. Look to improve your skills and make yourself a more valuable asset to others.

Lapis has been called the gemstone of kings. It's a blue, opaque stone, with flecks of pyrite that sparkle like gold. It's often made into jewelry, but you can also find small, tumbled pieces to carry your pocket or purse. Wear or carry the stone to remind yourself of your value and worth. Wash the stone with soap and water about once a week to clear it. This will help re-energize the stone. You can also carry this stone with you when you're going on job interviews to give you a boost in that area. If you prefer not to carry the stone with you, then place it on your desk at work or at home or put it where you do financial matters in the home.

Education

At the beginning of the year, you may be completing a school program. You might not have a lot of interest in continuing towards your degree even if you are only short some credits at this point. Taking a break is okay. During your time off consider learning something fun and completely unrelated to your field. You could look into cooking classes, pottery, acting lessons, photography, or find a foreign language tutor. Whatever you study this year will prove more useful than you expected.

That said, it is very likely you'll find support while you're in school if you continue towards that degree. This can take the form of money from an obscure scholarship, or it's you can ask for time off work for study. Your family supports your decisions regarding education, and you can count on them all year.

If a new computer is needed for your studies, don't buy it during Mercury retrograde.

Legal Matters

Monkey natives have a lot of good luck and positive energy around legal matters, contracts, and agreements this year. You may have the opportunity to negotiate not just for yourself but for several family members as well. It is likely you will win lawsuits initiated this year.

Even though you are lucky, do read carefully and understand any contract before you sign your name on the dotted line. The lucky energy you have indicates you can negotiate for better terms if you choose.

Health and Well-Being

There's a little disconnect happening with you this year. You have habits which you know are not beneficial or helpful to you and yet you seem to be rationalizing about why you keep doing them. Monkey natives are smart, but this time you might be too bright for your own good. You may be scouring the internet for "evidence" your position is right, while deep down you know you're fooling yourself. (Ketchup and french fries are not vegetables).

You're less energetic this year when it comes to exercise. You find yourself spending a lot of time at your desk or in front of a screen. Don't let your bike get rusty or your gym membership go unused. You may have to put exercise into your schedule, or bring your gym bag to work and set it on the chair next to yours to remind you to get some daily exercise in.

Your biggest stressor this year is your finances. This doesn't mean your money situation is bad. It simply means you're looking at the world and listening to the news, and it's gotten you worried about the future. Consider shifting this energy by reminding yourself how resilient you are. You have skills and are endlessly resourceful!. You will prosper even if times get bad.

This year to best shelter and safeguard yourself and your family, place seashells on your bedroom window sill. Seashells represent protection, a comfortable home, and a sense of safety. This will attract positive energy for health and vitality.

Rooster

January 22, 1909–February 9, 1910: Yin Earth Rooster

February 8, 1921–January 27, 1922: Yin Metal Rooster

January 26, 1933–February 13, 1934: Yin Water Rooster

February 13, 1945–February 1, 1946: Yin Wood Rooster

January 31, 1957–February 17, 1958: Yin Fire Rooster

February 17, 1969–February 5, 1970: Yin Earth Rooster

February 5, 1981–January 24, 1982: Yin Metal Rooster

January 23, 1993–February 9, 1994: Yin Water Rooster

February 9, 2005–January 28, 2006: Yin Wood Rooster

January 28, 2017–February 15, 2018: Yin Fire Rooster

Rooster Personality

When considering the qualities of a Chinese Zodiac animal, it's a good idea to examine the traits, behaviors, and personality of the mythic creature we are discussing. While most animals in the Chinese Zodiac do not differentiate between male and female, the Chinese sign of the Rooster is the male. (No one ever says they're born under the sign of the hen or the chicken.)

When we look at the personality of this creature, we think of Rooster as the boss of the hen-house. Roosters are polygamists; they can have many 'hens' under their care. He also will guard and protect all he sees as his from any interlopers. He will oversee from a high perch, keeping a sharp lookout, sounding his distinctive alarm if predators approach.

Because of the substantial duties a Rooster always seems to have (particularly that of keeping an eye out for others) the Rooster personality is to be a perfectionist, someone with a sharp eye for detail and the ability to keep an accounting of everything (and everyone). In matters of money, Rooster excels. Roosters are adept at handling finances, protecting assets, and making good investments.

As perfectionists, Roosters are intolerant of even the smallest error. They will aggressively go after what belongs to them, from a small overcharge at the bank to a raise or bonus they believe is owed them at work. (It's best not to owe a Rooster money unless you can pay them back.)

Roosters like to look good, and they equate looking good with respect from others. So when Roosters open their pocketbook, it's to add things to their lives to make other people take notice. Money is well spent when it's for a flashy car, or a nice suit, or a piece of sparkling jewelry.

Roosters prefer routine over surprises. Surprises are seen as a warning of danger and are perceived on a range from merely irritating to stressful. Those born under the sign of the Rooster like to be prepared. They will keep extra things in their home or their handbag just in case—everything from extra change for the parking meter, to remedies for headaches, to extra pens.

Rooster likes to be seen as the person who has it all together. Because of this, they can be convinced to take part in projects which prove to be impossible tasks.

Rooster natives are very inquisitive. They end up taking on more and more and still find the energy to do it all. They give parties, volunteer for groups, and decide to make their own bread, possibly all in one day. Overall, they keep a calm demeanor—unless things go very wrong. Then you will witness their extreme distress and hurt, seemingly erupting from out of nowhere.

If we can find fault with Rooster, it would be their sense of entitlement. Roosters do a lot it's true, but then they also want a lot of praise and compliments for their actions. Roosters can be given to jealousy when others seem to be in the limelight. This can cause the Rooster to take actions which don't benefit him, like being insensitive or even vengeful.

When a Rooster falls in love, it's serious business. He follows his practical manner in his approach. This can lead to great disappointments in Rooster's love life as it's hard to categorize and schedule emotions.

Many Roosters find that being in a relationship is preferable to being alone. It's not that they need the romance, it's more their life and the house just seem to run better when there's two. Rooster loves an orderly and tidy house. To romance a Rooster, just share kitchen duties, and he'll pronounce it, "true love."

How to use your Lucky Days: *On these days plan to take essential actions, make necessary phone calls, send emails. These are days when your energy and luck are high.*

Rooster: Predictions for 2019

January: *[note: This month there is a Solar Eclipse on January 5th and a Lunar Eclipse on January 21st. Check out the section on Eclipses for more details. Your Lucky Days this month are 3, 9, 15, and 27.]*

The New Year brings a career opportunity to light. You could make a change in your position/title or transfer within your current company. If you're job hunting, you will make good progress this month. If you own your own business, you feel new energy and enthusiasm based on the sales results of the previous quarter. It's full steam ahead.

You're inspired to make changes in yourself, your wardrobe and your appearance. You receive encouragement and support for your choices. This renews your spirit and passion for life—plus you do it while staying on budget.

Changes in the home, home improvements, renovations, etc., are also highlighted. If you've been thinking about moving, you'll find a great place and could start the buying process. It may be a little bumpy at first, but there is a happy ending. If you're making changes to the home, you will find a lot of help making design decisions—even help with decluttering. Any changes you make now bring in positive energy for the whole year.

February: *[note: Happy Lunar New Year on February 5th! Your Lucky Days this month are 2, 8, 14, 20, and 26.]*

This month we enter the Year of the Earth Pig. This is better energy for Rooster natives. Now, after a couple of challenging years of seed planting, you are starting to see your efforts sprout and take root. New things you've tried over the last couple of years are paying off. This year, you may be finishing up some education, looking for a better job, or expanding your business. You can move forward with confidence. This is going to be a good year.

A friend with a very unique take on life shares some wisdom with you; you need to hear this message. It's good to listen.

This is a perfect month to sit down with your family and review the family finances. It may be difficult to get everyone together (as some do not want to have this meeting at all) but once you're all on the same page, you will make significant progress. This will also open the door to a conversation about other family matters such as travel, use of vehicles, and issues with neighbors. Keeping the lines of communication open within the family is key to the great year you have in store.

March: *[note: Mercury is retrograde from March 6th to March 29th. See the section on Mercury retrograde for more information. Uranus moves into Taurus on March 6th—Time for change. Your Lucky Days this month are 4, 10, 16, 22, and 28.]*

This can be an emotional month for usually confident, decisive Rooster. You may feel offended by an offhand comment (perhaps unintentional). It's a sign that you're feeling vulnerable in that area of your life. But instead of attacking the messenger, look at this event as a sign from the Universe that's it time to take an honest look at what you're doing. You are hardworking and rarely sentimental about the behaviors or habits you have, but in this case, there is some aspect of yourself you've been unconsciously holding on to. Bring it front of mind, and decide if you want to continue holding on.

You can gain recognition for something written this month. Put your words out in the world.

Clearing out any negative thinking as you are doing currently, helps you remove blocks to new sources of income. You are at the end of these blocks, and just need to expend a little bit of effort now to clear them away. When you are as practical and pragmatic as you are, it's hard to imagine that a change of attitude is anything more than wishful thinking. But any creation starts with an idea and the belief something is possible. Believe and take action, and you will see the money flow in over the next few weeks.

If you're looking for a relationship, you are not feeling very motivated right now. The last few dates have been less than inspiring and you're ready to chuck the whole idea. It is probably a good idea to take a break right now, but don't give up on love altogether. Opportunities are coming.

April: *[note: Jupiter goes retrograde n April 10th, Pluto goes retrograde on April 24th and Saturn goes retrograde on April 29th. Your Lucky Days this month are 3, 9, 15, 21, and 27.]*

The restrictions of the past month fade away and you're spreading your wings with a sense of freedom. As you've been kinder to yourself, you've found it makes you more productive and better able to handle the whims of others.

You are complimented for seeing the other person's point of view on several occasions.

There's actually some fun this month as a result of participating in a water-related activity. The time away from your routine renews your spirit and boosts your attitude.

Money is flowing in, and while you always would like more, you're feeling optimistic about your prospects going forward.

A change in transportation or a shift in the driving route is needed in the middle of the month, but Rooster natives are good at handling practical changes. If you've been waiting to buy a new car, this is a good month to make a deal.

Your relationship has improved, and communication between the two of you is more engaging and helpful. The air has been cleared and both parties are feeling listened to and appreciated. Now is not the time to "impart wisdom." no matter how useful it could be to their circumstances.

If you're looking for a relationship wear bright colors this month and go out where you will be seen.

May: *[note: Your Lucky Days are 3, 9, 15, 21, and 27.]*

For some reason, you feel like you want to just stay home. You're stuck on the sofa for hours (very uncharacteristic for you). Taking a break may feel necessary, but look at what has driven you to this couch potato state? Are you overworked? Are you not happy with some aspect of your life? Find the reason and start visualizing a change.

Much of your finances are focused on your home this month. This could mean a move is about to happen, or renovations are beginning at home. You may be adding a person to your household either by moving a romantic partner in, or seeing an adult child moving back home.

Overall this month is positive for you financially—but the greatest benefit comes from creating change. Take a look at what you can do differently in the way of dwellings and real estate.

There's a lot of activity in the area of relationships. This could be related to all the previously mentioned changes going on at home. You may actively be pursuing your relationship now, charming them with your dashing manners and entertaining banter. Plus you still have time for wining and dining your beloved.

If you're looking for a relationship, this is one of the best months to put yourself out there. Ask your friends to be on the lookout for you, too. Do prayer, meditations or light a candle to call love into your life. Join an online dating site. Really make an effort this month and you will see results.

June: *[note: Neptune goes retrograde on June 21st. Your Lucky Days are 2, 8, 14, 20, and 26.]*

Rooster natives are known for their bravery but sometimes you are more talk than action. Roosters can be seen or in some way described as small, flightless birds with no real teeth or claws, so some hesitation is understandable. This month, however, you are protected when you take action—so just can go for it!

Your finances are directly connected to how you're feeling about yourself this month. If you've been slipping back into negative attitudes about self, you will see your finances nosedive (as though to confirm your thoughts). But begin once again to treat yourself with respect and kindness, and your income rises accordingly (if you're on a fixed income you will see outside money opportunities come to you).

Your relationship is strong, but you can get into an argument that shakes the walls of the home. You can be abrasive when trying to make your point and you're so sure you're 100% right that you're not really seeing how being right isn't the goal, it doesn't really make either of you happy. This relationship can last, but you must lead the shift in its energy by keeping your ear tuned to the emotions behind the words your partner is saying.

July: *[note: Mercury is retrograde from July 8th to August 1st. See the section on Mercury retrograde for more information. There's a Solar Eclipse on July 2nd and a Lunar Eclipse on July 16th. Check out the section on Eclipses for more details. Your Lucky Days are 14, 20, and 26.]*

This is a disruptive month for everyone so don't think the universe has singled you out. This is a time when you discover something you've counted on, some part of you that you considered vital to who you are, was never really there in the first place. At the first shock of finding out, you may be left feeling naked and exposed. But then you realize you don't need it. You're fine just as you are.

This period of change will lead to some fascinating projects and people, and a better understanding of yourself. At some point in the future, you will look back on the experiences of this period and feel both satisfaction and pride in your personal growth.

Depending on how much change you make early in the month you will experience an increase in finances. The process of clearing past blocks brings you new sources of money—and an increase is possible from existing sources. This all can mean you're working more hours, but this is paid work rather than the spec work you may have been doing in the past.

Your love relationship could go through a change this month. There is an argument, and a healing follows. The air is cleared and you both can happily move forward, knowing you have been heard.

If you're looking for love, this is the month when lightning can strike. You could find the person you fall head over heels in love with. While Rooster natives are sometimes cautious, this is a good time to put on your brave face and say "Yes" to the invitations as they arrive.

August: *[note: Mercury moves forward again on August 2nd. Both Jupiter and Uranus move forward again August 11th. Your Lucky Days are 1, 7, 13, 19, and 25.]*

This is a month of adjustments. Adjustments are usually in order when there's no obvious solution. It's like being hungry for both salmon and ice cream—there's no such thing as salmon-flavored ice cream (or at least there shouldn't be). Evaluate all possible choices: you know that choosing one thing means you will have to forgo the other. This is the challenge right now.

This month listen to a friend. They have valuable advice for you.

There is a possible math error in your checking account, or there is a cash flow problem, perhaps a deposit into your account didn't make it in a timely fashion. The overarching message here is to make sure you have a safety net as well as flexibility in your finances.

Look for where you can increase your savings by letting go of some recurring charges. Increase your auto-deposits when possible so money is flowing into investments. Look at insurance and banking expenses. Visit your financial planner if you haven't seen him or her in a while.

In your love relationships, you or your partner is very focused on the intimate aspects and what's going on (or not going on) in the bedroom. There can be some medical issues that are causing this rift, or it just may be a matter of shifting your schedule around so you have more play time. Rooster natives are known for their work ethic and can often skip leisure time. But work/life balance is beneficial now for keeping you and your partner in a romantic mood.

September: *[note: Saturn moves forward again on September 18th. Your Lucky Days are 6, 12, 24, and 30.]*

This month there's a lot of energy around education for you. You might be going back to school or teaching a class. You may find your job requires certification of some sort, or installing a new computer system brings some new software for you to learn to use. If you don't have a mandatory class to take, you should find something to study.

Finances are good this month with opportunities for receiving money from several sources. There is a monetary source connected to travel or a foreign country. You may consider importing merchandise or applying for contract work with an overseas company.

This is an excellent month to expand your influence by posting professional articles or tips on websites like LinkedIn, or your company's blog.

You need to ask for payment or a raise sometime soon, and this month you have positive energy around such a request.

If you are in business for yourself, you may consider raising the prices of your products or services.

This is a great month for a planning a getaway for the two of you. Think about taking your beloved for a quick weekend to a leisure location, or even just making a day trip to an upscale part of town. The break in your routine is beneficial for both of you. You are more in harmony now than you have been in months. Communication is good and you receive reciprocal support in a similar way to the way as you have supported them.

October: *[note: Pluto moves forward again on October 3rd. Your Lucky Days are 6, 12, 18, 24, and 30.]*

Friendships are very prominent for you this month. Among your friends, you're often seen as the high achiever, very focused on duty and accomplishment. This can mean you are quick to tell others what they should do. You're known for giving enthusiastic support to your friend's projects.

If you own your own business think about how you can expand at little or no cost. This often means you need to connect with the Universe and ask for through prayer, meditation or the use of Feng Shui remedies. In a world of so much information and so many voices, all speaking at once, you can best reach the people you want to talk to by first visualizing that connection.

Your lover is your best friend right now, there for you when you need a sounding wall for your thoughts and feelings. This is a marvelous time to be social with other couples, perhaps even gather parties of two or three couples for games, bowling, or just a good conversation. Your life is better right now when you both get out of the house and see people you haven't seen in a while, or connect with potential new friends.

If you're looking for love, you are quite easy to find this month (that is if you leave the house). You can find someone at places where there is dancing, hiking, or other physical activities.

November: *[note: Mercury goes retrograde from November 1st to November 21st. See the section on Mercury retrograde for more information. Neptune moves forward again on November 27th. Your Lucky Days this month are 5, 11, 17, 23, and 29.]*

Life suddenly feels like there's so much to do and you're not really interested in doing most of it. You just want a break and you're tired of not only doing your share but other people's jobs as well. This has made you cranky.

This can still be a stellar month, just a really busy one. You must let go of the concept life should be fair. That will drive you crazy. Some people (Roosters for instance) are very responsible people and get tasks done.

Several projects are coming to an end—and if they are not, perhaps it's time to abandon them! Letting go of something not viable will free up energy for other things.

If you work for someone else, either as an employee or contract worker, you have opportunities to increase your paycheck this month. This may be just a one time increase, or a bonus or, with some negotiation on your part, it can become a permanent increase. Rooster natives are superb negotiators. Plan your talking points ahead of time and find a way to make it a win-win for your company.

If you work for yourself, you show some challenges with your top few customers. There may be a new competitor in town, or perhaps there was some ball-dropping on a previous order. Either way, your personal touch is needed now to keep your best customers happy and paying.

You are a bit more emotional and sentimental now than usual. It could be the approaching holidays, but for some reason, you're anxious to be with family and friends. Your intuition is correct. There is a possible separation from a friend due to a choice, a move, or new relationship of theirs.

If you're looking for love, consider making some new friends first. Join a social club or find a local coffee shop to spend time at on a regular basis. Be open to unexpected connections.

December: *[note: There is a Solar Eclipse on December 26th. Check out the section on Eclipses for more details. Your Lucky Days are 5, 11, 17, 23, and 29.]*

Give yourself some time for emotional healing with a visit to an art gallery or another beautiful place. Clear your brain with daily meditation (even if it's just five minutes a day).

While your finances are good this month, it feels as if money is tight. This is because you've been really generous with the gift-giving; and while nice gifts put a smile on your face, these smiles are emptying your wallet at the moment. No worries. You'll attract more money soon.

A funny thing happens this month. As you spend time and energy taking care of yourself (for a change), you find others going out of their way to help you as well. You haven't received this much love and support from friends, family members, or even strangers in a long while. Your partner is quite interested in your wellbeing at this time and taking extra steps to make your life easier.

If you're looking for a relationship as you feel better about yourself, you find you are attracting quality people who are absorbing to talk to—and available. What a great combination!

January 2020: *[note: There is a Lunar Eclipse on January 10th. Check out the section on Eclipses for more details. Uranus moves forward again on January 11th. Your Lucky Days this month are 4, 10, 16, 22, and 28.]*

This is a busy month for you. The requirements of work and home life collide, forming a long list of chores, tasks, and projects. You are a little disturbed to find someone in your life has let some vital matter go on past its deadline. This could be related to a contract, license or taxes. You need to rush in and save the day. (Fortunately, that's no problem for super-efficient Rooster!)

The year starts out well financially and you are encouraged by the flow you see happening. You've invested wisely, and when markets have fallen, you've picked up investments at a bargain. There may be rumblings in the financial news; it's imperative you don't buy into fear. Many a savvy Rooster has made a fortune in an uncertain market. Trying to control everything will get you nowhere. Instead, hedge your bets and study the downside before moving forward. Don't dwell on worst case scenarios. Just get a plan and stick to it.

Relationship energy is powerful right now. Going into the new year, you feel alert, decisive and super-efficient. Okay, these are both the most romantic qualities, but they do help you keep the household running like a clock. This, in turn, takes pressure off your beloved and you get heaps of praise.

If you're looking for love, consider visiting comedy clubs, music festivals, and art shows. Go where creative, unique people hang out.

Attract New Love

Take heart, Rooster natives, this is one of the best years to find new love you've had in a while. Perhaps you've been on the lookout for some time, or maybe you are just starting to look, no matter, love is about to knock on your door. Are you ready?

Rooster natives are known for being alert and decisive. You know what you're looking for (perhaps you've made lists, meditated, focused your energy) but at this time the more you can clear away reminders of the past, the easier it will be to find and secure this new relationship. So start to declutter. Get rid of memorabilia from past relationships, delete (or at least archive) photos on your phone, and when thoughts of someone from the past intrude on your thinking, visualize the scene shifting to the left (the past) and fading away.

Wear red and other bright colors this year to attract attention. Smile at the world and be curious each day about who you will meet for the first time, and who is someone coming back into your life. While the energy is quite strong all year long, there will be increased energy to help you find your next relationship at the beginning, middle and end of the Earth Pig year. Expect February, July and January 2020 to be highlight months.

When attracting a new love call that person's energy to you with the sweet sound of a bell. The bell can be made of metal or porcelain or any material, but it must have a sweet sound. You don't want to attract love with a bell that's off-key. Hang the bell from a yellow ribbon, yellow is the color of friendship and mutual understanding.

Put the bell in your bedroom where you can ring the bell at least once a day. (Do not hang the bell where you're going to bump your head into it.) If you want the relationship to start as a friendship and move slowly, hang your bell in the living room. Then move it to your bedroom when you want the relationship to become intimate.

Enhance Existing Love

While you're having a good year overall, your existing love relationship needs some work. Small irritations build within both of you. You may be justified in thinking your partner should change, but that doesn't mean it's going to happen. Rooster natives are experts at debating and making their point in a negotiation, but this doesn't always fly well in love relationships.

The family budget is a point of contention. If the two of you can find a way to get on the same page early in the year, you will do very well financially throughout the year. But if the spending patterns of the two you differ and this becomes a stress point, there could be quite a row in July and/or December. Try to defuse the situation with a sit down chat in February or March.

Despite this, overall you enjoy a sense of contentment this year. While there are aspects of this union you wouldn't call perfect, you are happy to be in this relationship. If you need more support, ask for it. If you want more recognition for what you do, point it out. Between a couple of challenges this year, there are many weeks of smooth sailing.

If your relationship is worth keeping and you want to make it better and stronger than ever, choose the crane as your symbol for love this year. The crane is a symbol of fidelity and marital bliss in many cultures. To bring greater happiness to your relationship, find or make some paper cranes. This origami bird is simple to do, and are said to bring fidelity and longevity. You can also hang a painting of actual cranes. Place the picture or the paper cranes in the bedroom where you can see them from the bed.

Looking to Conceive?

Looking to get pregnant this year? Herd a couple of terracotta elephants into the bedroom. Elephants are considered lucky in many cultures and for a variety of reasons. In India they are also seen as a fertility symbol—specifically when made from red terracotta clay (said to mimic menstrual blood).

If you can find mama and baby terracotta clay elephants with, perhaps, the little baby holding on to mama's tail with his trunk, you have found the ideal pair. Place them in the bedroom so mama is facing the door and so you can see them from the bed.

(From Donna Stellhorn's book, A Path to Pregnancy: Ancient Secrets for the Modern Woman)

Family and Kids

You may not be spending a lot of time at home this year. Perhaps you're traveling, or you may just be putting in a lot of time in at the office (maybe you're heading straight to yoga right after?). Overall you feel a little disconnected from your home at this time. This feeling is not strong enough to make you want to move per se, but it's also not drawing you home very quickly.

There's lots of activity going on at your house. There may be children bringing their friends over. There could be some construction, either on your property or nearby. The house seems noisy and full of life. This is good if you're having a party, it's not so good for sleep or spending quiet evenings after a long day. Soon you're off again, leaving the house behind.

There is some drama in your extended family this year. You are pulled in one direction and then another as various members ask you to choose a side. Rooster natives are self-assured and decisive. You have no trouble knowing where you stand on these issues and you may just wish people would take their drama elsewhere.

Coral, the beautiful, hard stony substance formed from certain marine animals, symbolizes growth and protection. It comes in a variety of colors and shapes, and it displays beautifully on tables. Place a piece of coral in your dining room or family room. Place it on a shelf or table where can be seen. You can also find a piece to wear when you feel you need some added protection.

Money

You have some remarkable opportunities for financial gain this year. However, there may be some ups and downs with investing. It's a good idea not to invest in things you don't understand,

2019 Year of the Earth Pig

or to invest in chancy prospects. Rooster natives are generally conservative in their dealings, but you can, on occasion, be quite headstrong and believe you're right. This is a fine time for sound investments, not get-rich-quick gambles.

There is money to made through your own actions, such as marketing your own services as a consultant or trainer. You might do this as a side business. There are platforms online for advertising your skills such as Fiverr.com and TakeLessons.com.

You can make money through real estate deals this year.

This is a good year to examine and remove personal blocks to money. You have a good understanding of your value, but you may have had trouble getting people to pay you what you know you're worth. This may mean you need to hone your negotiating skills, or find more places where you can negotiate. This is the road to having more.

You are probably familiar with lucky bamboo, i.e., sticks of bamboo growing in water, or small pots with bamboo growing in stones and water. There are about 10 species of bamboo grown in China. Some can measure a diameter of 3 feet and a height of 40 feet. Bamboo has many uses; it's been used for food, in the manufacture of paper, for making buckets and furniture; the leaves have been used to thatch roofs; the seeds and sap are used for medicinal purposes.

So this versatile plant is a perfect Feng Shui cure, a symbol of attracting money and benefit of all kinds this year. Place a lucky bamboo plant in your living room – in sight of your front door – to attract easy money opportunities.

Job or Career

This year you need to decide whether the career you're in is something that pleases you, or if you have this career it satisfies someone else. If you got into this field because your father encouraged you to do so, or because it was your mother's dream, it might be time to make a decided change towards what you've always wanted to do.

Some people search their whole lives for their "path," but Rooster natives know all paths are chosen. You can set out in any direction you want by working to acquire the skills needed to do what you want to do. If you want a creative job, you need to practice the skills required for that type of work. It's the same with management, it's a skill set you can develop.

You may not need formal study to put yourself on the new path. Confidence in your own ability to learn, working and doing your very best will help you more than having a degree (or several) on the resume. Make a list of what you love to do and a second list of what you know how to do. Find what's in common on these two lists and meditate on that. There will be opportunities throughout the year for you.

Even though you have lots of positive energy this year for career, you want the energy to flow smoothly and continuously. Hang a windsock or flag outside, either by your front door or on your patio/balcony. Choose a colorful one, something bright that makes you happy when you see it; you might also switch out the banner for each holiday or at the change of every season. Or, you can choose one in the form of a fish (fish represent abundance). This will attract a constant flow of energy and bring you more opportunities.

Education

This is a fortunate time to consider going back to school or completing the degree you have in progress. It's especially good if your course of study is practical and can lead to many job opportunities. Studying art history or sociology may help you grow but if it doesn't directly lead to employment then perhaps it's a good idea to wait a few years.

You do best this year in live classes. Prerecorded classes will not capture your attention or bring you the knowledge you are looking for. Look for hands-on practical courses in building, repair and maintenance, as well as classes on having/growing your own business, web design, or social media marketing. There is a surprising source of education funding available to you late in the year.

Legal Matters

While there's no danger involving lawsuits for you this year, legal matters can be a source of irritation at this time. You may have signed something on another's behalf (such as co-signing a loan for your son or daughter or another close relative) and now find out they are not living up to their end of the agreement.

Unless you take decisive action quickly, you may end up having a big bill you are forced to pay. You may need to enlist other family members to get this straightened out. But there's enough positive energy here for a proactive Rooster native to achieve good results.

Health and Well-Being

It looks like your gung-ho for exercise this year. You may have found a new method or routine you have just fallen in love with (hot yoga? Indoor rock climbing? Horseback riding?). But your enthusiasm won't help you if you get injured. Be cautious and make sure to stretch appropriately before jumping into strenuous exercise. Be extra careful in December.

You also appear to be caring for your body through clean eating. Your friends are impressed as they see you turn down foods and beverages you used to consume to excess. Your body is showing more muscle tone and you're looking years younger. Good job.

The biggest stress in your life this year is your relationships, not just with partner, family, and friends but with people you run into every day. It will be necessary to look at their situation with compassion even while you don't know their whole story. You'll recognize they are on their own journey this year and in their own time (which is on the road ahead of you, driving 20 miles an hour in a 35 mph zone).

One Feng Shui cure I recommend for Rooster Natives this year is the mirror; mirrors have many uses in Feng Shui. A particular kind of mirror is recognized as a very strong symbol of protection, stronger than an ordinary mirror. It's known as the "Bagua mirror." This cure most commonly consists of an octagon-shaped wood frame with a small circular mirror in the center.

Symbols designed to attract the energy of protection and harmony are carved into or painted on the wooden frame. This type of mirror is never used facing into the house; it is always used pointing out of the house. Place or hang the mirror in a window facing outward. Specifically, to help protect your health, hang it in your bedroom or bathroom window. This will keep negative energy at bay.

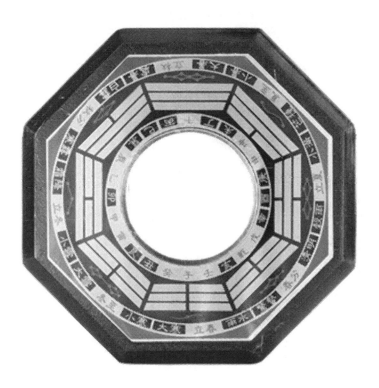

Dog

February 10, 1910–January 29, 1911: Yang Metal Dog

January 28, 1922–February 15, 1923: Yang Water Dog

February 14, 1934–February 3, 1935: Yang Wood Dog

February 2, 1946–January 21, 1947: Yang Fire Dog

February 18 1958–February 7, 1959: Yang Earth Dog

February 6, 1970–January 26, 1971: Yang Metal Dog

January 25, 1982–February 12, 1983: Yang Water Dog

February 10, 1994–January 30, 1995: Yang Wood Dog

January 29, 2006–February 17, 2007: Yang Fire Dog

February 16, 2018–February 4, 2019: Yang Earth Dog

Dog Personality

When looking at the qualities of a Chinese Zodiac creature, it's a good idea to consider the traits, behaviors, and personality of the animal itself. When considering the qualities of the Dog, many of us have some idea about dog personalities and behavior.

It said that dogs came to live with humans around 100,000 years ago. Humans found dogs to be very valuable; helping them hunt and herd. The dogs could pull loads, even protect their people from wild animals.

Sometimes we can confuse the personality of the dog in general, with the individual characteristics of specific dog breeds (most of which are only a few hundred years old). We want to consider the energy of a dog in general as we think about the personality traits of natives born under the Chinese Zodiac sign of the Dog.

The animal dog is known for companionship; similarly, individuals born during the Year of the Dog are usually very well-liked and friendly. They have a deep sense of loyalty and are willing to play fair. They are happier around people than they are on their own. They tend to go with the flow, not being overly demanding, always willing to meet others halfway so that everyone gets something of what they want.

Early humans brought dogs into their lives to increase their chances of survival. The dogs would help them find food, keep them warm at night, and protect them from dangers. Those born under the Chinese Zodiac sign of Dog are very protective of their friends. They watch over them and are willing to fight for them. Dogs are eager to take up a cause, whether on behalf of an individual, a group, or an organization.

Because they take loyalty so seriously, Dog natives choose their friendships very carefully. It can take a long time for them to accept a new person in their circle. At the same time, many people want to be their friends, as Dogs are often in positions of influence, connected with people of power. Dogs are rarely selfish, and when they crave power or money, there is usually a person or cause who will benefit from everything Dog creates.

Dog natives are known to work hard and to play hard. They have to be cautious to avoid overindulgence in food or overspending. They generally like competitive sports, and they often love a good hard workout. They don't mind a night out dancing followed by an early morning yoga session. They like a stylish home, but their home may not be neat—although it doesn't matter to them since they're not at home that often.

Dogs make good lawyers as they are always looking for justice and fairness. These characteristics also make them an excellent employee. They're particularly good at managing several projects simultaneously. They won't gossip at the water cooler, nor will they speak ill of others. Dog prefers to be a team player, and if you're part of the team, you can count on them.

Dogs alternate between aggressive spending and aggressive saving. When it comes to investments, they are better at investing in property, or in precious metals or stones, and other tangible things rather than intangible derivatives.

Most in life, Dog wants loyal, honest, intelligent friends, who will share a dinner or attend the theater, or join them on an impromptu trip to the Bahamas for the weekend. They love to be treated fairly and honestly; they don't like to be questioned too deeply about their reasoning and thinking processes. They'd love to have enough money—in fact, so much money they never have to think about what things cost!

Even when Dog seems happy, they are pessimists by nature, capable of worrying a great deal, including the small things. They can count the times when they were overconfident, and it led to disaster, and they use this information as a tool to confirm their need to worry.

They are very resourceful and resilient, and they can overcome any difficulty. However, Dog spends a great deal of time visualizing potential problems, and they tend to look for the storm clouds and never the silver lining.

How to use your Lucky Days: *On these days plan to take decisive actions, make essential phone calls, and send emails. These are days when your energy levels and luck are high.*

Dog: Predictions for 2019

January: *[note: This month there is a Solar Eclipse on January 5th and a Lunar Eclipse on January 21st. Check out the section on Eclipses for more details. Your Lucky Days this month are 4, 10, 16, 22, and 28.]*

Energy is calmer this month, and you welcome in 2019 surrounded by friends and family who love you. If only you could feel as confident and competent as they all think you are. This is one of your goals for this year: to feel you are the person others believe you to be. They are a better judge in this case than you are. Accept their compliments and focus your attention on building those relationships.

Speaking of relationships, your love life is improving significantly. If you're already in a love relationship, you will see it strengthen this month.

If you're looking for a partner, there's good news. You have several opportunities to meet someone who could become truly special in your life. Put yourself out into the world. Smile at strangers and start up conversations. Or get back onto the online dating sites. The energy is in your favor now.

There are possibilities for a new vehicle or mode of transportation (which could include something for fun like a scooter).

February: *[note: Happy Lunar New Year on February 5th! Your Lucky Days this month are 3, 9, 15, 21, and 27.]*

This month we welcome in the Year of the Earth Pig, and your life starts to feel much more comfortable. You enter the second year of your personal seed planting period, and you begin to see some results from all your hard work during 2018 last year. You can breathe a sigh of relief as you see money and opportunities come from directions you've actually been working on. This is not a sign to let go of other support systems yet, but it does show you are—for the most part—heading in the right direction.

You have lots of energy right now. Your brain is working overtime on a project. You are busy, busy.

You are fortunate this month. You may receive a financial windfall, or win some prize. But more importantly, you are lucky when it comes to friendships. One of your friends can introduce you to someone who will truly be a gift in your life. Say "Yes!" to invitations and see the people you love and cherish. Be happy and happiness will find you.

You have a good interaction with a new neighbor. This person may be helpful in the future or become a real friend.

March: *[note: Mercury is retrograde from March 6th to March 29th. See the section on Mercury retrograde for more information. Uranus moves into Taurus on March 6th–Time for change. Your Lucky Days are 5, 11, 17, and 23.]*

You are coming into a time when you are challenged to let go of anything that isn't working right now. You've completed one of three seed planting years, but some of the seeds you've planted (i.e., the new things you've tried) haven't shown any results yet. Some of these seeds you still have hope for and that's fine. Consider, however, things you've tried that were a bust right from the beginning. It's time to stop putting any time or resources into these projects. This may mean cutting your losses (subscription services?), selling off slightly used equipment or telling friends and family you're quitting. The energy you will save by letting go will be well worth it.

Your finances are highlighted this month. You show protection around your accounts. During protection periods it's a good idea to update passwords on financial accounts and empty your wallet of credit cards you don't use often. Pull your credit report and check it for errors. If you find something, start the paperwork to correct the issue. All this work will not only protect you now but help bring more money opportunities in the future.

Even Dog natives who are in relationships feel independent this month—which could mean your partner is traveling or very busy with other things. That's okay. This is an opportune time to get caught up with old friends.

Dog natives looking for someone to love can consider going to plays, concerts, and art shows and cultural events to meet new people.

You are catching up on your sleep which is healthy. It's now time to analyze your sleep patterns to see how you can get better quality sleep. Many apps and devices can measure your sleep and provide you with useful information to help you rest better.

April: *[note: Jupiter goes retrograde on April 10th, Pluto goes retrograde on April 24th and Saturn goes retrograde on April 29th. Your Lucky Days are 4, 16, 22, and 28.]*

At this time you are noticing and breaking old family patterns. This is a very good thing for you to do. Your loyalty to your loved ones doesn't mean you have to fall into the same negative behavior patterns as siblings or parents have done. The work you do on these issues is very beneficial.

Financially things are moving forward in the best direction possible—upwards. You have money-making opportunities from a new source. While this option isn't bringing you massive amounts now, it is starting to grow and could become quite viable in the future. You can make more this month by tapping into the prosperity energy of the Universe. This is done through prayer, meditation or lighting candles. Spend a little time every day to increase the energy.

When you see a feather on the ground, know it's a sign for you to communicate with others. This could mean sending out a newsletter or blog post, calling up a friend or emailing a distant family member.

When it comes to love relationships, you are having trouble getting out of your own way. You seem quarrelsome when you want to be agreeable. You are suddenly irritated by habits that have never bothered you before. A lot of this is that you're not happy in another area of your life that you haven't yet identified (or you've stopped your healthy eating, and you're reacting to consuming too much sugar). Some self-reflection and honest assessment will set things straight.

If you're looking for love, you are projecting skepticism rather than your usual optimism, and this is chasing away any prospects. Find your balance.

May: *[note: Your Lucky Days are 4, 10, 16, 22, and 28.]*

Your home life is wonderful now. You may be adding a pet, or there's a visit from loved ones. You may want to throw a party and bring even more positive energy into your place.

You're also sticking to your personal schedule, taking time for exercise and eating better. This results in big dividends for you: you have more energy and a brighter outlook on everything.

Time to focus on paying down debt and perhaps getting yourself to a debt-free place. This is one of your long-time goals, and it's achievable this year if you put the energy in that direction. Consider making a spreadsheet of what you owe and facing the truth of it. Debt doesn't make you a bad person. Be kind to yourself during this process. Debt does mean you have to cut way back on the shopping. It sounds counterintuitive, but as you get rid of excess stuff, you find you need less and shop less. Take the time to sell what you can and donate what you can't sell.

The harmony at home has spread to your relationship, and you feel happy with your partner. You're having fun together.

If you're looking for love, you're now on the right track. Expand your search by telling your friends (and friends of friends) that you're in the market for love. Accept their invitations to meet new people (even if you don't think it's a great match). Just going through the exercise of meeting a new person helps move the energy forward.

June: *[note: Neptune goes retrograde on June 21st. Your Lucky Days are 3, 9, 15, and 27.]*

Your excellent instincts tell you it's a time of reflection and to clear the energy in the home. You may use a traditional method of clearing, like smudging, or you might burn candles or use essential oils.

While you're at it, a spa day wouldn't hurt! Take care of yourself. After working on your body, take care of your heart and mind too, by giving yourself a few days of no self-criticism (or longer if you can manage it). It will benefit you greatly.

If you own a business, there is money flowing in, but you may not be experiencing the growth you were hoping to see. Money doesn't come because you work harder. It comes because of the contacts you have with influential others. Take some time each day to reach out to people you admire, people in your industry who can help you or mentors who understand what you are trying to do.

When it comes to a relationship, you may find your feelings are hurt this month by a careless remark from a friend or your partner. Dog natives can vacillate between feeling very confident to quite vulnerable, and during this time, your uncertain emotions are taking you for a ride. Clear the air as soon as you can. Speak up and get the healing started.

July: *[note: Mercury is retrograde from July 8th to August 1st. See the section on Mercury retrograde for more information. There's a Solar Eclipse on July 2nd and a Lunar Eclipse on July 16th. Check out the section on Eclipses for more details. Your Lucky Days are 3, 9, 15, 21, and 27.]*

There is a lot of change energy around you this month. You may have noticed a quiet feeling in the back of your mind for several weeks. Your intuition is letting you know the winds of change were coming. Now the wind is really beginning to blow. You may feel ready for action right now, but first, weigh your options. The road will become clear by the end of the month.

Time to focus on your money magnetizing ability. Dog natives are charismatic and resourceful. Visualize money coming to you. Each day you repeat this vision strengthens the energy and your ability to request from the Universe. You could start to see results after just a week or so of practice.

A friend who's always short on cash will ask for a loan at this time. If you've lent to them many times before, "gift" them a small amount—but tell them this will have to be the last time.

The eclipse energy could really affect your relationship this month. The love of your life could be going through a challenging time and need your support. Fortunately, they are in a relationship with a Dog native, the most loyal of all the signs. You always seem willing to sacrifice for others. You will receive love in return for your heroism even if all you are doing is listening.

If you're looking for a relationship, this is a powerful time. You can be struck by cupid's arrow when you least expect it. Be your usual friendly self, and this will be enough for them to find you.

August: *[note: Mercury moves forward again on August 2nd. Both Jupiter and Uranus move forward again August 11th. Your Lucky Days are 8, 14, 20 and 26.]*

This is your month to receive help and support from others. State what you want to the Universe and to everyone you meet. See who steps up to help you. Those who do will be rewarded by the Universe. If someone doesn't then just let them be.

Think big. Think of an action you can take, and then think of something even bolder. Dog natives have excellent instincts but can be given to worry (mostly about small details) so don't let yourself be stopped by your own brain now.

Your financial month is all about how many people you can reach. Get out your phone list and start calling. Reach out to people who want sales proposals, who have requested resumes or have job openings, and those who are leaders in your industry. Knock on doors and set up meetings (even a 5-minute chat on the phone is good). Think of ways you can benefit them as well as getting what you need.

If you own your own business, you can announce a price increase. Also, contact related companies to see how you can work together for the good of all.

Your partner is quite happy with you this month but not so satisfied with something about the home. If you live together, it may be time to think about changing the home in some way so you're both happy.

If you're looking for love, this is one of your best months of the year. Don't hide at home and don't spend all your time at work. Do fun things and meet new people. That's the way to find love.

September: *[note: Saturn moves forward again on September 18th. Your Lucky Days this month are 1, 7, 13, 19, and 25.]*

Your luck continues this month. People who promised to support and help you last month now come through. You feel blessed having all these great friends. Not feeling that? It's because you haven't asked. Dog natives sometimes get blocked by their own negative thoughts. Clear that energy by smudging, meditation, affirmations or by forming a new habit of encouraging a positive attitude. You can sometimes be a social introvert—the one who is always at the party, but standing unnoticed in the corner. It may feel risky to ask for help, but it's a way to see who really is there for you at this time.

Meet with your financial planner to discuss ways to make passive income.

If you've been considering buying a business or franchise, it's seriously time to do your due diligence.

If you have an employer talk to your HR department about retirement planning and maximizing a company match. Actions taken this month can send you down a path to prosperity.

In your relationship, the block that was holding one of you back is gone, and now you can enjoy your each other on a deeper level. Now is the time to explore some new options in the area of intimacy.

If you're looking for love, you can easily find a lover now. However, this person may or may not turn into a long-term relationship you hope for, no matter what they promise in the heat of the moment. So use your good judgment before going all the way.

October: *[note: Pluto moves forward again on October 3rd. Your Lucky Days are 1, 7, 13, 19, 25 and 31.]*

After a couple of high flying months, you are brought back down to earth. You're feeling somewhat irritated with several areas of your life. Some people have really come through for you, but others have been a disappointment, and now as the dust settles you're wondering if you should confront these individuals. Your feelings are hurt even if it was just by one person. You may feel like a confrontation would make the pain go away, but that is only if the other person is ready for some constructive advice. If this a habit with this person, just walk away.

If you took a lot of bold action in the last two months, you will be feeling the positive results this month. But you may be feeling irritated with yourself for missing opportunities. Don't wait another second. Face your fears (the fear of rejection mostly) and dive in.

This month an opportunity to speak in public or speak up at a meeting is very beneficial to you in the long run. You may also have the option to travel for business soon; this will be of help to you.

This month you and your partner are having some trouble syncing up your schedules. You may go days without having a real conversation. This can make Dog natives feel lonely and stressed. This is a temporary situation, as both of you are quite busy now (or if you're not then something is bothering your partner they haven't shared with you yet).

If you're looking for love this month, you need to change tactics. The methods you use or places you go are not working for you. If you're focusing on online dating, it's time to go out into real life. If you're hanging out at the bar, perhaps you need a change of venue.

November: *[note: Mercury goes retrograde from November 1st to November 21st. See the section on Mercury retrograde for more information. Neptune moves forward again on November 27th. Your Lucky Days are 6, 12, 18, 24, and 30.]*

As the year comes to a close, you feel proud of all you've been able to accomplish, and the many seeds you have planted. You've tried many new things, and while some didn't pan out, some are showing you signs of sprouts and good things to come. Don't think of any of this as wasted energy. When you are in the first years of your 12-year cycle, it's important to explore your options.

This month it's a good time to record some of this information. Consider journaling, writing "morning pages," or take some pictures of things you're grateful for in your life. Just the act of doing this will allow you to see more clearly what's working, and what needs to be left behind.

Money energy is stimulated by you being in the flow. That means balanced productivity by letting go of procrastination. You also don't approach tasks in a manic this-must-be-done mode. You see the task at hand and you do it. When you're tired you rest. This is releasing hesitation and the fear of putting yourself forward, and this brings money opportunities (as well as other options to benefit you as well).

You and your partner may be having a disagreement right now. This doesn't mean you don't love each other but there is a temporary divide forming between the two of you. It could be ideological, political or spiritual and left unchecked it could grow to be a real problem. The solution is to agree to disagree. This may feel like you are compromising yet again. But this is more about having your opinion and allowing your partner to have theirs.

December: *[note: There is a Solar Eclipse on December 26th. Check out the section on Eclipses for more details. Your Lucky Days are 6, 12, 18, 24, and 30.]*

Dog natives, more than any other sign, can find the balance between rest and alertness. Your gift is the ability to spring into action and fearlessly face what you must do. Be optimistic and find bold things steps to take on your goals. One move can lead to many opportunities now.

Finances could get a boost from something in connection with your home or real estate in general. You may be taking on a roommate, renting out your place as a vacation destination, or flipping a house. You may be starting a business out of your home and bringing in more money that way. You could be selling off excess stuff as well.

Like last month you benefit from tapping into the spiritual energy as you look for money opportunities. This means meditation, chanting, candle lighting on a daily basis, at least for a while. Money can flow in, in a big way, it just needs a clear destination.

While things are better at home, there may still be some hurt feelings resulting from the disagreements last month. Dog natives are great at helping others heal and so just by talking openly, you can fix a lot of the issues now. But that may not help how hurt you feel. Instead of waiting for your partner to say the right thing think about what you would like to hear them say and help them say it. Often times people mean well but they don't have the exact words you want to hear.

If you're looking for love, you need to change your thinking. If you don't want a person who drinks and parties, hanging out at Happy Hour isn't going to help you find someone to love! Look for places a compatible person might be.

January 2020: *[note: There is a Lunar Eclipse on January 10th. Check out the section on Eclipses for more details. Uranus moves forward again on January 11th. Your Lucky Days this month are 5, 11, 17, 23, and 29.]*

You feel the new energy already, even though we don't officially enter the Year of the Metal Rat until later this month. You can already feel the positive boost. This will be a rewarding year for Dog natives who have a firm plan for what they want to do and where they want to go. If you're vacillating between many ideas, still not sure what seeds are sprouting it's time to pick something and give it your time, energy and love.

You have access to power and negotiating skills now. You're worthy of more (money, time, consideration, etc.) but you need to let others know what you expect. Dog natives are naturally hard working and you are an asset wherever you put your efforts. This month, and as you go into the New Year, you will have the resources and support to make changes.

Love is strong this month. If you're already in a love relationship, you have reason to celebrate. Even though not every day is rainbows and roses, it's still great to have someone in your life. This month take a look at what irritates you about your partner and turn it around. See if there's anything you can change in your dealings with that person or others. A small change in yourself seems to quite magically change others.

If you're looking for love, you are very visible this month. Don't waste this opportunity by trying to hide. Lift your eyes from your phone once and a while and smile at the world. You will find someone there waiting to talk to you.

Attract New Love

You are known for being cautious until the need arises and then you jump in fully, immersing yourself in whatever you're doing. This year, in the area of love, you are likely jumping without a net. Love is at your doorstep, and you accept it (even though it's in a form you weren't quite expecting). This could be a past friend, someone you thought would stay in the friend-zone. It could be a neighbor you've known for years. It's possibly the sibling of someone you know well. But the spark is now lit, and you can follow where your heart leads.

Dog natives are known for their social skills and extensive network of friends. But you might have been wishing for a long-term exclusive love partner. This will take some work on your part because your friends need you, too. Make sure to bring any prospective lovers around to meet your friends fairly early in the relationship. If you feel hesitant, imagining your friends won't understand your choice, you might want to rethink the situation yourself. There are lots more opportunities to meet a special someone to love for you this year.

During the middle of the year, you need to pay attention to what your friends tell you about your dating choices. They may tell you to be more assertive, or perhaps they advise you to back off a little. Either way, they are correct. Trust their sage advice.

To attract lots of love possibilities get a heart-shaped bowl. The bowl can be made out of wood, stone or fabric. Choose red or hot pink. Avoid pastel colors as this can attract a very passive partner. Write your wishes for a new love on small pieces of paper and place them inside the bowl. This list can include the qualities of the person you're trying to attract, what a new relationship will mean in your life and how you will know that you've found the right person. Then place this bowl on your bedside table to attract love and romance.

Enhance Existing Love

While it may not be obvious, your current relationship is most likely quite stable. You can be sensitive to the changing winds of emotions, but this doesn't mean there are cracks in your foundation as a couple. Overall, this is a good relationship that, with effort, could be better. This is a good year to pick out one or two changes to make easily within your power, and to keep an eye out and pick up a few things about your partner which seem outside of your control that you are willing to accept.

One good thing about this relationship right now is "what you see is what you get." There isn't anything to hide. There's no secret rendezvous or hidden agenda. Everything is on the table. Feelings you have to the contrary are the results of old hurts—perhaps going back to relationships from the past. You can dismiss these current insecurities and get down to enjoying a delightful relationship.

There are some changes in the household which directly affect your relationship. These put a small strain on your communication in July and then again later in the year. You'll both survive this easily, as long as it's not blown out of proportion. Loyalty is an essential thing to Dog natives, so if you feel your partner is showing more attention to a relative or friend outside your relationship, you may feel a bit unloved. The key here is to talk about it until your feelings are acknowledged.

If you're in an existing relationship and you want to increase the fidelity energy and overall happiness, you can place a pair of Mandarin Ducks on your bedside table or dresser. These ducks are known to mate for life, and they are a symbol of marital bliss. These ducks can be so attached to each other that when separated they will pine away and die.

Mandarin ducks are primarily used as they are considered the best of the species in intelligence and beauty. Their energy symbolizes felicity. They are usually displayed with the lotus blossom, the flower that emerges from the mud pure and clean.

Looking to Conceive?

If you're looking to get pregnant this year, place gemstone eggs in the bedroom. You will be able to find gemstone eggs at rock and mineral shops, or check online where you'll be able to find a variety of stone carved in the shape of eggs. The egg shape represents a baby. Reasonably priced eggs carved from Agate, Jasper and sometimes Rose Quartz are easy to find.

(From Donna Stellhorn's book, A Path to Pregnancy: Ancient Secrets for the Modern Woman)

Family and Kids

What outsiders might think looks like chaos in your home actually feels pretty good to you. People constantly coming and going, friends or relatives staying for shorter visits, sometimes even for several weeks at a time. Or, perhaps you have a business at home, and clients are coming and going for meetings and consultations. You're bringing in good fortune and opportunity. All this activity makes you feel quite happy and simultaneously brings opportunities to the other members of your family.

Sleep is so important, and either you or someone in your immediate household is struggling to sleep well. This may mean you need a new bed, or to see a professional for help. Changes in the evening routine (such as limiting screen time) could help. Altering the diet may also be beneficial for this.

If there are adult children in the house, one may be moving in or moving out. A milestone has been reached, and things are happening—perhaps one member of the family is graduating or leaving home to start their career with a "real" job. These are reasons for celebration, so break out the bubbly and kick up your heels.

Even though there is no one brave enough to stand against you, a little protection never hurts. Kuan Kung with his sword is an example of a protection symbol that you can use just to ward off anyone who dares try to take something that belongs to you. Or you can just use the sword itself. Display the statue of Kuan Kung or his sword in your living room or family room. Dust it off about once a month to keep the energy active. This will help ward off negative energy

Money

The energy of money is quite changeable for you this year. This means you can go from rags to riches and then, if you're not careful, back to rags again. There's the possibility of a windfall this year, possibly money you've been expecting for some time; or maybe some unexpected money just shows up. You can receive loans and financial support from family members, too.

For Dog natives, money flow is connected to how much you feel you're worth. If you treat yourself with love and respect, you will find the flow of money is steady throughout the year. But if you are in the habit of berating yourself, putting yourself down or you just feel you're less worthy of support, the Universe will send you an amount that fits that energy. It is now to your advantage to work on positive self-talk.

There are opportunities for money in the area of transportation, travel, teaching, and communication. You may find some financial assistance with the help of a sibling. But be cautious about signing agreements or spending money you don't have, as things will not go well towards the end of the year.

The Jade plant, otherwise known as Crassula ovate, is a succulent with tiny white or pink flowers and round, deep green leaves. The flowers are not prized, it's the leaves that are important. It's called the Jade plant because the leaves resemble jade coins; a symbol of wealth and abundance. It's also called the "money plant." If the plant does happen to bloom in the Spring, it's said that friendship along with prosperity will visit your home.

Place your Jade plant in a sunny window near the front door or on your front porch. This will help you attract positive financial energy. Don't over water. This plant is a succulent and can withstand drought conditions. This represents money flow, even when the economy is challenging.

Job or Career

There have been lots of changes in your life and in the lives of the people around you; this has been going on for some time. Now this energy is starting to calm down, and you will enjoy a more peaceful, steady time in your career. You may still encounter some change energy around the middle of the year, but at this point, you're ready for any change. Something promised to cause a considerable disruption proves to be only a slight delay and irritation. Then things are back on track.

If you work for a large company, you can stay discretely behind the scenes. This will give you time and energy to focus on other aspects of your life. You can choose to work alongside others or close yourself off and work alone, whichever you prefer. Some work-at-home opportunities are available if you are willing to mount the campaign to make that program available to you.

You are well-liked at your job, and you will most likely receive support when you ask for it. If you're in your own business, you will find useful people to take on various roles in the company. You can also find reliable suppliers and delivery people this year.

The traditional red envelopes are used each year to give presents of money to people, mostly children. These envelopes are glossy red with colorful pictures and prosperity sayings printed on the front. You can use this energy to help you attract a new career.

Take a traditional red envelope and write down a description of your desired new career. You may name the profession or you may just describe some aspect of the work ("I get to use my creative abilities." "I work with enthusiastic people." "I leave each day with a sense of accomplishment.", etc.) Place a small amount of money in the envelope and place it near your front door, either on a table or in a drawer.

Education

You spent the last year exploring new avenues for yourself. Now you may find you want to get more education or complete a degree started in previous years. This is an excellent year to pursue an education, as you have both luck and support to help you.

There could be a disruption in your plans in July which is not traditionally a school month. This could mean that between semesters you shift majors, change schools or decide to really buckle down and get through school as quickly as possible. Whatever you choose, know that it's the correct decision. The Universe will step up to clear the path for your forward movement.

Legal Matters

You have hidden luck in the area of contracts, lawsuits, and negotiations. This means you may not be aware of how much power you wield in the situation. You may feel like you're walking blindly through the process. You do need to take it slow and get professional help when the legalese is indecipherable. However, positive energy and luck in these affairs, suggest fortune will smile on you if you put in the effort to make an agreement you're happy with. Don't sign anything if you're feeling rushed or coerced (even if a family member is involved). Take your time, read it carefully and you will be just fine.

Health and Well-Being

There is an abundance of energy available for you to make excellent headway on healing a health issue, or getting yourself into better shape. You have support from those around you (maybe not everyone, but some key people will be there for you) and you have the resources you need in the way of medical help, information and treatments. The opportunities you have available to you this year should not be ignored.

To improve your eating habits be aware of what you're drinking or not drinking. Add more water to your diet while reducing soft drinks or alcohol, and you will feel better in the first few weeks. Also, you can consider adding foods originating in the ocean. This may include fish as well as a variety of seafood and/or seaweed.

To deal with stress this year, you need to focus on getting restful sleep. If this has been an ongoing problem for you, consider bringing in professional help, you might go to a sleep clinic, or using special devices to measure the quantity and quality of the sleep you're getting. You might need a different bed, a new mattress, or for your bedroom the room to be a different temperature. Take a look at your evening routine as well, and see if there are changes you can make in your "wind-down" period before you go to bed.

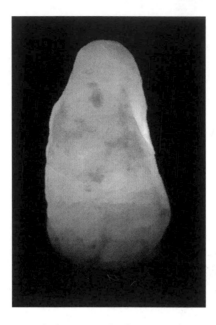

Consider adding a salt lamp to the home to bring in good health energy. Salt lamps are made from solid pieces of Himalayan rock salt. A hole is carved into the bottom of the block of salt, and a small light bulb is placed inside. When lit, the lamp glows with a soft peach-colored light. Also, the heated salt emits negative ions into the air, like a miniature version of the air at the ocean.

The combination of the heavy object (the rock salt) and the negative ions it produces will bring stability and peace to an environment. Place the salt lamp in the living room or bedroom and keep the light on for long periods during the evening hours. You can also display several salt lamps since they come in many interesting shapes and sizes.

Pig/Boar

January 30, 1911–February 17, 1912: Yin Metal Pig/Boar

February 16, 1923–February 4, 1924: Yin Water Pig/Boar

February 4, 1935–January 23, 1936: Yin Wood Pig/Boar

January 22, 1947–February 9, 1948: Yin Fire Pig/Boar

February 8, 1959–January 27, 1960: Yin Earth Pig/Boar

January 27, 1971–January 15, 1972: Yin Metal Pig/Boar

February 13, 1983–February 1, 1984: Yin Water Pig/Boar

January 31, 1995–February 18, 1996: Yin Wood Pig/Boar

February 18, 2007–February 6, 2008: Yin Fire Pig/Boar

February 5, 2019–January 24, 2020: Yin Earth Pig/Boar

Pig Personality

There are two Signs of the Chinese Zodiac that nobody ever seems to want to be, and one of them is Pig (or Boar) (in case you haven't guessed it already, the other is Rat). Even so, you should understand Pig is one of the best signs to be! Pig is the symbol of the prosperity and good fortune of the family.

When considering the qualities of a Chinese Zodiac creature, it's a good idea to examine the traits, behaviors, and personality of the animal and associate our traditional knowledge about the animal with the metaphorical or symbolic creature who is part of the zodiac. Throughout history and in many cultures there are traditions and stories about the pig.

The ancestor of the domesticated pig is the wild boar. While the male wild boar is usually solitary, the females and piglets live in groups and welcome the males at breeding season. For this reason, the Chinese zodiac sign of Pig (sometimes also called Boar) represents one of the most sociable signs. This sign is known for being community-minded and gregarious.

The animal pig is an omnivore, consuming both plants and animals. Natives born under the Chinese Zodiac sign of the Pig/Boar are known for their culinary abilities (or at least their love of great food). They are also delightful hosts, who provide their guests with lots of comforts and splendid meals.

The animal pig is known for his exceedingly acute sense of smell. People born under this Chinese Zodiac sign are known to be very discerning, able to suss out what's really going on. Scientists tell us that in social situations when we are connecting with others whom we may not know (or not know well), we often use our sense of smell to determine friend or foe. People born in the Year of the Pig (or Boar) are better able to access this ability in their daily lives.

At home, Pig loves a social gathering. The kitchen is always filled with ingredients—should they be needed for an impromptu party. At the sound of the doorbell, Pig is ready to greet guests. The people who come to the party are lucky; Pig does whatever he or she can to make their guests feel welcome and comfortable. This doesn't necessarily mean that the house is spotless, some Pig natives keep a very messy house, but they will still welcome guests with open arms.

In the business world, Pig is often underestimated. On the outside they seem "sweet," gullible; and almost never seem to be able to say "No!" However, Pig is quite smart, is ready to take on a leadership role whenever called upon to do so.

Pigs do not like confrontation and are always looking for a win-win situation; they also dismiss insults and easily shrug off negativity. Should you hire a Pig to work for you in your struggling business, and they will devote their time and energy to building your success.

Pigs are generous. They like to see a smile on someone else's face. They love the good things in life, gourmet food, designer clothing, the upscale or even exotic car. They are looking for a life of luxury, comfort, and ease, and they're willing to put some effort into your being comfortable, too.

On the other hand, Pigs can trip themselves up with the excessive rules and limitations they put upon themselves. When others cross them, they can respond very aggressively, which can be quite a shock to the person on the receiving end.

Pig natives are susceptible to lawsuits and can become entangled for years. Because they like to see the best in people, they can be swindled, and they need to watch out for con-men. Pig has a warm heart, and when things don't go well in their lives, they can be subject to depression. Their desire for perfection can overwhelm them, resulting in increased stress.

How to use your Lucky Days: *On these days plan to take essential actions, make necessary phone calls, or send emails. These are days when your energy level and luck are high.*

Pig: Predictions for 2019

January: *[note: This month there is a Solar Eclipse on January 5th and a Lunar Eclipse on January 21st. Check out the section on Eclipses for more details. Your Lucky Days this month are 11, 17, 23, and 29.]*

As we enter the New Year, you find you are not too clear about your priorities. Things you wanted to do just a few months ago now don't seem nearly as exciting or compelling. You're finishing up your 12-year cycle, so the old goals are passing away. If you have uncompleted projects, things you haven't touched in months or even years, it's time to let them go. Clear the slate and your schedule. Leave time open for the new that's coming.

When you encounter the number 99 or 999, know this is a signal from the Universe to let go of something. Think of what you were doing just before you saw the number—this activity is related to what you need to release.

There is good energy around finances this month. Money is flowing in from a couple of different sources. You may be receiving a raise or bonus or, if you own your own company, you might be making more money in general.

Even though you already have a list of things you want to buy, try to hold off for a few weeks longer. As you enter into the new energy next month, there's a good chance you'll want something entirely different.

February: *[note: Happy Lunar New Year on February 5th! Your Lucky Days this month are 4, 10, 16, 22, and 28.]*

This month we enter the Year of the Earth Pig, and for Pig natives this means the beginning of a new 12-year cycle. Now you will look around and easily release that which is no longer serving you. You'll want to let go of more than just 'stuff.' You'll be letting go of old fears and negative attitudes. You will also drop people who are not supportive. The process will start this month and continue throughout the year.

This month the sighting of a hawk or other bird of prey indicates a time to focus on your goals.

The best thing to do during a seed planting year (like the one you're now in), is to try new things. These new represents the seeds of the future, and by trying the new things, you find out what you like and what you don't like. Sometimes Pig natives can be overly wary of the new. But this month, and indeed this whole year, as you try new food, products, go to new places and meet new people, you easily find out who and what will support you going forward. This what to focus on.

March: *[note: Mercury is retrograde from March 6th to March 29th. See the section on Mercury retrograde for more information. Uranus* *moves into Taurus on March 6th—Time for change. Your Lucky Days this month are 12, 18, 24, and 30.]*

This is an ideal month to slow down and take care of you. While you are quite good at taking care of others, making them feel welcomed and loved, sometimes you get overlooked. This doesn't have to be complicated or take up a lot of your time. Consider giving yourself a spa day or even a half day. Take yourself fishing or for a leisurely hike in a beautiful place nearby.

You can also renew your energy by doing something creative. This may be getting involved in an art project or doing something fun at home. It might be related to cooking, painting or decorating. Better still, find a good friend who wants to take care of you for a day. Let them drive you around and buy you lunch.

Pig natives can find some parts of dealing with their financial wellbeing challenging, but this month you'll have a lot of opportunities to increase your income. Visualize ways more money can come to you through your employment, business, or a side venture. Picture the money easily finding it's way to you. Once you have the vision in your head then gently initiate the appropriate conversation, or ask for the sale.

If you're in a love relationship, expand the number of friends you have as a couple and consider getting together with other couples on a regular basis.

If you're looking for love, you can have luck through online dating sites now. Set your intention by writing out some of the qualities you would like to attract in a partner and then put a profile up on one of the dating services.

April: *[note: Jupiter goes retrograde on April 10th, Pluto goes retrograde on April 24th and Saturn goes retrograde on April 29th. Your Lucky Days are 5, 11, 17, and 23.]*

The energy of change will seem to come in waves. Suddenly everything will seem to be tossed about. But give it a day or so and it will smooth out again.

Changes will be suggested around your home situation this month, but it may just be a notification from the Universe about a shift sometime this year being beneficial. If that's the case, then it's a good time to declutter and lighten the load as you prepare for this change.

When there's change energy around you, there's a temptation to spend money. This month you may feel justified making a big purchase you've been wanting to make for some time. However, be cautious. You don't want to rush into buying something you may not really need, or you may not have budgeted for just yet. Money opportunities are still strong. Do prayer or meditation work to attract the funds you need for this purchase.

You are particularly attractive to others at this time. If you're single, this can work to your advantage. You just need to get out of the house, and you will meet some new and interesting people.

If you're already in a love relationship, things could get complicated. Your general kindness to another could be seen as more than just being friendly. It could bring you an offer you weren't expecting. You may also find yourself attracted to a person who is, like you, already spoken for. All this can be fun if not taken too seriously or too far. Be mindful of your partner's feelings (you usually are anyway) and if they're the jealous type then keep this all to yourself.

May: *[note: Your Lucky Days are 5, 11, 17, 23 and 29.]*

The first year of your 12 year cycle can be a challenging year. You can look back 12 years ago, 24 years ago, even 36 years ago and see the kind of changes that were going on in your life during those times. Recognize you are now older and wiser. It won't be as difficult this time if you remain open to change.

This month it feels like people want to pick a quarrel with you. You are very conscientious and considerate of others, and so this has you a little mystified. It's probably the Universe nudging you in a different direction. So when someone seems to lose their temper around you, see if you can find the message while getting out of the way of the messenger.

Sit down and meditate on your overall goals. If you are offered an opportunity to do something brand new during the first year of your 12 year cycle, it's a good idea to consider it because the timing is perfect.

You are quite busy now and not having as much time as you've had previously to take care of your love relationship. This can make you feel as if you're not as connected to your partner as before, or that the relationship is fading. This is a temporary situation and solved easily through a conversation or two. Even just sitting on the sofa holding hands one evening will go a long way toward helping you feel connected again.

If you're looking for love, you might feel as if it's time to give up because you're not interested in anyone who's been showing up so far. But don't give up. Love is close by.

June: *[note: Neptune goes retrograde on June 21st. Your Lucky Days this month are 4, 10, 16, 22, and 28.]*

This is the most significant month of the year. The changes you make this month will create ripple effects that last your entire 12-year cycle. It's nothing to be nervous about. You will do just fine. Just approach all of your options with curiosity, and choose the path that takes you out of your comfort zone (even if it's just by a little bit).

Consider whether an option being offered is about doing the same old thing you have been doing, because then it's probably not the right choice for you right now. But also realize that even though this is a pivotal month, you will get more invitations to change this year. If you take a running leap at this now, then great things will happen down the road, but if you're not ready then just use this time to get used to the new ideas.

You have a lot of amazing qualities: courage, endurance, patience, tolerance, but you may not be good at personal accounting (the financial kind). That's okay, but to really make some gains this year financially it's a good idea to create/outline a budget you can stick to. If you can't find a person to help you, consider finding an app.

If your partner is also born in the Year of the Pig, they are going through significant changes the same as you are, and this could take you both in seemingly different directions (like a job offer out of state for one or the other of you, or an educational opportunity elsewhere). This will take at least one good family meeting to sort out.

If you're looking for love, you can find the person close to home. Attend events in the neighborhood, hang out at the local coffee place, or take walks near your home.

July: *[note: Mercury is retrograde from July 8th to August 1st. See the section on Mercury retrograde for more information. There's a Solar Eclipse on July 2nd and a Lunar Eclipse on July 16th. Check out the section on Eclipses for more details. Your Lucky Days are 4, 10, 16, 22, and 28.]*

The people around you are feeling a lot of intense energy this month. You've now had several months of change energy flowing in and out of your life, and at this point you're going with the flow. But other people you care about may be feeling adrift right now, calling out to you for love and support.

If you've been following the energy along the lines of your finances, getting a budget in order, monitoring the outflow, this month can bring you a sizable financial opportunity.

If you have been sliding on these preliminary steps then any shifts this month may give you a reason get your financial house in order. Nothing to fear here. It's just a wake-up call. Gather the needed paperwork and make the necessary phone calls or send the emails and collect the information you need to get things straightened out. You are good at getting the job done, and once you get started, you have no problem completing the task.

If you're looking for love, you have many opportunities this month. If you've been looking for a while, however, without success, then this is the month to return to the drawing board and ask yourself if you are deep down afraid of being in a relationship. What is the real block here?

August: *[note: Mercury moves forward again on August 2nd. Both Jupiter and Uranus move forward again August 11th. Your Lucky Days are 3, 9, 15, 21, and 27.]*

After last month you're ready for a vacation, however, it just might not be on the schedule. You're a bit frazzled and about at the end of your rope when it comes to everyone around you needing your energy and attention. You must give yourself a break and take some time to heal and re-energize. Pig natives have lots of stamina, but everyone has their own breaking point, and now it's your turn.

Also, it's time to share the chores. If you live alone consider hiring some temporary help. If you have a house full of family members, it's time for a sit-down chat to divvy up the list of things to do.

You are quite busy this month, and while this is beneficial to your pocketbook, it's not really that sustainable. What you want to meditate on this month is how to make more money by working less. Pig natives can be a little fatalistic, so you may have gotten into a situation and believe you're stuck, or perhaps you feel this is the best things will ever be! But things can always improve with a little effort.

Be cautious about lawsuits now. This is not a lucky time for you to be suing someone.

Some parts of your relationship are going so well. This is helping you overlook the irritating things about your partner right now. You've been quite understanding thus far, but you're watching your partner slip back into some old bad habits—ones you thought were done a while ago. This has your teeth set on edge. It sometimes feels like they don't care about your feelings. This is more a matter of their priorities not all being the same as yours. There will have to be some adjustments on both sides.

If you're looking for love, check out opportunities near your work or related to your profession.

September: *[note: Saturn moves forward again on September 18th. Your Lucky Days this month are 2, 8, 14, 20, and 26.]*

Your reputation is highlighted this month. Avoid posting anything negative or even controversial online as it could affect your job or social standing.

There is a lot of energy around parents or older relatives this month. You may consider a visit, or you may have relatives descending on you. That's probably okay as Pig natives are great entertainers and love a good party.

There are rumblings at work, and a change could be coming. If you want to stay put, you can use positive energy and Feng Shui cures to retain a job but remember in a seed-planting year it's better to make a change than try to hold on to the old.

This is an exhilarating month for relationships. If you're in a love relationship but haven't tied the knot, you might want to make it official now or at least set the date and let friends know. You may take your relationship to another level by moving in together.

You may be looking for even more significant changes in your life and this could mean putting your relationship on notice. You're not one usually to test others, you accept faults in others as well as in yourself, but with so much change energy around you, the relationship you're in could be swept away unless some deep, meaningful conversations take place now.

If you're looking love be brave and ask someone out. Make the first move and exciting opportunities will follow.

October: *[note: Pluto moves forward again on October 3rd. Your Lucky Days are 2, 8, 14, 20, and 26.]*

After the intensity of last month here comes the calm after the storm. Some cleanup may be needed, hurt feelings may need soothing, rest and recovery but overall things are much better. If you've been true to yourself, following your heart, and trusting in the power of the Universe, you are doing just fine. If you've been trying to hold back change, well, this is the time to reevaluate your position. This month, energies are aligned to give you more help and support than at any other time this year. Ask and help will appear.

When money is easily accessible, you always find someone in need and very soon the money is gone. This is an outstanding time to put something away for your future. To make a little extra this month, sell off things you don't need. There may be an additional windfall coming your way.

Energies are quite positive around love relationships this month. You have opportunities for intimacy and closeness.

If you're looking for love, you have opportunities to find an interested party for a physical relationship. This person doesn't want to take things slow. This may not meet your definition of romance, and if so say it openly. If this is real love, the person will stick around and love will grow.

November: *[note: Mercury goes retrograde from November 1st to November 21st. See the section on Mercury retrograde for more information. Neptune moves forward again on November 27th. Your Lucky Days this month are 7, 13, 19 and 25.]*

This is an excellent month to challenge some of your limiting beliefs. You have an opportunity to free yourself and move forward in an area where you've been stuck for some time. These beliefs have possibly stemmed from childhood or been taught to you in school. You can find the information you need by paying attention to the signs you are receiving, and your intuition.

There is a lot of financial activity this month, some of it beneficial and some of it needs your attention. You may be making plans for the end of the year, holidays and travel. You may be setting up your budget for holiday shopping. Keep your attention on your credit cards and handbag now. Put some extra protection around your valuables (you can do this through prayer, meditation or lighting a candle and making a wish).

You are likely to have opportunities to secure a good end of year bonus now. You can expand your business at this time.

Look for money you thought was lost (or unavailable to you) to return to you now.

The shift of energy at home is a welcomed one, as you need to stir up the chi every once in a while. Consider finishing up home renovation projects before the guests arrive. Pig natives are consummate entertainers, and you can show off your skills by inviting a large party.

If you're looking for love, find other single friends to join you on your journey. Take a trip. Have an adventure. You will meet interesting people along the way.

December: *[note: There is a Solar Eclipse on December 26th. Check out the section on Eclipses for more details. Your Lucky Days are 1, 7, 13, 19 and 25.]*

This could be one of the best months of the year. While the year has had its challenges—and all seed-planting years do—you are already seeing the benefits of the growth you've accomplished and the new connections you've made.

You are quite busy now. There are charitable events to can attend, professional parties, and friends sending messages and greetings.

If you are working a contract job, it's likely you will find additional contract work or your current contract will be extended.

How you make money is going well, but there still may be some struggles when it comes to accumulating money. This is not Pig natives' strong suit. However, you do possess both fortitude and patience. Accumulating money is a particular skill and you will just need more practice. So, for now, adjust your budget to something you can live with, and try to stick to it.

You are surrounded by loving people this month, but if you're in a partnership, your partner may be hard to find. Perhaps they are traveling to see relatives, or they are in a seasonal job requiring lots of overtime, but you're feeling a little lonely and forgotten in your crowd of friends and well-wishers. Pig natives don't usually wallow in sadness, though. You focus on giving and that brings you special joy.

If you're looking for a love relationship, it's a good idea to advertise. This could be done using an online service or by reminding all your friends and relatives you are in the market for love.

January 2020: *[note: There is a Lunar Eclipse on January 10th. Check out the section on Eclipses for more details. Uranus moves forward again on January 11th. Your Lucky Days this month are 6, 12, 18, 24 and 30.]*

As the first year of your 12-year cycle comes to a close, you look back know this wasn't an easy year. Now sit down and write out two lists, one listing the things that seem to be working, and the other a list of what needs to be dropped or discarded. Set the energy in motion with a little ritual, placing the positive list in a particular area of the house where you'll see it, and decorating it with effective Feng Shui cures. This will give you a sense of direction and energy going forward. Burn the other list.

If you count up the valuable skills you gained this year, the money and better investment choices you made, you can truly assess this year as a success. Sometimes you are too hard on yourself, and this can really zap your motivation. Make a point to be kind to yourself, and you will have more energy to do the right thing when choices (especially financial or purchasing choices) arise.

Make a commitment to reduce the amount of stuff you own to the things that truly bring you happiness (or at least is very useful). Get rid of duplicates and excess. You can sell off unneeded items and bring in a little additional money.

If you're in a love relationship, this may be a superb start to your year. You have the opportunity to cement your connection with your beloved through open and deep conversation.

If you're looking for love, notice if you keep finding the same type of person. If you're attracted to a personality type that hasn't been good for you previously, it's time to make a change. Date someone who's not like anyone you've ever dated before. Be being curious about someone entirely new to you.

Attract New Love

This is your year, the start of a new 12-year cycle, and this can mean you are starting fresh in the area of love. If you were seeing someone last year and are still thinking about them, realize the new cycle will bring you new opportunities. Thinking about the past and wishing it to return isn't helpful at this time.

There's so much going on in your life right now, so much change at the beginning of the year you may on the other hand not be giving your love-life much thought. Of course, Pig natives naturally thrive in relationships. Their intuitive ability to know what their partner needs is legendary. So if you want a new love now, the energy is positive for "calling in" love into your life.

To "call" love, you need to spend some quiet time thinking about the type of person you want to connect with. Focus more on the attributes of the person rather than a name or a specific person or physical attribute. Notice if fears or insecurities come up when you think about being in a real relationship. Make of note of those fears as you will need to address them at some point. Then return to visualizing. You will start meeting new people in just a few weeks of beginning this process.

You can enhance relationship energy and bring a bit of art and beauty into your home. Place a figurine or statue of a couple in love in your living room, family room, or bedroom. Place this figurine in a prominent place, so it is easily seen. This will help pull the love energy into your space and your life all year long.

One additional tip is to hang a small bag of cardamom seeds from the love figurine. Cardamom has been used in passion/ lust potions for centuries. To make a bag take a small piece of cotton cloth about four inches square and lay it out on the table. In the center place about a teaspoon of cardamom seeds. Gather the corners of the fabric and tie it together with thread or embroidery floss leaving a bit of extra string for hanging the bag. Adding this touch of spice will help bring in the romance.

Enhance Existing Love

This year the energy of your love relationship seems to swing back and forth from really marvelous to what-the-heck is happening here. This is quite common during the first year of a 12-year cycle as you attempt to gain your footing with the new energy. You are testing new options for your life, and even if you have no intention of changing your relationship, you are becoming a different person. This can leave your partner confused, and they can respond more emotionally than usual.

You are a sensitive, sensual soul and it would be wonderful to feel in love again. But you're busy, your partner is busy; seemingly effortless love actually takes a lot of planning. Use small things to put the fun back into your relationship. A loving note tucked into a jeans pocket hidden there waiting to be found, a single flower in a vase on their side of the bathroom or just turning over control of the remote can bring joy to the union.

Often when people start a new 12-year cycle, they question continuing everything/anything in their life. You may be tempted to chuck everything, including your relationship, in order to grab onto something new. If this is something you've been planning for years then the beginning of this new cycle signals it's time. But if this thought is recent, know it's actually about letting go of something else. Search and you will find what you truly need to release.

For those of you born in the Year of the Pig promote love energy in your home by adding orchids. Orchids have gained great popularity in recent years. You can find orchids in garden shops as well as the local grocery store. Orchids have long symbolized love, luxury, and beauty.

Choose an orchid with beautiful blooms and place the plant in your bedroom or family room. When the orchid loses its blooms and goes into it's resting phase, continue to water and care for the plant.

When temperatures drop, a cared for orchid will develop a bloom spike. They will continue to grow in cold weather, then produce blooms as temperatures turn warmer. Most orchids bloom once per year. If you can't wait for the new blooms to appear just buy another orchid to display.

Looking to Conceive?

One of the gemstones associated with pregnancy is the geode. A geode is a hollow mineral mass with gemstones growing inside the shell. On the outside, a geode often looks like an egg, and when it is cracked open, the inside reveals the sparkling gemstones.

Geodes range from a couple of inches in size to several feet in diameter. When you find a geode you like, place it in your bedroom to enhance the pregnancy energy.

(From Donna Stellhorn's eBook, A Path to Pregnancy: Ancient Secrets for the Modern Woman)

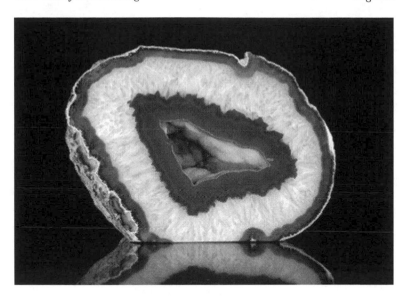

Family and Kids

This is your year, and while you don't usually gravitate towards change, you find it hard to say you truly love the place where you live living. It might be the house or the neighborhood, or it just may be the climate is not to your liking anymore. You may not move this year, but you can do things to start thinking about a move. Start decluttering and visiting potential places to live.

Despite not being in love with your home right now Pig natives are natural homebodies. You find it hard to get out of the house on time. This can be due to your own procrastination or it just takes forever to herd everyone in the direction out the door. The benefit is you do more cooking at home, spend more evenings with the family or working in the garden.

You have a desire to clear out the old. This means digging deep into the garage or attic to remove the really old stuff. Perhaps it's time to let go of your grandmother's china or your mother's rocking chair. Family heirlooms may need to be distributed to younger relatives or to distant cousins living far away. As you let go of each piece, you let go of past disappointments. You will feel a healing when you are done.

Blue is a power color. It represents the energy of the sky and the ocean. It represents strength, loyalty, and wisdom. This year, to help bring positive protection energy into your home, burn a blue candle about once a month. You can choose a large candle or a little tea light. Find a holder and burn it safely in the house. If you don't like burning candles, then hang a picture of a lit blue candle in your bedroom or in the hallway near your bedroom.

Money

With all the change energy you're experiencing this year you'll be happy to know that money coming from employment or contract work from an employer looks strong. You may even have several sources of income this year due to picking up some work. Also, the completion of one employment contract directly leads to the next, so income will continue to flow.

Money is also increased by finding people to inspire you. Consider joining a mastermind group or business networking group, not so much to sell something to them, but more to spur you towards taking on more challenging projects and finding better ways of making money. Look even to elders in your family who amassed money and sit down with them for advice and counsel.

There is a strong desire this year to spend some money on new technology or a new vehicle. These represent trying a new path. If these purchases are within the budget, then go for it. But if this is something that's going to be a stretch for you or it puts you in debt, consider waiting or finding a way to raise the funds you need to make the purchase.

When you want to attract money in abundance, hang or display a pair of fish by the front door. The fish may be crafted out of fabric, glass, wood or metal. The symbol of the two fish represents the saying, "May you have so much money, you have left-over money!" In Feng Shui, fish are used to attract wealth because the Chinese word for fish sounds like the word for "abundance." Displaying a couple of fish this year will help the money flow in effortlessly.

Job or Career

You have a great deal of luck related to your career this year. Luck means you have more protection than usual, but this doesn't necessarily mean things aren't changing. You might have a job change this year, but you will most definitely find a new position. You may have a setback in your own business and then come back much stronger than before. Trust in your luck.

Over the past 12-years, you've been building a set of skills. Now it's time to showcase what you can do. Take a good look at how your abilities and experience could translate into employment you really enjoy. If you are unsure what the ideal position for you would look like, then consider at least heading towards a job in an industry you're interested in.

You might be considering studying for a new type of position entirely. You will find you make more career progress by enlisting "who you know." to help you or offer a referral. Build your list of contacts, perhaps through sites like LinkedIn, or through membership in professional organizations. Take people to lunch who are in similar positions as you are in (or would like to be in) but who work for companies you admire. Reach out to headhunters in person or online or sit down with managers and talk about what you're looking for in the future.

Sometimes in Feng Shui, we combine multiple symbols to create a powerful cure. The symbol of a bowl is to "welcome something new into our space." If the bowl is made out of brass, we have the energy of success and prosperity.

So, for this cure, place a small brass bowl on your entryway table. You can leave the bowl empty or put coins and crystals in it. You can also place a list of your wishes describing your new, awaited career.

Education

There's a lot of positive energy around education this year. You may decide to go back to school or to complete a program you started years ago. You may want to try online courses, even if you don't receive a formal university credit, you will definitely improve your skill set. If you are studying online make sure to avail yourself of all the one-on-one help available from your teachers/mentors; and connect if possible with other students for virtual study sessions.

There is a real opportunity for you to receive some funding for education. This may be a reimbursement from work, a grant or scholarship or some other program you uncover as the result of a thorough search. Look for ways to cover education costs this year without having to incur debt.

Legal Matters

You have positive energy and flow around legal matters. This means delays in contracts will be brief and lawsuits have an opportunity to be settled out of court.

There will be a temptation to co-sign an agreement for an adult child but only do this if there is absolutely no other way to move this forward—because there is a likelihood this could go south in a few years. On the other hand, agreements involving employment, contract work, and creative work are likely to go well and result in future beneficial contracts with these same parties.

Health and Well-Being

This year marks a new cycle, which means you have an opportunity to incorporate new health routines. You may find the remedies you need for chronic issues you've been struggling with. But change is hard, even small changes, and so it will require mindfulness on your part to keep from falling into old habits.

This year, the key to success is change. Look at even the little things like changing your toothpaste, using a different type of toothbrush, or brushing your teeth with your other hand. At first, it won't seem like such a small change will bring much of a difference but the little things are the microcosm representing the big things. Small changes lead to big results.

The area of your life stressing you the most now is your vision of the future. Perhaps you're not good at seeing what's to come, or like many Pig natives, you have a hard time deciding which path you want to take. It's time to stop trying to know if what you're doing now will bring you the results you want. Instead, shift your energy to knowing you can excel at whatever you set your mind to. You have willpower, courage and lots of friends to help. Remove the stress by staying in the present and doing your best today.

Historically Jade was considered more valuable than diamonds in Asia. Jade is most commonly found in the colors green and purple. Green jade represents longevity. Jade can be carved into many things, from lucky charms to fine jewelry. Hang a Jade charm in your bedroom to protect your health, or find a Jade pendant to wear. Jade has a protective quality, but it is fragile. If your Jade piece breaks, make sure to replace it..

Compatibility Between Signs

In this section of Chinese Astrology: 2019, Year of the Earth Pig, I will explain a little about compatibility between the Chinese Zodiac signs with regard to love and friendship. Sometimes a pairing of two signs isn't the most promising. We can often improve the energy by placing a Feng Shui Crystal cure to support the relationship.

Feng Shui Crystals are round, cut glass crystals which have a prismatic effect. When light hits the crystal, a rainbow of glittering, shiny light prisms twinkle around the ceiling, walls, or floor. Shiny things attract energy, so the sparkling crystal attracts energy to balance the relationship.

Cut glass crystals come in many shapes, but round is the most balanced and harmonious shape, so it's used to balance relationship energy. Whenever a Feng Shui Crystal is called for, you can use a clear one (clear crystals are the easiest to find), or you can use colored crystals to bring in the energy of one of the five elements.

Use green to represent the Wood element if you want to increase growth and prosperity.

Use blue to represent the Water element, to activate good communication, flow, and harmony.

Use amber or yellow to represent the Earth element, to bring stability and longevity.

Use red to represent the Fire element, to stimulate energy and passion.

Use clear to represent the Metal element, to attract resources and business success.

Along with the compatibility listings below, you will find suggestions about where to place the crystal if your relationship needs some help. Choose a green crystal if troubles in the relationship are because of finances. Choose a blue crystal if the problems in the relationship center around communication.

Choose an amber or yellow crystal if there has been infidelity and you want to try to heal the relationship. Choose a red crystal if there's been a lack of passion, romance, and sex. Choose a clear crystal to come closer together, and to receive help and support from your partner.

To find the correct direction for placing the crystal, think of your home and the rising sun. The sun always rises in the east. The sun sets in the west. If you know where the sun rises and sets in relation to your home, you will be able to identify the other cardinal directions, north and south very easily. (Hint: Google Maps aerial view can make this task very easy, as it always shows north as up, south is down, to the left is west and to the right is east.).

To find the inner directions such as north by Northwest, find north and find west. Halfway between these two is northwest. North by Northwest is halfway between north and northwest.

Place the diagram (facing page) on the floor, east pointing towards the rising sun. The diagram will help you find the right direction for placing appropriate crystal.

If you can place the crystal in a window, it will catch the most light. If there is no window in that direction, hang the crystal on a lamp, on a plant, on a drawer pull, or simply from a hook on the wall. To see all the different ways to use Feng Shui Crystals and how to hang them, go to www.fengshuiform.com.

We can divide the 12 animals of the Chinese Zodiac into four groups. Each group has some key personality traits:

Rat, Dragon, Monkey are the action-oriented ones. The Rat takes care of the details; the Dragon has the big ideas, and the Monkey is able to improve the skills of others.

Ox, Snake, and Rooster are the deep thinkers. The Ox is methodical, thinking things through thoroughly. The Snake is wise and sees things from various perspectives. The Rooster is alert and aware of everything going on around him.

Tiger, Horse, and Dog are the freedom lovers. The Tiger is impulsive: he sees what he wants and pounces. The Horse runs across the prairies and lands with power and grace. The Dog can work alone or within a group, and still retain his independence

Rabbit, Sheep/Goat, and Pig/Boar are the peace lovers. The Rabbit is diplomatic and can bring opposing forces together. The Sheep/Goat is the humanitarian, wanting to bring peace to the world. The Pig/Boar is the homebody, wanting to create comfort and peace for the family.

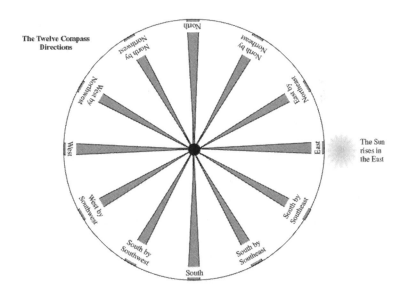

Chinese Zodiac Signs and Compatibility

Rat Compatibility

Rat with Rat: Well suited and lots of fun. Always busy, doing things, making deals, and making money. You'll need to respect each others' time and secrets. Occasionally you'll need time apart as much as you need to be together. If you find one of you is too bossy, or you both need to focus a little more on the big picture and the future, hang a Feng Shui Crystal in the North side of the house.

Rat with Ox: A happy and long-lasting relationship. You will benefit from Ox's stability and strength. You are both optimistic, and enjoy the little things in life. You can start the job and know that Ox will be there to help you finish it. If you find your partner is stubborn and not open to your ideas, hang a Feng Shui Crystal in the North by Northeast part of the house.

Rat with Tiger: Hot and cold, with lots of energy and excitement in this relationship. Sometimes the Tiger will ignore the little Rat, and sometimes the Tiger will be surprised at how loud a Rat can squeak. If Tiger's unpredictable ways get on your nerves, you can steady this relationship by hanging a Feng Shui Crystal in the East by Northeast part of the house.

Rat with Rabbit: Arguments after the fling is what we have here. You are both clever, but a little too clever. One wants commitment, and the other wants freedom, and neither wants the same thing at the same time. If you find Rabbit too passive and you're looking for more dedication to this relationship, hang a Feng Shui Crystal in the East side of the house.

Rat with Dragon: Happiness abounds when the Rat joins with the powerful Dragon. The relationship can be very intense. But use caution (and flattery) because if you break the spell, there is no putting the broken relationship back together again. If you find Dragon's head in the clouds and need a more grounded partner to help you with the day to day parts of the relationship, hang a Feng Shui Crystal in the East by Southeast side of the house.

Rat with Snake: Volatile pair that sometimes can be a good relationship... at least until the Snake gets hungry. Avoid being on the menu. This is more of a learning experience than a love match. If you find Snake too secretive and a little on the manipulative side, hang a Feng Shui Crystal in the South by Southeast part of the house.

Rat with Horse: Unhappy pair that can't see eye to eye. You find Horse's needs exhausting. If you get into this relationship, keep a life raft handy. You'll be paddling to shore in no time. If you insist that this is the relationship of your dreams and you want Horse to settle down and be not so restless, hang a Feng Shui Crystal in the South part of the house.

Rat with Sheep: Poor match because the sensitivity of the Sheep is no match for your quick tongue. Communication starts out well, but there will be problems with words, and that will be the end of the relationship. You would think with horns; he wouldn't have such thin skin. If you only see eye to eye when pampering your Sheep partner and want to have things be a little more equal, hang a Feng Shui Crystal in the South by Southwest part of the house.

Rat with Monkey: Very lively meeting of people from different worlds. Monkey can take Rat on the trip of a lifetime and open new worlds. It's the unlikely pair in love. You will give each other new perspectives on life and living. But if all the excitement and Monkey's high energy starts to wear on you, hang a Feng Shui Crystal in the West by Southwest part of the house.

Rat with Rooster: Need to work hard at this to make it work at all. You are natural barnyard enemies, both hunting for the same big prize—and not just chicken feed. So you're better off avoiding this cage-match. If you find yourself with an overly critical Rooster on your hands, hang a Feng Shui Crystal in the West part of the house.

Rat with Dog: Lots of energy and togetherness; this is good for you, you both enjoy being out and about, enjoying others and each other. However, you may find you have trouble finding personal space. Dog will tag along wherever you go, and keep trying to pull you back home. If you feel your life restricted by

Dog's constant bark, hang a Feng Shui Crystal in the West by Northwest part of the house.

Rat with Pig: Picture this charming pair of homebodies, both taking care of the other. There is optimum togetherness when you want it, and alone time when you need it. Pig keeps the house cozy and warm. If you find all this happiness and optimism is maxing out your credit cards, hang a Feng Shui Crystal in the North by Northwest part of the house.

Ox Compatibility

Ox with Rat: You are a happy, practical pair that compliment each other. You have the potential here for a very stable relationship with benefits for both partners. Rat sees the details, and your tireless energy can envision what will become of them. If you find Rat is too picky about the small things and can't get the big picture, hang a Feng Shui Crystal in the North part of the house.

Ox with Ox: A caring pair where each is interested in the comfort and security of the other. Not exciting to others, perhaps, but you can be quite content. You can enjoy decades of holding hands and feeling safe, as the cold winters blow outside. While you can remain content for long periods, should you want to add some fun (or at least a break from the constant work), hang a Feng Shui Crystal in the North by Northeast part of the house.

Ox with Tiger: Your goals in life are entirely different, as are your methods of pursuing outcome. This cat doesn't come when he's called (what cat does). There are quarrels that lead to nowhere. Build a stable home, and Tiger looks for the door. If you want this temperamental kitty with claws to be your lifelong partner you have some work ahead. Hang a Feng Shui Crystal in the East by Northeast part of the house.

Ox with Rabbit: A so-so match. You want stability and clear rules, and Rabbit wants some pampering and kindness. It takes a while to get this one to work, but when it does, it lasts. He can be your lucky Rabbit in the end. But if you honey-bunny spends his or her time sulking in the corner and being overly sensitive, hang a Feng Shui Crystal in the East part of the house.

Ox with Dragon: Tricky pair; expect battles to start from day one. These are two powerful forces with two different ideas of what a relationship is and should be. Ding goes the bell, and the fight begins. If you can see the strong qualities in each of you, there's hope. Hang a Feng Shui Crystal in the East by Southeast part of the house.

Ox with Snake: Supportive, though there can be some conflicts. This is the strong Yin and Yang: together, opposite sides of the same coin. You need each other, and over time with Snake's clever thinking and your perseverance, you both can prosper. While Snake can make an attractive partner, if they are draining your bank account on clothes and toys, hang a Feng Shui Crystal in the South by Southeast part of the house.

Ox with Horse: Difficult match for you. The Horse is fast and careless, compared to your slow and thoughtful ways. There is little Horse can give you that you really want, and so you're more likely to send him on his way. If you want to stable this pony and try to make this restless soul settle down, hang a Feng Shui Crystal in the South part of the house.

Ox with Sheep: Steer clear, this one is trouble from beginning to end. You will have to be exceptionally patient to ride this one out. After butting heads for a while, heartbreak is the most likely ending. You can make this work if you have deep pockets, but it's more likely he/she will spend the money when they're feeling hurt or insecure. To balance the energy, hang a Feng Shui Crystal in the South by Southwest part of the house.

Ox with Monkey: Love and joy can abound with this combo. Monkey will bring you fun times and surprises every day. That will make your steady life more interesting. Once the Monkey settles down, the match can be good for both. If you find Monkey is only interested in him- or herself, and too independent for your peaceful dream of a relationship, hang a Feng Shui Crystal in the West by Southwest part of the house.

Ox with Rooster: Good match for these barnyard pals. You both understand the need for hard work, and Rooster appreciates your patience and understanding. You like having someone around who can mind the details. Together you're the soul of productivity, if you would like to have a bit more romance or at least the occasional cuddle, hang a Feng Shui Crystal in the West part of the house.

Ox with Dog: Possibly good, but too many compromises will be required. This is too much Yin energy together; communication will suffer. Both of you are hesitant to lead. Let the Dog go and see if he comes back of his own accord. If you are tired of coming home and always finding a house full of people, or your partner is always on the phone, you can hang a Feng Shui Crystal in the West by Northwest part of the house.

Ox with Pig: This needs effort and adjustments on both sides. If there is chemistry (and good cooking), the relationship may last. But most likely the Pig won't respect your goals and effort. You get frustrated with his/her play-all-the-time attitude. There can be harmony if there is an understanding of the work and sacrifice it takes to create a financially stable home. If overspending is a problem, hang a Feng Shui Crystal in the North by Northwest part of the house.

Tiger Compatibility

Tiger with Rat: Hot during the chase, and cold when caught, Rat is not a great match for you. Rat is too cynical to see your splendid qualities, and it will need to be taught how to behave. This is more work than you want to do. If you think this is a mouse you want to keep, but the pettiness and demands are hurting the relationship, hang a Feng Shui Crystal in the North part of the house.

Tiger with Ox: Needs effort to keep from being a boring relationship. You might think that Ox will help you settle down and get serious, but in the end, you are just bitter from having all the fun taken out of your life. But if you long for an established relationship that will withstand a bitter winter or a wild party, hang a Feng Shui Crystal in the North by Northeast part of the house.

Tiger with Tiger: Happiness… with claws. As long as you both retain your thick skins, this will be a happy, fun relationship.

But arguments can get nasty, so be ready to forgive each other later—and keep bandages on hand. Of course, making up can be the most fun, and what's life about but having fun? So hang a Feng Shui Crystal in the East by Northeast part of the house.

Tiger with Rabbit: Can be good, but Rabbits are not known for their decisive action. You'll have to be patient with this one and prepared to leap into the fray of this relationship without waiting for the careful Rabbit to make the first move. If this Rabbit keeps sprinting away and you want to lure him/her back, hang a Feng Shui Crystal in the East part of the house.

Tiger with Dragon: The explosive power of you and the Dragon is legendary, making for either the most exciting relationship ever, or you'll both knock the world off its axis. If you want to be looked up to, this is not your match, but if you can work things out and share the leadership roles, giving credit where credit's due, this can work. Hang a Feng Shui Crystal in the East by Southeast part of the house.

Tiger with Snake: Steer clear no matter how attracted you are! You are not going to get the Snake's attention easily, and as soon as your back is turned, he's moved on. You can chase again, but after a while it just gets tiresome. When you leave, Snake chases you; and when you are available, Snake is off without a care. To get this match together, hang a Feng Shui Crystal in the South by Southeast part of the house.

Tiger with Horse: Good ally out in the world, but there may be a conflict about who has to stay home and do the dishes. If you can accept and be happy with an unstable relationship, then grab an apron and give this one a try. Or, better still, pool your creative minds and social nature and make enough money to hire a maid. Stimulate this energy by hanging a Feng Shui Crystal in the South part of the house.

Tiger with Sheep: Can work it out over time, but the Sheep will be cautious. You will have to follow the rules given to you by the Sheep, and this can bring conflicts into the relationship. Mr./Ms Planner will not appreciate your impetuous nature. If you find

Sheep too clingy (which surprises you, you thought you were the one with claws), and you wish he or she had more confidence, hang a Feng Shui Crystal in the South by Southwest part of the house.

Tiger with Monkey: It's very difficult to catch a Monkey who's swinging from tree to tree. You might be attracted to one playing hard to get, but after a while, it's no fun always being the one who has to chase... even for a Tiger. If you want to make this work but Monkey's loud, know-it-all behavior is grating on your nerves, hang a Feng Shui Crystal in the West by Southwest part of the house.

Tiger with Rooster: You come from different worlds, so once at home, there's not much to talk about. You feel bossed around by the nagging Rooster who's frustrated that you don't seem to fall in line like the other chickens. If you find he or she is always on you about your spending and your inability to do the laundry right, smooth things over by hanging a Feng Shui Crystal in the West part of the house.

Tiger with Dog: Strong ally and a good match for you. The Dog can keep the home fires burning while you prowl the world for wealth to acquire. There are a few differences of opinion, but the good definitely outweighs the bad. Sometimes it's hard to get Dog to agree to quick vacation or a last minute party, but you can bring some energy to this partnership by hanging a Feng Shui Crystal in the West by Northwest part of the house.

Tiger with Pig: Good match if you take it slow. Pigs can be a little nervous facing Tiger's mandibles of death (actually that's just your smile). But if you approach Pig with gentle understanding, Pig will comfort and take care of you. You both have a tendency to help others before yourselves, so if you find you're giving away too many resources to hapless friends, hang a Feng Shui Crystal in the North by Northwest part of the house.

Rabbit Compatibility

Rabbit with Rat: You may argue and fight, and this doesn't make your peace-loving nature euphoric. Rat will have too many demands on you so a long-term relationship will be very challenging. You may seem similar, but your differences are huge. If your Rat partner is running you ragged with work and social plans, temper the energy by hanging a Feng Shui Crystal in the North part of the house.

Rabbit with Ox: If you want a long term relationship, this one can work—after you get past the boredom of the stable Ox. However, if you are looking for a fling, look elsewhere. Be in this one for the long haul, or not at all. If you find your Ox partner is not the one to sit down and have a good discussion about feelings and the relationship, hang a Feng Shui Crystal in the North by Northeast part of the house.

Rabbit with Tiger: Can be good if you like being pursued, and what Rabbit doesn't. If the Tiger catches you, you can have a happy relationship... after you teach him to behave. Tip: Play hard to get even after you've been got. If you find this energetic Tiger keeps you up all hours discussing life and relationships and you just want a peaceful time to hold hands, hang a Feng Shui Crystal in the East by Northeast part of the house.

Rabbit with Rabbit: The pair of you are truly loving and having endless fun. You will play and laugh and bring each other tokens of your affection. You can cuddle in front of a fire or talk until you fall asleep in each other's arms. If you find, however, your bunny-buddy is not doing his or her share of the home duties, hang a Feng Shui Crystal in the East part of the house.

Rabbit with Dragon: Hard going at first, but things get easier over time. The Dragon is a bit of a show- off and hogs your stage. He may think you're small, but you're packed with power and easily a match for any Dragon. Your Dragon has big ideas for both home and business, and if you want to bring him or her back down to earth, hang a Feng Shui Crystal in the East by Southeast part of the house.

Rabbit with Snake: It'll take hard work to get this to be a happy match. The Snake may want you for a relationship, or just for dinner. Once you're in this relationship, you will be looking for a way out of it. You both have good taste and a desire for a good life, but if you're keeping secrets from each other, trouble is ahead. Hang a Feng Shui Crystal in the South by Southeast part of the house.

Rabbit with Horse: Can work it out as friends, even if it doesn't work out as lovers. There are a few conflicts here and there, but in the long run, there are many possibilities with this match. Just don't try to possess this one. Horse may want to run free, but he'll keep coming back. Trouble can come when your Horse partner does everything by intuition rather than as a result of a discussion between the two of you. If more sharing is needed, hang a Feng Shui Crystal in the South part of the house.

Rabbit with Sheep: Great fun at times, because you'll always win against a Sheep. The Sheep will love you and keep trying. If you give a little to this relationship, the Sheep will give a lot. This could be the peace and happiness you've been waiting for. Your Sheep partner will be quick to depend on you, and this can make you feel great, but if the dependence becomes a burden, hang a Feng Shui Crystal in the South by Southwest part of the house.

Rabbit with Monkey: You'll need effort to understand the changeable and tricky Monkey. This is not a match that happens easily. You could be in danger of getting your heart broken by bad Monkey if you're not careful. If he or she is not understanding your feelings and is glossing over your anxieties, you may feel this Monkey's mocking you. Balance this relationship by hanging a Feng Shui Crystal in the West by Southwest part of the house.

Rabbit with Rooster: Many conflicts with this noisy bird who's constantly pecking and prodding you. Rabbits are the silent ones, and these Roosters are constantly making noises at you—too much so to make you happy. If your Rooster partner is telling all the friends and neighbors the intimate details of what works and doesn't work in your relationship, you can create a tighter bond between you by hanging a Feng Shui Crystal in the West part of the house.

Rabbit with Dog: More chasing than actually having fun. The Dog will make lots of demands on you, and you may find this relationship quite tiring in the beginning. If it lasts, it can grow into a real loving relationship, but it will take quite a bit of work. The loyalty of this partner can make this match worth it, but if you find the communication just not flowing, hang a Feng Shui Crystal in the West by Northwest part of the house.

Rabbit with Pig: Superb match; both of you can have a lot of fun. But if you get bored, you may try to create a little drama in the relationship just to stir things up. That could backfire big time! Once Pig's feelings are hurt, it will hard to tempt him back. Count your blessings, as your Pig partner can be devoted to you; and if you find his or her attention on you is not strong enough, hang a Feng Shui Crystal in the North by Northwest part of the house.

Dragon Compatibility

Dragon with Rat: Suitable match where both feel compatibility and interested in one another. You can explore the world together. You will have secrets, and so will Rat, but the secrets won't hurt the relationship. Learn to trust, and Rat will take your grand ideas and turn them into reality. There is much the two of you can accomplish, although sometimes Rat will keep a tight hold on the purse strings. If you need to balance this energy, hang a Feng Shui Crystal in the North part of the house.

Dragon with Ox: Tricky times with the stubborn Ox will make the relationship rather exhausting. If you hold on, you can smooth things out and have a good long term relationship. This can happen because Dragons are said to live a thousand years. You love to dream up new ideas, but your Ox partner could be unsympathetic if he or she doesn't see immediate results. To temper this energy, hang a Feng Shui Crystal in the North by Northeast part of the house.

Dragon with Tiger: Requires patience and understanding, as together you represent two powerful Yang forces. Those around you might not believe the relationship will work out, but if you don't make too many demands on each other, you have a chance at a happy time with the Tiger. With two leaders and no followers there can be some fights, even out the "eventful" energy by hanging a Feng Shui Crystal in the East by Northeast part of the house.

Dragon with Rabbit: Hard going at first, but you will soon find the Rabbit admires your good qualities. Rabbit also helps you strengthen some areas where you are weak: like being calm and quiet. You can help Rabbit be more detached and able to deal with the world. If you can let Rabbit have a soft place to land you two will get along just fine, in the meantime hang a Feng Shui Crystal in the East part of the house.

Dragon with Dragon: The best or the worst relationship for you. You love to be the center of attention and so does your partner. This [airing will work if the two of you can share the stage. It can be glorious, or it can be a battle. You could make an enviable couple and rule the social scene. Agree now that you, together, will hang a Feng Shui in the East by Southeast part of the house to make this happen.

Dragon with Snake: Can be good as friends, but as lovers things tend to break down. Snake wants you to try harder in the relationship, but your attitude is, "It will work if it's meant to be." This causes the Snake to slither away eventually. If you feel that holding on to this relationship is going to benefit you both, you can hang a Feng Shui Crystal in the South by Southeast part of the house.

Dragon with Horse: Lively pair; this combination can bring both fun and fights. You may become irritated that the Horse always thinks you're up to something. There will be more physical compatibility than intellectual or emotional. You both have a lot of energy but no patience for mundane tasks; create enough income to hire help by hanging a Feng Shui Crystal in the South part of the house.

Dragon with Sheep: Sheep thought he was on top the world until he saw you flying overhead. You may want this relationship to work, but Sheep may get frightened by your power and energy. Coax him in slowly before you reveal all your greatness to him. If you feel strongly about this relationship, you can put in the effort to help temper your Sheep partner's moods by hanging a Feng Shui Crystal in the South by Southwest part of the house.

Dragon with Monkey: Good pair because you admire Monkey's cleverness. You have the inner strength to get Monkey to behave; so this can be a good match. Monkey will amuse you every day! Take this act on the road, and you can be stars, or keep it close to home and be the toast of the neighborhood. Adding a Feng Shui Crystal to the West by Southwest part of the house will bring you some exciting opportunities.

Dragon with Rooster: The legendary Dragon and Rooster (okay, Phoenix). This pair feels a lot of attraction to one another. You can have a long term happy relationship as long as the Rooster doesn't look for reasons to be suspicious of all the happiness. If your Rooster partner starts snapping at you, hang a Feng Shui Crystal in the West part of the house.

Dragon with Dog: Not suitable, unless you like putting oil and fire together. This is a battle waiting to happen! Dog doesn't care how powerful you are; he's willing to take you down a notch. If your Dog partner wants to curtail your freedom and put you on a leash, hang a Feng Shui Crystal in the West by Northwest part of the house.

Dragon with Pig: It's hard not to like being at home with your Pig partner, nothing but comfort and good food abounds. But to keep Pig happy, you'll have to pitch in and do your share of the chores. Ever the peacemaker your Pig partner will support you on your goals. Attract what you both want by hanging a Feng Shui Crystal in the North by Northwest area of the home.

Snake Compatibility

Snake with Rat: Is it love you're feeling? Or, is it just casual amusement? You may feel common interests at first, but unless you want to commit, Rat will flee the first chance he gets. You can have a very profitable relationship if you set the right tone from the beginning. Keep things moving upward by hanging a Feng Shui Crystal in the North part of the house.

Snake with Ox: Can be so supportive of each other, but someone has to make the first move. If you two get together, you are likely to enjoy a long and happy relationship. Set your boundaries and then take a chance. You both have the drive and interest in making this work. To keep the lines of communication open, hang a Feng Shui Crystal in the North by Northeast part of the house.

Snake with Tiger: Steer clear, this is a battle waiting to happen. The Tiger is seductive, and you might be tempted, but it's you who should be doing the tempting. This is a match destined for a breakup. If you're determined to stay together, and yet you're both suspicious of the other's actions and intentions, hang a Feng Shui Crystal in the East by Northeast part of the house.

Snake with Rabbit: It's hard work to find the balance here. Rabbit will bring out your deeper qualities, but his thin skin won't stand up to your assessments. There could be pain on both sides. On the other hand, if you can see the best in the other, you will both benefit from your refined sense and mental acuity. Hang a Feng Shui Crystal in the East part of the house to stimulate this positive energy.

Snake with Dragon: Can make a good couple—from dating to a long term relationship. There is fun to be had by both. Keep your demands light, and you and the Dragon will fare very well. Keep in mind how much you admire the qualities of the other and communicate this often. To bring more harmony, hang a Feng Shui Crystal in the East by Southeast part of the house.

Snake with Snake: Wonderful pair that can balance each other. If you share leadership with your partner, you can expect a long and happy relationship. You can work together to bring yourselves power and success. Hang a Feng Shui Crystal in the South by Southeast part of the house to increase success energy.

Snake with Horse: This combo is difficult. You might be afraid of being stepped on, but you should be more worried about being forgotten or left behind by the popular Horse. Keep your eyes open because Horse may not be all that faithful. If Horse's impulsive nature starts to drive you around the bend, hang a Feng Shui Crystal in the South part of the house to calm that energy.

Snake with Sheep: Needs concentrated effort, but by taking a thoughtful approach, you can find happiness together. Sheep's feelings need to be considered, and you will have to tread lightly at times, but you can work this out. This relationship may start out with you both in a constant embrace, but after a while, Sheep's clingy behavior may put you off. To ease this energy, hang a Feng Shui Crystal in the South by Southwest part of the house.

Snake with Monkey: Long-lasting match, once you get past the game-playing. You are both very clever, and you can learn much from each other. There is fun and romance for both here. But if this relationship is punctuated with fights and competition, temper that energy by hanging a Feng Shui Crystal in the West by Southwest part of the house.

Snake with Rooster: What seems impossible at first turns into a wonderful pair. Rooster may be lots of talk and fussy behavior, but deep down he truly cares for you. Try not to get irritated, don't take things too seriously, and things will work out. Turn your attention to business, and you two will be the dynamic duo. For wealth energy, hang a Feng Shui Crystal in the West part of the house.

Snake with Dog: Quite charming match with you being both friends and lovers. But try not to be too possessive, Dogs need to run and play sometimes. (Know that Dog always comes home afterward.) On the other hand, when Dog is out of sight, you can do some of the things you may not be able to do under Dog's keen nose. Hang a Feng Shui Crystal in the West by Northwest part of the house for harmony in this relationship.

Snake with Pig: Not a good match, as your temperaments are entirely different. You are a deep thinker, and the Pig is looking for a comfortable, non-drama home. You might appreciate all that Pig can do for you, but the conflicts will be challenging. If you find your Pig partner being loving and supportive not to just you but the whole neighborhood and every charity he or she can find, you can bring Pig's attention back to you by hanging a Feng Shui Crystal in the North by Northwest part of the house.

Horse Compatibility

Horse with Rat: Poor match, because neither wants to compromise. Things may start out fun, but they will for the most part end badly as you exert your desire for freedom, and Rat extends his desire for control. Your Rat partner may be a big help to you at home, but often you will find you're not on the same level. Balance the energy by hanging a Feng Shui Crystal in the North part of the house.

Horse with Ox: Difficult to balance this relationship. You are impressed with Ox's stability, yet also bored by it. You wish Ox would not be so demanding, and pretty soon you break out of the paddock to run free. If you're trying to get your Ox partner to drop the workload and live a little, you can try hanging a Feng Shui Crystal in the North by Northwest part of the house.

Horse with Tiger: Both enjoy good times! You and Tiger are the life of the party; you are always where the action is. As long as neither of you thinks the other should sit at home, you will have a great time. Instead of fighting about who does the housework, attract more money to pay for the help by hanging a Feng Shui Crystal in the East by Northeast part of the house.

Horse with Rabbit: Given time, this can be a good relationship. At first, you will enjoy a lot of passionate fun with Rabbit; this can easily grow into trust and companionship. But keeping up the romance will take some planning. If Rabbit feels lonely at your wanderings and starts to kick up a fuss, you can balance the energy by hanging a Feng Shui Crystal in the East part of the house.

Horse with Dragon: Lively discussions and dates for these two. You are likely to be involved in the best fun together, or the biggest fights. Both of you are powerful and energetic beings, and together you are unstoppable. Try to base your relationship on what you have in common. Look for the partnership to extend to business as well as personal, and you can attract much success. Hang a Feng Shui Crystal in the East by Southeast part of the house to attract opportunities.

Horse with Snake: This is a tough match. There's a lot of finger pointing (at each other), yet both are guilty of something. Too much complaining leads to more fights. You might win, but that just results in a squished Snake. If you're Snake partner just seems like a stick in the mud, you can loosen up the energy by hanging a Feng Shui Crystal in the South by Southeast part of the house.

Horse with Horse: Caring and sharing and having a great time, frolicking through the pastures without a care in the world. You are beautiful together, and the world is your happy playground. Sometimes you're so alike it's uncanny... and a little boring. Spice things up by hanging a Feng Shui Crystal in the South part of the house.

Horse with Sheep: If you get past the first couple of months, this can work out just fine, but Sheep's sensitive nature may take offense when you try to be honest and straightforward. Give him time to cool off, then try again. If you find your Sheep partner glum and lifeless at times, you can stimulate the positive energy by hanging a Feng Shui Crystal in the South by Southwest part of the house.

Horse with Monkey: Quite a painful duel can result from your mixing with the tricky Monkey. But if the Monkey cares about you, he will make an effort, and things may work out over the long run. You're both smart enough to understand each other. Sometimes that makes things better, but sometimes it breeds contempt. Bring in the positive energy by hanging a Feng Shui Crystal in the West by Southwest part of the house.

Horse with Rooster: There are some pluses and minuses to this pair. You may feel that Rooster is leading you around by the nose, then dropping you without a moment's notice. Guard your heart if you're interested in this chicken. If you're feeling a little hen-pecked, hang a Feng Shui Crystal in the West part of the house.

Horse with Dog: Running and playing, two hearts beating fast, this is a great match. Dog is faithful and forgiving and looks up to your power and grace. You feel gratitude and dedication in this positive puppy. But if you feel your Dog partner snapping critically at your heels, you can hang a Feng Shui Crystal in the West by Northwest part of the house.

Horse with Pig: You can't help kicking up a fuss with the fussy Pig. Pig doesn't want to do battle, but an argument usually ensues. This can be a long term relationship if you don't mind a knock-down-drag-out every few months. If your Pig partner's clingy-ness is starting to bore you, spice things up by hanging a Feng Shui Crystal in the North by Northwest part of the house.

Sheep/Goat Compatibility

Sheep with Rat: Always starts well and ends badly, as both are under the impression they have a lot in common. But it doesn't take long to figure out that Rat is not a Sheep, and you just don't see eye to eye. If Rat seems nicer over time, you might take a chance—but don't put too much money on the bet. If you are determined to make a go at this, hang a Feng Shui Crystal in the North part of the house.

Sheep with Ox: Steer clear of this steer. You're both too stubborn to compromise, and butting heads with this giant will only give you a headache. Ox is too clingy, and you want balance; this just won't work. On the other hand, Ox will get a lot of the work done before you have even stirred, so if you want to smooth out the bumps in this relationship, hang a Feng Shui Crystal in the North by Northeast part of the house.

Sheep with Tiger: Can work it out—if you can house-train this kitty. Tiger wants worship, and you usually have more sense than that. But if you can stomach giving out all that flattery, this relationship will work just fine. If you need a little something to balance out the Tiger temper, hang a Feng Shui Crystal in the East by Northeast part of the house.

Sheep with Rabbit: Hot romance is possible with this pair. Rabbit wants to go have fun, and you are more than willing. It may be a hot date night after night. If you're a Sheep who likes to stay home, you may have a little trouble convincing this bunny, but everything will work out if you exercise some patience. To ensure this positive energy, hang a Feng Shui Crystal in the East part of the house.

Sheep with Dragon: Be prepared to be completely overwhelmed by Dragon's power and enthusiasm. Later, you may feel claustrophobic in this relationship. You will have to reach a compromise to make this work, and it will have to start with you. If you want to have Dragon share in some of the relationship responsibilities, hang a Feng Shui Crystal in the East by Southeast part of the house.

Sheep with Snake: Requires a good grip to hold onto slippery Snake. You might be a little shocked at the verbal matches you are drawn into with this forked-tongued lover. If Snake cares about you, he will tone it down, and you'll work it out in the end. The solution here will be a joint effort and real understanding of the other's position. To facilitate compromise, hang a Feng Shui Crystal in the South by Southeast part of the house.

Sheep with Horse: A fabulous time filled with banter and playful kicks at each other. This can be a wild ride if you don't take things said too personally. You both want to run; try not to run in different directions. To have the thrill of running off into the sunset together, hang a Feng Shui Crystal in the South part of the house.

Sheep with Sheep: Your friends might think this is the dullest match ever, but you feel delight as both of you do kind and thoughtful things for the other. You're happy, dancing on cloud nine. Combine your strengths and learn you can rely on each other by hanging a Feng Shui Crystal in the South by Southwest part of the house.

Sheep with Monkey: You can work anything out if you can forgive some of Monkey's antics in the beginning. Let the past be the past, and you will find that you have a lot in common. Love will bloom after a time. To encourage the love and romance, hang a Feng Shui Crystal in the West by Southwest part of the house.

Sheep with Rooster: No one is as confusing as a Rooster. You seem to have similar beliefs, and yet you go about doing things so differently. You can become a depressed little lamb if you think that Rooster will ever see your point of view. If you find the energy of your Rooster mate a bit too dizzying, hang a Feng Shui Crystal in the West part of the house.

Sheep with Dog: It's a tough life with a Dog nipping at your heels. You're not sure you want to be herded. Dog is trying to show you loyalty and love, but sometimes it feels like you are penned in at the farm just when you want to climb mountains and be free. Soon you'll be looking to unlatch the gate. If you want to stay in this energetic match, hang a Feng Shui Crystal in the West by Southwest part of the house.

Sheep with Pig: What a pretty couple you make; and you're both so nice. Sometimes Pig is too casual and you have to do all the heavy lifting in the relationship. But if you can let it slide, this could be a very nice romance. However, if you're finding that Pig has overbooked your social calendar and you just want a break, then hang a Feng Shui Crystal in the North by Northwest part of the house.

Monkey Compatibility

Monkey with Rat: If you've got your eye on a Rat it's because you're intrigued by his clever, money-making skills. Rat is easily flattered and impressed by your ability to take chances and fly through the trees. You can find yourself in a happy relationship with no effort at all. Boost your financial prospects by hanging a Feng Shui Crystal in the North part of the house.

Monkey with Ox: This can be a great match as long as you understand that an Ox can't climb trees. Come down to share Ox's domain every once in a while, and things will be just fine between you. Ox will give you the stability you crave while not curtailing any of the fun. But if this ends up being a contest of wills, you can balance the energy by hanging a Feng Shui Crystal in the North by Northeast part of the house.

Monkey with Tiger: Very rocky, so stay out of Tiger's reach. Tiger's impulsive nature and desire to be respected above all else rubs your fur the wrong way. Consider swinging past this potential disaster. If you've already been snared by this fellow jungle creature, you can bring more love to the relationship by hanging a Feng Shui Crystal in the East by Northeast part of the house.

Monkey with Rabbit: You can have a good time if you hold back on the tricks and teasing until Rabbit is in a happy mood. An unhappy bunny will take out their pain on you, so don't push. This can be a good combination, so save your witty remarks for someone else. If you're trying to coax this Rabbit out of the house for social occasions, you can hang a Feng Shui Crystal in the East part of the house to increase the energy of fun.

Monkey with Dragon: The perfect balance between power and intelligence, even your fights are fun. Dragon will show you the big ideas, and you will show him how it can all be done. There is so much potential for this relationship. There is also potential to extend this partnership into money-making activities. Attract wealth energy by hanging a Feng Shui Crystal in the East by Southeast part of the house.

Monkey with Snake: A long-lasting match filled with intimacy and strong feelings. Emotionally, as time goes on, you bond more and more with the wise Snake. Anytime you want, he will wrap himself around you and gently squeeze. But although there are tumultuous times due to jealousy on either side, you can temper this energy by hanging a Feng Shui Crystal in the South by Southeast part of the house.

Monkey with Horse: Is this a relationship or a competition? Sometimes you're supportive of each other, but the inflexibility of Horse means that you have to do all the compromising and understanding. After a while, this rodeo is less and less fun. If you feel like you're always coming in second place, you can hang a Feng Shui Crystal in the South part of the house to brighten up the energy.

Monkey with Sheep: This may be fun in the beginning, but Sheep has a whole bunch of rules and regulations for you to follow to stay in this relationship—rules that are sure to drain the fun right out of it. But if you can stay, it could become a happy, loving, long-lasting relationship. Balance this uncertain energy by hanging a Feng Shui Crystal in the South by Southwest part of the house.

Monkey with Monkey: Full of fun and play, this is an easy, happy relationship. There may be times when you don't see eye to eye, but keep those times brief, or one of you may find someone else to chase. Work out some boundaries, and you will be laughing together for a long time. To bond you two into a strong partnership, hang a Feng Shui Crystal in the West by Southwest part of the house.

Monkey with Rooster: Like magnets, you feel pulled magically together, but at any moment the poles can shift, and you will find yourself repelled by each other. This is a pair born to fight, and yet should the two of you have a long relationship; it will at least be interesting. More prosperity would help you both be happy in this match, so hang a Feng Shui Crystal in the West part of the house to attract more money.

Monkey with Dog: At first it just doesn't seem to work. You swinging in the trees, and the Dog barking and dancing around on the ground—but if you both persist, suddenly, one day everything falls into place. If you get to that point, this can be an excellent match. Remember it's a partnership, not a competition. To blend the skills of you both, hang a Feng Shui Crystal in the West by Northwest part of the house.

Monkey with Pig: This may be the easiest relationship you'll ever find: no hassles, no commitments, just comfort, and joy. Pig would love a commitment, but he's too much in love to ask, afraid you'll run for the hills. Consider settling down with this one; this could be one you cherish. To balance and harmonize this energy, hang a Feng Shui Crystal in the North by Northwest part of the house.

Rooster Compatibility

Rooster with Rat: You might work well together with Rat, but avoid getting into a relationship with this little mouse. He discovers all your weak spots, and he'll take you down a peg or three. If you're serious about your future happiness, kiss the Rat goodbye. But if you're committed to staying, temper the little mouse's petty complaints by hanging a Feng Shui Crystal in the North part of the house.

Rooster with Ox: Potentially a very good match, because even though you're both stubborn by nature, you are stubborn about different things. There's strength in unity, and as a united front, you can have a very happy relationship. Even your fights turn out okay. Strengthen this relationship further by hanging a Feng Shui Crystal in the North by Northeast part of the house.

Rooster with Tiger: This relationship will take a lot of effort because you both have different values. You have strength, but so does Tiger—and there will be communication issues. Your friends will try to help you stay together until they get tired of trying, and then they'll suggest you part. If you want to stay together and have fun instead of fights, hang a Feng Shui Crystal in the East by Northeast part of the house.

Rooster with Rabbit: A relationship between you and Rabbit just makes for one angry bunny. You try to use logic and reason, but you just make him madder. Even though initially you felt a kinship, you're just too different to have any harmony. To get your Rabbit partner to pitch in and pull half the weight of this relationship, hang a Feng Shui Crystal in the East part of the house.

Rooster with Dragon: The perfect pair, representing the Dragon and the Phoenix, this relationship is liberating and strengthening for both. With this winged creature, you revel in feeling on top of the world. Dragon feels like he's finally got his feet on the ground. Great times ahead. Hang a Feng Shui Crystal in the East by Southeast part of the house to capitalize on this successful union.

Rooster with Snake: You may have some differences in your daily routines, but that can be to your benefit as you will enjoy the times you are together all the more. Snake may like to argue with you, but you can hold your own. In the long run, this could work. Balance the extremes in this relationship, and you can make some serious money. Hang a Feng Shui Crystal in the South by Southeast part of the house to help.

Rooster with Horse: You are probably more interested in making this work than Horse is. When you fight, it will be you who has to say, "Sorry," first. This may be fine in the beginning, but after a while of eating crow, you may just give this one up. If you insist that this is the one for you, hang a Feng Shui Crystal in the South part of the house to sooth your differences and create harmony.

Rooster with Sheep: You are probably the more impatient one so Sheep can outlast you anytime. This will cause conflicts at home and with raising children. Sometimes you're both playing a game to see if you can get what you want, but neither of you shares your rules with the other. If you find that Goat/Sheep has a hard head and way too soft feelings you can hang a Feng Shui Crystal in the South by Southwest part of the house to balance the energies.

Rooster with Monkey: Hard going at first, but things can be smoothed over. You may be fascinated with Monkey's clever antics, and so you keep working on it. Over time there can be progress; it depends on how much you want to sacrifice to get this to work. If you start to think that Monkey is just in it for what he or she can get, you can hang a Feng Shui Crystal in the West by Southwest part of the house to bring the scales into balance.

Rooster with Rooster: Intense passion and intense fights will typify this relationship. Feathers will fly, and lots of words will be exchanged—but what you dish out you can receive. In the end, you will stick it out because you have put so much effort into it. If you both are too focused on being right rather than being happy, hang a Feng Shui Crystal in the West area of the house to remedy this.

Rooster with Dog: A Dog around the barnyard chases the chickens rather than being guided by one so you may find this relationship is about who gets to be in charge. This power struggle will continue and getting out may be your best bet. This is not an easy time for either of you. If all this relationship has become is two people snapping at each other, hang a Feng Shui Crystal in the West by Northwest part of the house to bring in loving, harmonious energy.

Rooster with Pig: You have a true admirer in this relationship, yet you doubt, thinking this is too easy. Pig wants to make you feel comfortable and happy, and yet your eye is ever wandering. Learn to respect the Pig, and this could be a dream match. Or, toss it all away and get chicken-scratch in return. Things can be good here if you can welcome in the positive energy. Hang a Feng Shui Crystal in the North by Northwest part of the house and be prepared to be happy.

Dog Compatibility

Dog with Rat: It will take cool nerves to make this match work. There's a lot of nervous energy between the two of you, and you may find Rat running for the door. Keep the lines of communication open to make progress long term. You may find you only fight over little things. Ease the disruptive energy by hanging a Feng Shui Crystal in the North part of the house.

Dog with Ox: You two can be great together because you're both stable and want to protect your partner. But power struggles can ensue. Your best bet is to lean back and allow Ox to drag the relationship forward. Ox can hold on to hurts from past fights for a long time. Heal the energy by hanging a Feng Shui Crystal in the North by Northeast part of the house.

Dog with Tiger: After a rough beginning, a relationship of mutual respect and admiration blossoms. The attraction to each other runs deep, and both can feel great happiness here. There are good times ahead for this cat and Dog. Together you can do a lot a good out in the world. Hang a Feng Shui Crystal in the East by Northeast part of the house and bring in the opportunities you desire.

Dog with Rabbit: After an exhilarating chase you could end up with a perfect match between you and the happy Rabbit. You both bring something to the relationship that the other lacks, and together you make a good team. It's the tiny things, like how he or she squeezes the toothpaste, that irritates you about your partner. Hang a Feng Shui Crystal in the East part of the house and find some peace.

Dog with Dragon: This is a star-crossed pair, intense love followed by severe pain. You may be tempted by Dragon's power, but he'll just fly away at some point. At some level, you know this, and so you may try to leave first. Save yourself the pain and avoid this match. If you insist on staying together, you must alternate with each other on who will lead. Hang a Feng Shui Crystal in the East by Southeast part of the house to find a truce.

Dog with Snake: If you do get together—which is not easy—you will need to work on your communication with each other. You are both smart but in different ways. You are much more loyal than Snake; don't give all your loyalty until you know it will be returned. If you stay realistic this can work, so hang a Feng Shui Crystal in the South by Southeast to improve communication.

Dog with Horse: Dating will be an exciting chase, and if you do rope this Horse, you may end up with a very happy relationship. But Horse won't be caught easily. Be prepared for some work. Once you break this Horse of running, the romance will blossom. Hang a Feng Shui Crystal in the South part of the house to encourage cooperation.

Dog with Sheep: There is such strong attraction at first, but Sheep doesn't like being herded, and you are having trouble putting up with his not agreeing with anything you say. After quarreling constantly, you may not find anything to save in this relationship. If you find you're more irritated than in love, hang a Feng Shui Crystal in the South by Southwest part of the house and smooth over the differences.

Dog with Monkey: At first sight, you didn't think this was going to be a match... and you were right! Monkey's antics and different ideas can hurt your feelings deeply. Even when it seems to be working, the timing will be off, and the gestures you offer each other are misunderstood. But if you want to make a go of it, hang a Feng Shui Crystal in the West by Southwest part of the house to attract money which will, in turn, attract a Monkey.

Dog with Rooster: Lots of chasing can make the beginning of this relationship a little rocky. Be patient, because there is more to this than meets the eye. There is a genuine compatibility here if you can get past some of the surface irritants. If you want to do more than just coexist, hang a Feng Shui Crystal in the West part of the house to bring out the best qualities in both of you.

Dog with Dog: You can run and play together, and you'll always be competing. You may even compete to show how much you'll sacrifice for the other. If you don't mind the constant quarreling, bickering, and barking this will work out just fine. Hang a Feng Shui Crystal in the West by Northwest part of the house to promote mutual respect and material success.

Dog with Pig: You find that Pig is a blissful partner, and have never felt so happy. This makes you nervous, which in turn makes Pig nervous—and that could bring a breaking point. But in general this is a great match, just lie down and enjoy it. Celebrate and hang a Feng Shui Crystal in the North by Northwest part of the house to attract the resources for a comfortable and happy home.

Pig/Boar Compatibility

Pig with Rat: This is an interesting match, you share many interests. You see the world in a similar way and value similar things. The little mouse may need some puffing up sometimes, but flatter him, and together you will build a comfortable house, with lots of money in the cookie jar. Hang a Feng Shui Crystal in the North part of the house to bring abundance and happiness to the relationship.

Pig with Ox: This works at first, but if you think you will get your way, you're wrong here. You may be obstinate, but nothing beats an Ox for sheer stubbornness. The more you push, the more he will not budge. Save yourself the effort and pass on this match. If you plan to stay in this relationship, hang a Feng Shui Crystal in the North by Northeast part of the house to relieve some of the friction.

Pig with Tiger: You may think the hungry Tiger will have you for dinner on your first date but after the initial nerves of a new relationship, you two can settle down and make a good match. Tiger's possessiveness will feel comforting and protective. Hang a Feng Shui Crystal in the East by Northeast part of the house to bring joy, laughter, and good times.

Pig with Rabbit: Once you get past the well-meaning criticism by this little bunny, you have a thoughtful, interested partner with whom you can share much. Rabbit may be slower to realize how good a match this is, so be patient. Rabbit will happily receive the outpouring of your affection, so to get some in return, hang a Feng Shui Crystal in the East part of the house.

Pig with Dragon: You are dazzled by the power and vision of your Dragon partner. He loves coming down to earth to be with you. While your friends may not understand this match, you are in heaven. You are sailing on the back of a Dragon. At times one or both of you will get carried away; balance out the energy by hanging a Feng Shui Crystal in the East by Southeast part of the house.

Pig with Snake: You have so many differences that you can't even begin to communicate. You are naturally nervous around the clever Snake, and so you become rigid and critical. It's not you; it's just a bad match. If you're staying in the partnership but can't stand all the secrets, hang a Feng Shui Crystal in the South by Southeast part of the house and let what's been hidden come out.

Pig with Horse: Horse feels this is a great relationship and that nothing needs to change. You, on the other hand, have a list of what needs to happen to start making this a happy relationship. But none of your subtle signals or overt signs will be a clue to over-confident Horse. To get your pony partner to pay attention, hang a Feng Shui Crystal in the South part of the house.

Pig with Sheep: Can work, but certainly not the most exciting relationship you'll ever have. This feels like the backup date for New Year's—maybe someone who might be a friend, but the passion's not there. If you want commitment, demand it; otherwise, let this one go. Stir up the romance here by hanging a Feng Shui Crystal in the South by Southwest part of the house and watch the magic happen.

Pig with Monkey: You and Monkey are so different, but somehow it works. This relationship is like fine wine; it needs to age—and you both will occasionally need some time to breathe. Some irritations on both sides can make this relationship feel sour. Hang a Feng Shui Crystal in the West by Southwest part of the house to sweeten up your love life.

Pig with Rooster: As barnyard buddies, this is tough in the beginning as Rooster wants to be in charge. You will find it hard to get respect from this bossy boss as he is sure he rules the roost. But deep down, there is more love here than you may think. Give this a try before saying goodbye. Between the two of you, there is a solution to every problem. Hang a Feng Shui Crystal in the West part of the house to attract the solutions easily.

Pig with Dog: You feel secure and safe with Dog (and nipped at, and barked at, too). There are some strong positives in this relationship and a big helping of irritants. Give nervous Dog some time to settle into the relationship, and you will feel safe and loved in no time. If you find your lively pup too quick with the criticism hang a Feng Shui Crystal in the West by Northwest part of the house to soften his or her words.

Pig with Pig: Hand in hand, here's a perfect match. You both share great depth of feeling and compassion for the other. Communication is fun and easy, and you spend many nights just staying up and talking. This may get to be a little routine after a while, but the deep feeling of happiness will last. Together you both give too much and may find others taking advantage of your kindness. Hang a Feng Shui Crystal in the North by Northwest part of the house to protect your finances.

Eclipses

Eclipses, both Solar and Lunar, happen six times between January 2019 and end of January 2020. Eclipses signal times of change. Even for those who are unaware of an eclipse, its energy can throw a wrench into your plans. Fortunately, we often feel the energy of an eclipse up to a couple of weeks prior to the actual event.

It's always a good idea to find an astrologer to offer you some personal advice around the time of an upcoming series of eclipses. Or, if you can find a reliable resource for information about the effects of a specific eclipse, you may be able to determine what does need to change in your life. This gives you a chance to take action.

It makes a difference, believe me! It's as if you have a choice between being hit by a wave, versus being on your surfboard, ready to catch a wave and ride it all the way to the beach.

Eclipses are noted in most of the daily news websites and in the weather section of a newspaper so you can see when one is about to happen. But it takes an Astrologer to tell you exactly where the eclipses hit in your chart, so you can be aware of the approaching energy, and keep an eye out for potential surfboards to grab hold of as you get ready to ride.

There will be a partial Solar Eclipse on January 5, 2019. This eclipse will be at 15 degrees of Capricorn. If you were born between December 31st and January 10th, this eclipse will have a strong effect on your life.

There will be a total Lunar Eclipse on January 21, 2019. This eclipse will be at 0 degrees of Leo. If you were born between January 16th and January 26th, this eclipse will have a strong effect on your life.

There will be a total Solar Eclipse on July 2, 2019. This eclipse will be at 10 degrees of Cancer. If you were born between June 28th and July 7th, this eclipse will have a strong effect on your life.

There will be a partial Lunar Eclipse on July 16, 2019. This eclipse will be at 24 degrees of Capricorn. If you were born between July 11th and July 21st, this eclipse will have a strong effect on your life.

There will be an annular Solar Eclipse on December 26, 2019. This eclipse will be at 4 degrees of Capricorn. If you were born between December 21st and December 31st, this eclipse will have a strong effect on your life.

There will be a penumbral Lunar Eclipse on January 10, 2020. This eclipse will be at 20 degrees of Capricorn. If you were born between January 5th and January 15th, this eclipse will have a strong effect on your life.

Tip: It's a good idea to consider challenging areas of your life, and choose to make some changes. For instance, if you have been thinking about changing jobs for a time, it would be an excellent idea to get your resume ready. If you've been thinking that you're unhappy with your home, it's probably a good idea to start looking around for a new place. Or, if you've been thinking your relationship is unsatisfying, this may be the right time to sit down and have a chat with your partner (or consider packing your bags).

While eclipses may sound scary, you've actually been through many of them in your life. You've been through at least four eclipses each year since you were born. Every 8-9 years the eclipse hits your chart with a bang like ringing a very loud bell. This is a signal that something in your life needs to change. The best course of action is to challenge yourself in whatever area of life you may feel "stuck." For more information on Eclipses, check out Diane Ronngren's book by the same name.

Mercury Retrograde

Each element of the five Chinese elements is ruled by a planet. The Chinese elements associated with the planets translate into the Western tradition as follows:

Wood is ruled by Jupiter, the largest planet in the solar system (named for the Roman king of the gods).

Fire is ruled by Mars, the red planet (named for the Roman god of war).

Earth is ruled by Saturn (named after the Roman god of agriculture).

Metal is ruled by Venus (named after the Roman goddess of prosperity).

Water is ruled by Mercury (named after the Roman winged messenger god).

2019 is an Earth year, so the energy of the planet Saturn will figure prominently. Fire is necessary to feed Earth, so Mars is an important planet this year. Mercury is not directly involved with the main elements this year so it will be somewhat easier to navigate through Mercury Retrograde periods.

Mercury Retrograde is an astronomical phenomenon that happens three or four times a year and has a very disruptive effect on those of us living on planet Earth. Things we rely on in our daily lives and work (such as our computers, cell phones, vehicles, email, snail mail, etc.) all seem to go a little haywire during Mercury Retrograde. Specifically, Mercury Retrograde can cause you to need to repeat something.

During this Pig year, Mercury Retrograde periods will be:

March 6, 2019 to March 29, 2019

July 8, 2019 to August 1, 2019

November 1, 2019 to November 21, 2019

A few weeks before Mercury goes retrograde each time, it's a good idea to back up your computer, and while you're at it, back up your cell phone contacts. If you're planning to have some work done on the car, try to get it finished before Mercury goes retrograde.

In fact, anything you don't want to repeat soon, such as: moving, lawsuits, root canals, elective surgery, expensive repairs, custody battles, break-ups—well, let's just say you will be better off if you can avoid doing them during the Mercury retrograde period.

If at all possible, avoid purchasing electronics during the retrograde, especially ones you can't return. Make copies of important documents before you send them, as they may not reach their destination. If you are issued one traffic ticket, you're likely to get a second ticket during this period, so drive safely.

If you have to return your cable box, renew your driver's license, or make a doctor's appointment, take a book with you (something long, like one by Tolstoy). It's going to take a while.

During the retrograde, plan and do things you don't mind repeating. Take a vacation—but beware, sometimes Mercury Retrograde can send your luggage to Baltimore (even if you're going somewhere else). However, if you do carry-on, you'll probably be fine.

Visit a spa, have a massage, enjoy a romantic dinner with someone you love, or have a party with good friends. These are all things you might enjoy doing multiple times.

Start exercising. If you drop the program, you are very likely to be inspired to pick it up again at the next retrograde. Or, buy yourself some jewelry or a new pair of shoes, that's something none of us women mind repeating!

For more information on Mercury Retrograde, check out the booklet by Diane Ronngren. http://amzn.to/2geLmGI

What Is Feng Shui and How to Use Cures

This book is different than most Chinese Astrology books, as this book contains information on Feng Shui cures you can use to help turn bad luck into good luck and make stuck, negative energy start to flow and be positive.

Feng Shui is the ancient Chinese art of placement. Feng Shui is based on the concept that everything present in our environment affects us: the colors, shapes, symbols, building layout, furniture, and décor affect our energy, mood, and decision-making process.

Consider for a moment two buildings which both represent how we connect with money: a casino, and a bank. When you walk into a casino, your head spins with all there is to see. There are flashing lights in every direction, ringing bells signaling a win, the sounds of coins falling. You can feel the abundance of good fortune and money, money, money.

Looking down at your feet, you'll see the floor carpeted in a busy, colorful pattern. Look up, and you will see moving lights, curved ceiling soffits guiding us in different directions, and huge rooms filled with aisles of machines, tables, and open chairs inviting us to be seated. There is an overwhelming feeling originating from this décor; it tantalizes: "You'd be a fool not to sit down and try your luck," it tempts us.

Contrast this feeling with the one you have in a bank. The environment here is also a large room, but this room is nearly silent. People speak in lowered voices. A velvet rope guides us to a waiting teller who sits (or stands) behind a marble counter (perhaps even behind a plexiglass shield).

Behind her is a large round door made of shiny metal, a foot and half thick, standing open to reveal a few safe deposit boxes. Even though we know there are no stacks of money in the vault and it's mostly a prop, the image created by all of it still gives us the impression that our money is safe.

We're all affected by the décor of a place. We may not think so per se, but run down areas in need of repairs cause us to feel less hopeful. We are more apt to believe it's not worth the effort to try something new.

When we see a neighborhood with flowers and manicured yards, we become more optimistic. We feel a sense of possibility, the desire and willingness to take on new projects. When we face a desk topped with clutter, disorganized, it's more likely we'll avoid working on our finances, and instead check out what's on the television (or on Facebook).

A messy kitchen can cause us to gain weight because it's so much easier to run out quickly and pick up some fast food or call for pizza delivery. A bedroom filled with old garage sale furniture or family hand-me-downs can cause us to avoid looking for a new relationship.

Thousands of years ago it was found that if you set up a particular environment—often a temple or a palace—in a certain way, the people in these environments would make better decisions. They would become more prosperous and happy. Scholars of the time collected this information and created a system they called Feng Shui. In the West, we know this system as well, nowadays we call it Environmental Psychology.

Feng Shui is much more complex than merely cleaning up the clutter in your home or office—though this is what many Westerners think about when they hear the term. Clearing away clutter is almost always a beneficial activity to carry out when we want to improve our environment. But it's important to understand that to achieve the best effect from our Feng Shui efforts, we must learn to place certain objects in specific places with the intention of creating harmonious change in our lives.

There are many schools of Feng Shui. Different schools emerged at different times and in different areas of China and the Far East. Some schools were formed in mountainous regions and were based on the topography of mountains, rivers, and lakes. Some schools were more focused on Astrology and timing, and these practitioners would predict the future and change things around as the seasons changed. Some schools used a compass to measure the quality and quantity of energy from each direction.

All of the schools of Feng Shui are valid. They all work. For our purposes, we're going to focus on a school called *Form School* which has straightforward principles we can readily apply to a western way of thinking about traditional and environmental practices.

Your Front Door: The front door is where all new energy will enter the home and therefore your life. Even if you never use your front door, this is the traditional area of a home where all new energy is welcomed into the lives of the people who reside in the home. (If you found stranger coming through your back door you'd call the police). If you invited the CEO of your company to dinner you wouldn't say, "Just go through the garage, squeeze past my car, past my boxes of Christmas decorations and old skiing equipment, until you find the door into the kitchen."

Important people are greeted at the front door and invited to enter a home or place of business. Many deliveries are made to the front door of a home or apartment residence. Using this principle, when we want something new, such as a new job, new love, money from a new source, etc., we will concentrate on the area around the front door (inside and out).

Your Bedroom: Your bedroom is where the love happens. If you want to attract a new relationship or you want to improve your existing relationship, then your bedroom is the area of the home we are going to focus on. We also look at the bedroom when you want to conceive a child, to rest or recover from illness. So, if you have trouble sleeping, or if you are recovering from something, we want to focus our attention on your bedroom.

The Kitchen: Your kitchen is your source of health and weight loss. Kitchens tend to be the most powerful rooms of the house. You can confirm this by observing that when you have a party, often your guests want to gather together in the kitchen. Kitchens are where we cook and prepare our food; food is the key to our health and well-being.

The Living Room: If you want to attract new friends, but not necessarily an intimate partner, focus on your living room. The living room represents a public area of the home where we can welcome and entertain people without revealing the private areas of the home (like a bedroom). Thus, when we entertain people in our living room, we can enjoy people, yet safeguard the private things in our lives.

The Family Room: If you have a separate Family Room, we can focus on this area to enhance family relations overall—both between members of the family who live with you and those who live elsewhere. So if your family fights (or is dysfunctional in some other way), or the teenagers are sullen and uncooperative, this is the area your Feng Shui practitioner will focus on. (If you only have a Living Room, then we would focus on that area for family relations.)

The Home Office: If you have a separate room where you take care of bills and investments, or a room from which you run your business from home, we focus on this room when we seek to increase prosperity. If you don't have a separate office, then we consider the area where you do pay your bills—whether it be at the kitchen table, in your bedroom, or in the dining room. (Or, we can focus on enhancing the area around your front door for bringing in money.)

The Dining Room: If you have a separate dining room, it affects not only family relations but also your weight, and the weight of all who live in the home. If you are trying to lose (or to gain) weight we will consider this area, even if meals are seldom served in this room.

The Bathroom: There are a lot of Feng Shui rules and misinterpretations around the bathroom. The bathroom is an area for health, but it can also be an area which affects the prosperity of all who dwell in the home. When things are not going well in your life, this is the first area we consider.

Other rooms like garages, media rooms, craft rooms, guest bedrooms and more, all have energy linked to their use. In general, they are not as significant as the rooms previously mentioned.

There are, however, some exceptions. If you run a classic car business out of your garage, then the state of your garage will affect your success in your business. If you have a guest who is driving you crazy and won't leave your home, the state of your guest room will affect how your guest is treating you—even how long they'll stay. For tips on these and other more specific situations, contact me for a personal consultation, or see my book, Feng Shui Form.

Now that we have examined the energy of the various spaces in a home, let's define the concept of a Feng Shui cure. If you've ever experienced acupuncture, you know the doctor uses tiny needles, placed in very specific areas of the body to stimulate your body's energy and natural healing ability.

Feng Shui cures are similar to these acupuncture needles—they are intended to stimulate your home's energy and help create benefit, good fortune, and natural harmony by working within the environment of your home, instead of your physical body. Cures are objects which represent a certain energy: such as love or money. For example, a heart-shaped pillow would be a representation, a cure, of love energy. (The heart shape is a universal symbol of love.)

Universal and cultural symbols make the most powerful cures in Feng Shui. This may all sound a little strange, but Feng Shui cures do work, just as the acupuncture needles stimulate specific body energy and facilitate our natural healing ability. If you want to know more about the science behind Feng Shui energy, keep reading; otherwise, you can skip to the next section.

Why Feng Shui Works

It may sound strange to you that placing a gold cat bank in the far left corner of your home would attract money, but it does. The Feng Shui cure is based on two principles. The first is the idea of collective consciousness.

Collective consciousness is a shared idea which creates a unifying force in the world.

One example might be the number of people who are afraid of spiders. Spiders shouldn't be scary; they're tiny, and they tend to mind their own business. But some people are so afraid of them that they are classified arachnophobic, even when they have not had personal, life-threatening encounters with spiders. In mankind's past, spiders have been perceived to be dangerous in many cultures. So today, many, many people have this innate fear.

Likewise, most people in the world have for centuries considered round metal discs to be money. Even currency from a foreign country is still seen as valuable, even when it cannot be spent at the neighborhood store. Many objects not only have a universal meaning but also evoke an emotion. They are potent symbols in our collective consciousness.

Besides universal symbols, there are also cultural symbols— symbols which are particular to one culture, but not another. These also can be used very effectively (in fact I have found using symbols from a different culture is particularly effective).

A symbol such as a gold cat bank (a.k.a. Lucky Money Cat), is a popular symbol in Asia and works very well here in the U.S. If you have enjoyed a meal at a Chinese restaurant recently, you have probably seen one of these symbols next to the cash register, Lucky Money Cat waving his little golden arm, calling in money.

The reason cultural symbols work is there are enough people in the world who understand the symbol and connect to it emotionally; a mini "collective consciousness" is formed.

Our Reticular Activating System

The second reason Feng Shui cures work is our Reticular Activating System. This is a system within each of us, which allows us to filter the information reaching us through our five senses. If we were actually aware of all of the information bombarding us all the time, we would go mad.

For instance, just sitting here at my computer, if I were also listening to the computer hum, and the traffic outside, and the ticking clock, while watching the sun go down, observing the computer screen, not to mention all the things I'm touching, smelling, and tasting simultaneously, I would be completely overwhelmed. But fortunately, my Reticular Activating System allows me to focus only on the task at hand.

Your own Reticular Activating System activates when you place a Lucky Money Cat somewhere in your space. When you place your Lucky Money Cat in the far left corner of your home, also known as "the wealth corner," your subconscious awakens and begins to look for money opportunities.

When the money opportunity is detected, your RAS-system alerts your brain. These opportunities were around you already, but you were unable to identify them specifically. Therefore, it was impossible for you to grasp them or focus on taking necessary action. But when your Reticular Activating System uncovered the opportunities around you, they became clear to your conscious mind, and now it is easy to welcome in the new money.

Because of these two reasons, Feng Shui cures work. It is essential to understand why we use universal or cultural symbols, rather than just any old item/personal symbol. For example, you might tell me that for you, the vulture is a symbol of love because your beloved had a vulture tattoo on his right shoulder.

But this symbol is only a love symbol for you (and this particular relationship). So all the energy behind this symbol must be generated by you alone. If you're interested in focusing on vulture-tattoo-guy, you can fill your house with vultures, and it will possibly attract his energy to your door.

But let's say you want to attract a new man—maybe one who is vulture-free. In that case, it will be much easier to attract the new love energy if you choose to use a universal or cultural symbol of love. Many other people recognize these symbols. When you choose to use one of them, the combined energy of all of these others who acknowledge this symbol as a sign of love combines with your energy to attract what you want.

The peony flower is a cultural symbol of love. In Chinese art, this symbol is used to represent love and beauty. So if you choose to use this symbol, your energy combines with a couple of billion other people who also use this symbol to attract love. By using the collective consciousness and your Reticular Activating System you can use specific objects to attract wealth, love, and other things you want into your life.

As we talk about the individual predictions for each sign, I will be suggesting specific Feng Shui cures for creating the most positive energy for your year. You can substitute these cultural symbols for universal symbols if you choose. If you have questions about these concepts or substituting cures, you can write me at donnastellhorn@gmail.com

2019 Flying Star

9—Northwest	4—North	2—Northeast
Future Prosperity Star: lucky	Romance Star: lucky	Illness Star: unlucky
To increase achievement and growth add wood like a green, healthy plants. To have good luck add fire by burning purple or gold candles.	To have romance and better education and career choices, add the color red and pairs of ducks. To protect against bad investments, divorce or family pressure, add silver or Chinese coins.	To protect from illness and loneliness reduce the negative energy by adding plants, dried medicinal herbs or pictures of flowers. To balance health, pregnancy, and communications, add a sixrod metal wind chime.
1—West	**8—Center**	**6—East**
White Star: very lucky	Prosperity Star: very lucky	Luck Star: Lucky
To increase wealth, fame and improve career, add earth by adding granite, marble, or citrine. To balance spirituality and thinking, add metal in the form of a music box or Ipod dock.	To increase happiness, wealth, and family unity, add fire by burning white or gold candles. To balance career energy and have good relations with kids, add earth by placing a clear quartz crystal.	To increase success in career, military, science or technology, add large crystals like citrine, amethyst and smoky quartz. To balance energy of health and wealth, add brass vases or bowls
5—Southwest	**3—South**	**7—Southeast**
Misfortune Star: very unlucky	Conflict Star: unlucky	Violent Star: unlucky
To protect from accidents, illness, or lawsuits, remove stone and heavy objects. To balance mental energy and have happier children, place coins	If problems with career, lawsuits, or arguments, burn off the excess energy by burning a blue or yellow candle. If you need a job or require lots of change, add a string or pile of coins.	To decrease bad luck, add water. To protect from robbery, legal issues, burn off excess negative energy by burning black or dark blue candles. Add exterior lighting or keep porch light on.

2019 Flying Star

Each year the energy changes and "stars" fly into new locations. Some directions which may have indicated positive, lucky energy last year, become weaker and unlucky this year. Some which had vibrated with weak, unlucky energy in the past, have found strength and become more positive for us now.

In other forms of Feng Shui, we are concerned with the directions of our home, based on the position of the front door, but not with Flying Star. With Flying Star, we are concerned with compass directions.

The general principle of Flying Star is to increase energy in the directions of good stars and reduce energy in the direction of bad stars. If you live in a giant mansion and your bedroom is now on a negative star, you can choose a new bedroom to sleep in. But for the rest of us, we use "cures" to mitigate the negative energy and to increase the positive energy. Here's the forecast for 2019:

Flying Star 1—The White Star: Luck finds its way to the West of the house with the 1-Star. This is a star whose energy has changed over the last few thousand years. It has become more lucky, although it's a good idea to keep its history in mind as you increase the energy of this star.

If you find, after placing the cures, things are not going as well as you hoped, switch from increasing the energy (by adding water or metal cures) to reducing the energy (by adding wood cures).

That being said, to increase wealth and fame and improve career, increase the earthy energy by adding granite, marble, or citrine (a gemstone) to your space. To balance spirituality and clear thinking, add metal in the form of a music box, or an iPod/radio.

Flying Star 2—The Illness Star: A somewhat unlucky star, the 2-Star, flies to the Northeast. I say this star is somewhat unlucky because years ago in China this was a lucky star for those people working in government. Therefore, if you have a government job, you can receive some benefit from this star.

But, for the rest of us, this Star can cause health problems, especially digestive and intestinal problems. To protect from illness and loneliness, reduce the effects of the negative energy by adding live plants, bundles of dried medicinal herbs, or pictures of flowers to the Northeast part of your home.

If you are or become pregnant, you can support and protect the pregnancy by adding a six-rod metal wind chime outside of the Northeast part of the house.

Flying Star 3—The Conflict Star: The somewhat unlucky 3-Star flies to the South this year. This is the star of quarreling and disputes, but its energy can be directed positively to help you keep a job and pay your bills. Balancing the energy of the 3-Star is important.

If you are having problems with career, lawsuits, or arguments, burn off the excess negative energy by burning a blue or yellow candle in this area once a month on the full moon. If you are in search of a job, need more work, or wish to preserve a source of income, set a small pile of coins (choose an odd number of coins) on a windowsill facing the South of the space.

Flying Star 4—The Romance Star: The 4-Star lands in the North this year, and brings with it mixed luck. This star is both associated with positive romance and career opportunities, but it is also known as "The Six Curses." Like the 1-Star in the West, as you enhance the energy in the North, notice how your luck changes.

If you find that your experiences in the area of romance are not as positive as you would like, add fire (by burning candles or wood in a fireplace) to reduce the 4-Star energy. Also, be cautious about participating in games of speculation, or signing off on risky investments.

To enjoy more romance, add the color red, and pairs of Mandarin ducks as cures. To protect against bad investments, add silver or Chinese coins. For better education and career choices, add green plants with round-shaped leaves.

Flying Star 5—The Misfortune Star: Trouble comes as the 5-Star flies to the Southwest this year. This star represents illness, potential disaster, and lack of knowledge. To protect from accidents, illness, and lawsuits, remove stone and heavy objects from the Southwest area of the house.

If heavy objects are attached to the house (such as a stone fireplace), channel some of that energy away from the Southwest of the house by adding objects made of wood, like a wood bowl, wood furniture, or a picture of trees. To balance stressful energy and to have happier children, place pictures of them in metal frames in this area.

Flying Star 6—The Heaven Luck Star: The 6-Star flies to the East this year, and luck comes with it. To increase success in career, military service, science, or technology, add large crystals (over 2 inches) like citrine, amethyst, and smoky quartz to the East part of the home.

To balance the energy of health and wealth, add brass vases or bowls. You can place messages and wishes for your family's health and prosperity in the bowls each New Moon.

Flying Star 7—The Violent Star: The unlucky 7-Star flies to the Southeast this year, and brings the very unlucky energy of robbery, legal troubles, fire, injury, and arguments. To decrease bad luck, add the Water element. Good Water element representations are fountains, fish tanks, pictures of moving water, or decorative objects made of glass.

To protect yourself from robbery, legal problems, injury, and health issues, it is best to 'burn off' excess negative energy by burning black or dark blue candles once a month. Because this is the Violent Star, adding exterior lighting or installing a motion detector porch light wouldn't hurt.

Flying Star 8—The Prosperity Star: Luck moves to the Center as the 8-Star finds it's home there for the year. This is the area of your home or space to enhance and to experience increased happiness, wealth, and family unity. Do so by adding representations of fire: for instance, you can place red pillows, or art that depicts a distinct triangular shape; or burn white or gold candles in this part of the home.

To balance career energy and enhance good relations with children and young people, add earth to the 8-Star area by placing clear quartz crystals on a table at the Center of the house.

Flying Star 9—The Future Prosperity Star: This star brings us more lucky energy. The very lucky 9-Star flies to the Northwest this year. This is your success area for the year. Try to do things like goal setting, meditating, beginning new projects, or making important contacts by phone from this area of your home or office.

To increase achievement and growth, add wood energy to the space with things like green, healthy plants, pictures of forests and greenery, or add a new wood floor. To increase good luck and good fortune, add fire cures by burning purple or gold candles once a month.

For more information on the cures mentioned in this book, refer to the Feng Shui cure guide at the back of my book, "eng Shui Form." In it, you will find an 80-page guide to how to use Feng Shui cures.

The Grand Duke (or Tai Sui) lives in the Northwest area this year between 322.6 degrees and 337.5 degrees. You can use a compass to find these exact degrees.

The Grand Duke doesn't like being disturbed. The Grand Duke is like the King of all the Kings. It's said that you cannot confront him, only show him deference and respect. This year, those born in the Year of the Snake should keep a protective Feng Shui cure by their bed. This could be a Pi Yao (winged lion) statue or a Tai Sui plaque.

This year you can plant a tree in the Grand Duke's section of your property to show your respect. But beware, you cannot cut down a tree in this direction, or there will be misfortune. Also, be cautious about doing construction or renovation in this area of your home or your property this year, as the process can be plagued with problems, and bring trouble to the household.

The Five Elements

Pig's natural element is Yin Water. With the subtle, quiet Pig energy this year we feel the calming nature of this element. In 2019 we are in a Yin Earth year. With this combination, we feel a lot of desire to wait and see what happens, to hold back to let others go first and to be mindful of the present moment. This year there will be a focus on gratitude, meditation and a desire to celebrate with delicious food and drink. We'll gather friends together and enjoy each other's company.

Earth and Water are just two of the elements. The ancient Chinese philosophers looked at the world and categorized all they could see into five elements, five building blocks which are the basis of all things. The five elements and their representations are

Wood – represents growth and all things that grow.

Fire – represents energy itself, and all of the things energy creates or produces.

Earth – represents stability and things in a state of rest.

Metal – represents resources and things which make up the material of tools.

Water – symbolizes connectivity, things that help connect some one thing to another.

As mentioned previously, each of the five elements can be either *Yin* or *Yang*. Yin represents the more subtle and flowing energy, and Yang represents the more "in-your-face" direct energy. The Yin/Yang symbol is probably familiar to you. The black part represents Yin, and the white part is Yang.

The dot in the opposing color in the Yin/Yang symbol represents the concept: "One cannot exist without the other." To understand the concept of larger, we must be familiar with smaller. For us to understand the essence of weaker, we must know stronger.

Each of the five elements exists in a state of Yin or Yang.

Yang Wood is like a forest of the tallest trees, growing in the wild. Or, energetically, it is expressed in the life of the student who studies all the time. It is like the feeling of being on a new job, where you have to learn everything as quickly as possible (and you love every moment of it.)

Yin Wood is like a seedling, just popping out of the dirt to see the sun for the first time. It's the realization that you've grown as a person and don't need as much help as you did when you were younger. It's the act of tweaking a favorite recipe with just one new ingredient, to see what it will taste like.

Yang Fire is a forest fire burning out of control. It's like celebrating a college spring break at a beachside resort, daddy's credit card in hand. Or, it's like driving in a NASCAR race, exhilarating, demanding your entire focus and all your attention, simply to keep from crashing.

Yin Fire can be represented with the image of a match or a single candle. Imagine the energy of taking a stroll down a beautiful path and having the time to enjoy nature. Or, think of the amount of energy our body uses to digest food: it happens automatically, without effort or thought.

Yang Earth is a tall mountain, majestic and still. It's like a lazy retirement, one where you enjoy your time sitting on the porch, day after day, in a comfortable chair. There are no worries about finances. There are no obligations to create stress in your life.

Yin Earth is like a sandy beach, flat and smooth. It's like a Sunday afternoon in Summer, nothing pulling at you, your list of chores is completed. You take a restful, peaceful nap.

Yang Metal is similar to the power of collecting gold bars, having them stacked, and representing greater abundance than you will ever need. It's a world filled with unlimited resources. You can present a Black Visa card and purchase anything you wish. Or, it's like becoming CEO and receiving or having access to all the perks.

Yin Metal is like possessing a stack of coins or receiving a regular paycheck: you have just enough to feel secure; you can count on support to arrive as expected, week after week. It's like having just the right amount of cash in your pocket to buy what you need at the store.

Yang Water is a springtime waterfall, rushing downhill and churning up the body of water below. It's water bursting from a dam and rushing towards the town. Or, it's like melted snow pouring down the mountainside to flood the fields below.

Yin Water is like a still pond on a summer's day, no movement on the surface, it appears to be as still as a sheet of glass in the sunlight. Or, it's like a peaceful lake in the quiet of a moonlit night, the reflection of the moon glimmering on the surface. It's a glass of water, the exact perfect amount you need to drink to quench your thirst.

When the ancient people who brought us Feng Shui looked at the world, they divided every existing thing into these Five Elements. They also observed how one element could interact with another. This interaction can be seen in a Creative Cycle or a Destructive Cycle.

The Creative Cycle is: Wood creates Fire, Fire creates Earth (by producing ash), Earth produces Metal (because when we dig into the earth we find metal), Metal produces Water (when metal becomes cold it pulls water from the air in the form of condensation) and Water produces Wood (when water is poured on the ground, things grow).

The Destructive Cycle is: Wood depletes Earth (Trees and plants take nutrients from the earth), Earth blocks Water (dams can be made of earth), Water puts out Fire, Fire melts Metal, and Metal chops Wood (when metal is formed into an ax or other sharp tool, it can cut wood).

In Feng Shui, we are always looking for the larger to support the smaller. For example, if you as a single individual need to feed and clothe your entire community, you would soon become depleted of energy and resources. But if the community helps feed and clothe you, there would be an abundance of food and clothing for you.

This year is an Earth Year. Your individual element may be in harmony with this year's element being part of the Creative Cycle; or, your individual element may be in disharmony with this year's element by being part of the Destructive Cycle. Check the list at the beginning of the book and find your element.

If your element is Wood: Your element is Wood, and the element this year is Earth. Wood depletes Earth. There are many opportunities for you but you must reach out and take them. Nothing will be handed to you this year. However, there will be many ripe, juicy opportunities for the easy picking if you choose.

For example, if you want a new job there are many you are qualified for. You may need to tweak your resume to suit the job or fill out online forms to get the interview, but the opportunities will be there for you. In the case of love, suitable partners are waiting. You will need to get out into the world, attend social events or let your friends know you're looking. But once you do you will soon be meeting interesting people and have several to choose from.

If your element is Fire: Your element is Fire, and the element of this year is Earth; Fire creates Earth. You are the spark the world is searching for. But you must be cautious that your supply of Fire (energy, time, money, etc.) isn't used up too quickly.

This can manifest as many people coming to you with offers and opportunities, but you have limited time and can't do it all. You're the perfect fit for their job, business idea or investment, but when you commit to one project you cut off your ability to commit to another, so choose wisely. Consider first what your goals are to determine if what is being offered really fits your wishes.

If your element is Metal: Your element is Metal, and this year's element is Earth. Earth creates Metal. This year the whole world is offering you what you need to make your wishes come true. This is a time when you need to use your power of organization and knowledge of resources to ask the Universe for what you want and ask for the awareness you need to recognize Opportunity when it arrives! What sign can the Universe give you to let you know this is what you've been waiting for?

This year is when you need to implement plans that have been brewing in the back of your mind for years. Now is the time to find someone or a group of people who can help make your plans into reality. This is also a year to expand your expectations. You can have more in your life. If your vision of more causes you stress, examine your vision and change it where necessary. In this manner, you will be able to take advantage of the positive energy this year.

If your element is Water: Your element is Water, and this is an Earth year. Earth blocks Water. This year the world wants to shape and mold you into what it wants you to be. Opportunities that show up may not seem to be right for you, and you may not think you have the qualifications for the task, but if even a small part of the opportunity lines up with your goals, take a chance and allow the process to make you stronger.

This year the world may seem like a very irritating place, but the irritation you feel involves issues that reside deep inside of you. By looking within and addressing what's really bugging you, you'll be able to rise above any blocks to reaching your goals—blocks that may have been holding you back for years. Try to imagine or visualize that the irritation you feel is a message of blocks that you can't go through but can easily flow around.

It will seem like everyone has suggestions to offer you this year; everyone wants you to change in some way. It's beneficial for you to slow down and consider what they are saying. Water is often in constant motion, only a dam or river bank holds it back, and this year the whole world is Earth; keeping you contained and helping you build your power.

If your element is Earth: Your element is Earth and this year the element is Earth so you are in harmony with this year's energy. You have an innate understanding of the energy of Earth and its desire to remain calm and still until action is needed.

You are admired for your poise and balance this year. It's important you cultivate your ability to see situations clearly, to meditate on what to say and when to say it, and to wait for the right moment to take action.

Your challenge this year is to avoid getting bogged down doing so much research and thinking that no action takes place. You can gain much insight through journaling or meditation, but if you don't let the world know your insights, it doesn't bring you value. Don't hold back when you have something to say. When you know it's time to act—don't hesitate.

Using and Clearing Feng Shui Cures

"Okay, I did what you said, and it worked for a little while, but now it's not working."

When we place an object to attract new energy—and we place it correctly—we will get results within the first week. But after that, the energy will start to dissipate. There are several reasons for this.

Mainly, we are very quick to adapt to the new energy, and so even though new energy is flowing in; we cease to notice it. Also, when we first place the Feng Shui cure, we see it every day, but after a time it becomes part of the background and therefore is no longer activating our subconscious.

Often, the solution is to move the cure; or, if that's not possible, to take the cure down and dust it off and then replace it where was. I had a client who was using my "double lucky money fish" cure to attract money. She placed a pair of fish by her front door, and business started to flow in effortlessly. However, after a week or two, she would become overwhelmed by so many new clients.

So she would take the "double lucky money fish" cure away from her front door, and place the cure in her home office instead. The result of this was she would receive quick and easy payment from her clients.

Then, after a couple of weeks, she would find she needed new clients again. So she would take the "double lucky money fish" cure and once again hang them by her front door. By moving the fish over and over, she was always attracting positive money energy.

How to Clear Gemstones and Crystals

After a few weeks, gemstones and crystals have been absorbing energy, and it can seem they are not as effective as they were when you first placed them. Here is an easy solution. The gemstone or crystal needs clearing. There are several methods you can use. Each is very effective, choose the method that is most convenient for you.

Clearing with Sage: you can smudge the gemstone or crystal using Sage. Take your smudge stick and light it, then pass the crystal through the smoke several times. Turn the crystal so the smoke touches all sides. The crystal is now clear, and you can hang it back up where it was. You should see a bump up in the energy levels during the next few days.

Clearing with Salt: you can clear gemstones and crystals using salt. Some gemstones and crystals are sensitive to salt, so when clearing these with salt, place the crystal on a dish and draw a ring of salt around the crystal. (The salt should not touch the crystal.) Then place the dish where it will not be disturbed for 24 hours.

Once the 24-hour period is completed, remove the crystal from the plate and dispose of the salt in a trash can outside of your home. (Tossing the salt in the kitchen garbage will just release the energy back into the house.) Replace the crystal where it was. You'll see an increase in energy within the next few days.

Clearing with Sunlight: you can also clear gemstones and crystals in sunlight. Take the crystal down and wash it thoroughly in clear water and a gentle soap. Dry the crystal with a soft cloth. Place the crystal on a dish outside in the sunlight for a full day. In the evening bring the crystal back into the house and allow it to cool. Then re-hang the crystal where it was. If you don't see an increase in energy in the first week, use one of the other two methods to clear the crystal.

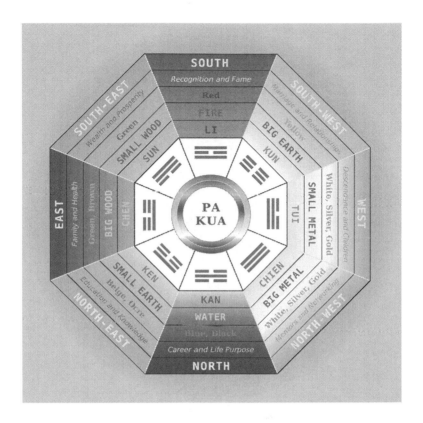

How to Identify the Wealth and Love Areas of Your House

To identify the Wealth areas of your home, stand inside the front door entrance to the house; take the above diagram, and place the side that says "Career" up against your closed front door. The diagram will show you the location of the Wealth area.

In fact, you will quickly identify two Wealth areas: one is the far left corner of the entrance area (or, the far left corner of the room where the front door opens into the home). The other important Wealth area in your home is the far left corner of the whole house.

To identify your "Love" areas, stand inside your home by your front door. Using the above diagram, place the side that says "Career" against your front door.

Now the diagram shows you the location of the Love area in the far right corner of the entrance area (or, the far right corner of the room where the front door opens into the home). The other significant Love area in your home is the far right corner of the house.

Bibliography and Recommended Reading

Bartholomew, Sarah, "Feng Shui: It's Good for Business," ETC Publishing, Carlsbad, CA, 2005

Brown, Simon, "Practical Feng Shui," Wardlock, London, 1997

Carus, Paul, "Chinese Astrology," Open Court, LaSalle, IL, 1974

Chuen, Master Lam Kam, "Personal Feng Shui Manual: How to Develop a Healthy and Harmonious Lifestyle," Henry Holt & Co, New York, 1998

Craze, Richard, "Teach Yourself Chinese Astrology," Arbingdon, England, Bookpoint, 1997

Cunningham, Scott, "Cunningham's Encyclopedia of Crystal, Gem and Metal Magic,."Llewellyn Publications, St. Paul, MN 1988

Cunningham, Scott, "Cunningham's Encyclopedia of Magical Herbs,."Llewellyn Publications, St. Paul, MN 1997

Cunningham, Scott, "The Magic of Food,."Llewellyn Publications, St. Paul, MN 1996

Eberhard, Wolfram, "A Dictionary of Chinese Symbols," Routledge, London, 1983

Gong, Rosemary, "Good Luck Life," New York, Harper Collins, 2005

Kwok, Man-Ho, "The Elements of Feng Shui," Elements Books Limited, Dorset, England, 1991

Lau, Kwan, "Secrets of Chinese Astrology: Handbook for Self-Discovery," Tengu Books, Trumbull, CT, 1994

Lau, Theodora, "The Handbook of Chinese Horoscopes," New York, Harper & Row, 1979

Lip, Evelyn, "Chinese Numbers," Heian International, Union City, California 1992

Lip, Evelyn, "Chinese Practices and Beliefs," Torrance, Heian International, 2000

Ronngren, Diane, "Color: A Secret Language Revealed," ETC Publishing, Carlsbad, CA, 1997

Ronngren, Diane, "Eclipses," ETC Publishing, Carlsbad, CA, 2001

Ronngren, Diane, "Mercury Retrograde," ETC Publishing, Carlsbad, CA, 2000

Ronngren, Diane, "Sage & Smudge: The Ultimate Guide," ETC Publishing, Carlsbad, CA, 2003

Ronngren, Diane, "Simple Feng Shui Secrets," ETC Publishing, Carlsbad, CA, 2005

Ronngren, Diane and Stellhorn, Donna, "Money and Prosperity Workbook," ETC Publishing, Carlsbad, CA, 1999

Rossbach, Sarah, "Interior Design with Feng Shui," Arkana, London, 1987

Skinner, Stephen, "Flying Star Feng Shui," Tuttle, Boston, MA, 2003

Stellhorn, Donna, "Feng Shui Form," ETC Publishing, Carlsbad, CA, 2006

Stellhorn, Donna, "How to Use Magical Oils," ETC Publishing, Carlsbad, CA, 2002

Stellhorn, Donna, "Sage & Smudge: Secrets to Clearing Your Personal Space," ETC Publishing, Carlsbad, CA, 1999

Sun, Ruth Q, "The Asian Animal Zodiac," Castle Books, Boston, MA, 1974

Tai, Sherman, "Principles of Feng Shui: An Illustrated Guide to Chinese Geomancy," Asiapac Books, Singapore, 1998

Too, Lillian, "Easy-To-Use Feng Shui: 168 Ways to Success," Collins & Brown, London, 1999

Too, Lillian, "Unlocking the Secrets of Chinese Fortune Telling," Metro Books, New York, 2006

Twicken, David, "Classical Five Element Chinese Astrology Made Easy," Writers Club Press, New York, 2000

Twicken, David, "Flying Star Feng Shui Made Easy," Writers Club Press, New York, 2002

Walters, Derek, "Chinese Astrology," Watkins Publishing London, 2002

Walters, Derek, "The Feng Shui Handbook," Aquarian Press, San Francisco, CA 1991

Williams, C.A.S., "Outlines of Chinese Symbolism & Art Motifs," Dover Publications, New York, 1976

Wydra, Nancilee, "Feng Shui: The Book of Cures," Contemporary Books, Lincolnwood, IL 1993

About Donna Stellhorn

Author, Astrology and Feng Shui expert, Donna Stellhorn, is a speaker, a supportive personal coach, and a practical business consultant, with more than 25 years' experience. In addition to building three successful businesses of her own and logging more than 20,000 hours of consultations with clients, she teaches a variety of classes, offers apprenticeship programs, leads workshops, and continues to write on a variety of topics. She believes in encouraging others to achieve success in their careers and their personal lives.

Donna has written 15 books. Her Chinese Astrology series, of which this book is the latest one (*2019 Year of the Earth Pig*) is the most popular Chinese Astrology book series according to Amazon.

One of her earliest books is *Feng Shui Form*. First published in Germany, it is a collection of many of her best and most popular concepts to help her readers create a supportive and comfortable living and working environment.

Her best-selling booklet for more than ten years, *Sage and Smudge: Secrets of Clearing Your Personal Space*, shares the concept of how to cleanse and clear space, objects, or environments.

A recent book is a Feng Shui expert's look at the puzzle of fertility, entitled: *A Path to Pregnancy: Ancient Secrets for the Modern Woman.*

She is currently working on a book that's a Feng Shui expert's guide to losing weight by changing how you eat, where you eat and how you store food in the home. This book is called: *Plate Size Matters* and is coming soon.

Donna lectures on both Chinese Astrology and Western Astrology as well as Feng Shui. Recently, Donna has lectured at Western Digital, Warner Records, Room & Board, the Rancho Santa Fe Water District, Brion Jeannette Architecture, and the San Diego Airport Authority. She's been on Coast to Coast AM with George Noory. She spoke at the 2018 United Astrology Conference in Chicago and she writes for Horoscope.com and Astrology.com. Donna is on the board of the International Feng Shui Guild and National Council for Geocosmic Research—San Diego.

For fun, Donna does improv and when she wants to be terrified, she does standup comedy. Donna lives in Orange County, California with her standard poodle, Giles and the magical cat, LaRue.

For more information check out Donna's blog, YouTube channel and her website.

Blog: https://fengshuiform.wordpress.com/

YouTube Channel: https://www.youtube.com/c/DonnaStellhorn

Website: http://www.fengshuiform.com/

or email her at donnastellhorn@gmail.com

One last thing…

Thank you so much for purchasing this book. I hope you found this information helpful, and if you did, please let your friends know about it. If you can take a moment and give it a review at your favorite retailer, I would be very grateful.

Giles crossed the rainbow bridge during the writing of this book. You were the best dog ever. You will be missed.

Made in the USA
San Bernardino, CA
05 January 2019